SCHOLARLY INFLUENCE IN CRIMINOLOGY AND CRIMINAL JUSTICE

CRIMINAL JUSTICE, LAW ENFORCEMENT AND CORRECTIONS

Additional books in this series can be found on Nova's website under the Series tab.

Additional e-books in this series can be found on Nova's website under the e-book tab.

CRIMINAL JUSTICE, LAW ENFORCEMENT AND CORRECTIONS

SCHOLARLY INFLUENCE IN CRIMINOLOGY AND CRIMINAL JUSTICE

ELLEN G. COHN
AND
DAVID P. FARRINGTON

Nova Science Publishers, Inc.
New York

For permission to use material from this book please contact us:
Telephone 631-231-7269; Fax 631-231-8175
Web Site: http://www.novapublishers.com

NOTICE TO THE READER

Additional color graphics may be available in the e-book version of this book.

LIBRARY OF CONGRESS CATALOGING-IN-PUBLICATION DATA

Scholarly influence in criminology and criminal justice / authors, Ellen G. Cohn and David P. Farrington.
p. cm.
Includes bibliographical references and index.
ISBN 978-1-62081-357-7 (hardcover)
1. Criminology--Research. 2. Criminal justice, Administration of--Research. 3. Bibliographical citations. I. Cohn, Ellen G. II. Farrington, David P.
HV6024.5.S363 2012
364--dc23
2012008886

Published by Nova Science Publishers, Inc. † New York

CONTENTS

Foreword		vii
Preface		xi
Chapter 1	Citation Analysis as a Measure of Scholarly Influence	1
Chapter 2	Citation Analysis in Different Fields	23
Chapter 3	Citation Analysis in Criminology and Criminal Justice	39
Chapter 4	Methods Used in Citation Analyses	59
Chapter 5	Most-Cited Scholars in Groups of Journals	69
Chapter 6	Most-Cited Scholars and Works in Nine Major Journals	97
Chapter 7	Citations in Twenty Major Criminology and Criminal Justice Journals	107
Chapter 8	Publication Productivity in Criminology and Criminal Justice	121
Chapter 9	Publications of Members of the American Society of Criminology	139
Chapter 10	Conclusion	147
References		155
Name Index		171
Subject Index		181

FOREWORD

In 1975, I was sitting in the foyer to Robert K. Merton's office when a package arrived at his secretary's desk. Soon thereafter, he emerged, opened the package, and excitedly looked through its contents: the *Social Sciences Citation Index*. As I recollect today, Professor Merton went directly to the M's to survey his citations. But this remembrance is approaching 40 years and could be an invention of mine—perhaps a projection of what I would have done in this circumstance! Regardless, I understood at the very beginning of my career the importance of citations and their analysis.

Criminologists know Robert K. Merton for his writings on anomie-strain theory. A few more might have learned that he coined the term "self-fulfilling prophecy" and "unanticipated consequences"—terms that find their way into criminological discourse on occasion. But what many criminologists might not realize is that Merton's commentary on crime and deviance occupied a small fraction of his sociological enterprise (although one that he revisited at various times deep into his career). Rather, Merton's main interest—starting with his dissertation research—was in the sociology of science, especially the factors that affect the invention and dissemination of ideas. In this regard, he grasped how science and social science citation indices could advance the sociology of science by allowing for quantitative analyses of the growth of knowledge.

As a small part of my dissertation, I conducted an analysis of citations to the work of Richard Cloward. It was my thesis—and one the numbers supported—that most scholars cited his writings as an example of "strain" theory. In fact, the innovative part of Cloward's work was drawn not from Merton but from the Chicago school of criminology. Their work showed that access to criminal roles—whether a professional thief or a jack-roller—was not universally available. From this insight, he formulated the construct of "illegitimate means," which he used to explain why individuals experiencing strain adapt in one way or the other. Adaptations are structured by the means available. Becoming a jack-roller, for example, depends on having associates who can teach youngsters the skills required to engage in this crime and then to help them perform the act. Citation analysis revealed, however, that this theoretical insight was ignored by nearly all scholars, who instead reduced Cloward exclusively to a strain theorist.

My decision to trace citations to Cloward's work was inspired by a wonderful account of the rise and decline in popularity of anomie-strain theory written by Stephen Cole in a 1975 festschrift for Merton, "The Growth of Scientific Knowledge: Theories of Deviance as a Case Study" (published in the *Idea of Social Structure*). This essay, which should be read even today, was an exemplar in how the quantitative analysis of citations could illuminate the contours of criminology within given periods of time and across time. For this reason—and due to my experiences at Columbia University—I have long appreciated efforts to understand our field through citations.

Over the years, therefore, I have welcomed and learned from the sustained contributions of Ellen Cohn and David Farrington, who have been the leading scholars in the use of citations to assess scholarly influence within criminology. In conjunction with Richard A. Wright in 1998, they published the pathbreaking volume, *Evaluating Criminology and Criminal Justice*. Now, in *Scholarly Influence in Criminology and Criminal Justice*, Professors Cohn and Farrington have, as the saying goes, "done it again." This work is an essential source for anyone wishing to understand the nature of contemporary criminology. Their analyses have value because the data are of exceptional quality—based on rigorous methods, a lengthy longitudinal design, and the meticulous attention to details.

Readers are likely to be intrigued initially by the rankings of most-cited authors. Who are the winners and the losers in the competition for the field's attention? But beyond this roster of scholarly influence, there is much more to be learned from Professors Cohn and Farrington. It is clear, for example, that today's winners may well be tomorrow's losers—that scholarly influence is difficult to sustain, even among the best scholars (although some scholars' influence enjoys a longer career). Not long ago, I asked my graduate students what they knew about Marvin Wolfgang. The best the students could share was the following: "Didn't he do something in Philadelphia?" I was astounded, but the data show why this might be the case: In the past two decades (he passed away in 1998), Wolfgang went from among the most influential authors to not being listed among the top 50 scholars cited in the field's leading journals. This is a sobering reminder that fame is fleeting. Yet this finding also cautions us to revisit the works of highly cited researchers from past eras—to learn what they so brilliantly illuminated and why their work was of consequence. There is some peril, as Herbert Gans argues, in our having a short "attention span" and, collectively, of engaging in a form of disciplinary "amnesia."

Notably, each chapter in Professors Cohn and Farrington's treatise broadens our understanding of the criminological enterprise. Thus, they use citation data to inform us about issues such as which scholarly works are widely cited, the proportion and rate of productivity among ASC members, and how citations can be used to establish the productivity of criminology/criminal justice departments. Most important, they end their work by showing the implications of citation analysis for understanding not only how criminological scholarship develops but also how these endeavors shape crime control policies and practices.

Finally, for over two decades, Professors Cohn and Farrington have provided an invaluable service to criminology by producing high quality data on the growth of scholarly influence and knowledge. I hope that it is not the case, but I suspect that *Scholarly Influence in Criminology and Criminal Justice* may be among their last contributions in this area. Regardless, it is perhaps time for the next generation of scholars, as the saying goes, to stand on the shoulders of these scholarly giants.

As is well known, new citation tools now exist—such as Google Scholar, Scopus, and Web of Science—that, though fraught with weaknesses, have inordinate power to assess scholarly publications and citation patterns. I can imagine that it would be possible to employ techniques such as network analysis to explore, in sophisticated ways, how ideas are invented, spread, and decline. The point is simply this: Building on the work of Professors Cohn and

Farrington, exciting opportunities to engage in the sociology of criminology—and to develop this area as a core specialty in our discipline—are at hand. I trust that the importance of this challenge will be fully appreciated and that serious, innovative research in the Cohn-Farrington tradition will be widely initiated in the time immediately ahead.

Francis T. Cullen
University of Cincinnati

PREFACE

As the title indicates, this book is about scholarly influence in criminology and criminal justice (CCJ). Most of the book is concerned with identifying the most-cited scholars in major CCJ journals over a twenty-year period (1986-2005), with an emphasis on changes over time. We also analyze members of the American Society of Criminology, to identify who published the most articles in CCJ journals in 1999-2000 and 2004-05.

The fundamental assumption underlying citation analysis is that, in general, scholars in a given field who are the most-cited tend also to be the most influential in that field. Citation analysis can be used to analyze the influence of scholars, works, journals, departments, and universities. It is an unbiased, objective, quantitative, and replicable technique. The raw data for citation analysis (names in the text and lists of references) are readily available to anyone who wishes to replicate our work. However, good citation analysis is extremely laborious, because it entails a great deal of checking and searching to resolve errors and ambiguities in references. While there are undoubtedly difficulties, citation analysis generally is a valid measure of prestige and influence.

Our analyses of scholarly influence began in 1988. Ellen was carrying out research on weather and crime under David's supervision in Cambridge, and was waiting to receive data on police calls for service. As she was somewhat at a loose end, David suggested that it would be interesting to analyze the most-cited scholars in major CCJ journals. At that time, few citation analyses had been carried out in criminology or criminal justice, and we thought that this technique would yield some objective, unbiased information about scholarly influence, in contrast to the highly idiosyncratic, biased and subjective "histories of the development of criminological thought" that were being written at the time.

Our first article ("Differences between British and American criminology: An analysis of citations") was published in the *British Journal of Criminology* (BJC) in 1990. Our second article ("Who are the most influential criminologists in the English-speaking world?") was published in the same journal in 1994. Since then, we have extended our research greatly and published a total of 21 articles and one book (*Evaluating Criminology and Criminal Justice*) on scholarly influence.

Unfortunately, citation analysis can arouse strong emotional reactions in scholars. A few people (those who are highly cited) are pleased with the results. Many others (those who are not highly cited) are annoyed. Many scholars find citation analysis threatening because of their concern that the results might affect their promotion prospects, salaries, or even the survival of their departments. A later editor of the BJC announced that he was not going to publish any articles on citation analysis!

Some scholars may feel that citations, unlike publications or grants, cannot be significantly affected by their own efforts. On the other hand, as scholars become more aware of citation analysis, we have heard about some undesirable developments, such as scholars selectively citing friends and departmental colleagues and deliberately avoiding citing works written by rivals and members of rival departments. Some scholars may even agree to cite each other as part of a "you scratch my back, I'll scratch yours" bargain. These developments constitute a challenge to the validity of future citation analyses.

We have found it difficult to publish papers on citation analysis in major CCJ journals. Some reviewers have said explicitly that CCJ articles on this topic, however interesting or competently executed, should not be published in major CCJ journals, which (they argue) should focus on CCJ topics such as the causes of crime, policing, sentencing, or imprisonment. And yet many scholars find our results fascinating and often beg us to send them the results of our latest analyses! We believe that our results do contribute to the development of CCJ knowledge over time. They have been cited as a partial justification for scholars receiving major awards from scholarly societies and as part of dossiers prepared for promotion applications.

And so we are left with a conundrum. Many scholars find the results of research on scholarly influence riveting, and our impression is that, when published, our articles are noticed and discussed more than many journal articles on more conventional CCJ topics. Many other scholars are hostile to the entire approach and do their best to prevent the publication of articles on scholarly influence. We will leave our readers to make up their own minds, and hope that they will find this book informative and thought-provoking, at the very least.

Circumstances were very different when we began our research in 1988. There was no internet and very little interest in citation analysis or any other research on scholarly influence in CCJ. In the last twenty years, the landscape has changed enormously. There has been a massive increase in interest in research on scholarly influence in general and citation analysis in particular. The internet and electronic resources make large-scale citation analyses a lot easier but, as we explain in Chapter 1, the results of mechanical citation analyses are full of problems and errors. The Journal Impact Factor, which is based on citations, is widely used, but again we will explain that it is highly problematic in CCJ.

The strength of our research lies in its very careful checking and correcting of citations, its exclusion of self-citations, and the longitudinal analyses (using the same methods) over a twenty-year period. We trace the waxing and waning of influential scholars and works between 1986 and 2005. We see how older scholars such as Marvin E. Wolfgang give way to younger scholars such as Robert J. Sampson, who in turn may be usurped by still younger scholars such as Alex R. Piquero.

We carried out this research without funding, because we thought that the results were very interesting. We were unable to obtain funding from agencies such as the U.S. National Institute of Justice because it was argued that our research had no policy implications. We disagree. We believe that our research, in identifying the most influential CCJ scholars and works in different time periods, has great policy implications. The works that CCJ scholars believe to be most important should indicate current policy concerns and should surely guide legislators in the development of new policies and influence the funding programs of government agencies.

We are very grateful to Maureen Brown for providing excellent secretarial assistance throughout the time period of this research.

Chapter 1

CITATION ANALYSIS AS A MEASURE
OF SCHOLARLY INFLUENCE

Citation analysis is a well-known and increasingly used technique for evaluating the impact and prestige of scholars, journals, and university departments in a discipline. It is also used for determining the impact of a particular article or book on subsequently published research in the field. Thanks to citation analysis, we know that up to 90 percent of papers published in academic journals are never cited, and it seems likely that many are never even read by anyone other than the authors, referees, and editors (Meho, 2007). Citation analysis has been used to study communication networks among scholars, has helped to identify new research fronts and the linkages among them, and may indicate links between two highly interrelated journals or topics ("co-citation analysis").

According to Meadows (1974), there are two main assumptions in citation analysis: first, that the most-cited works are those that were important in the research, and second, that citations indicate influence (so that several researchers working independently on the same problem would cite the same material). A wide variety of factors have been used to attempt to predict whether an article will be highly cited, including the article's methodological quality (Lee, Schotland, Bacchetti, and Bero, 2002), the amount of media coverage received by an article (Stryker, 2002), and, most commonly, the "impact factor" (see below) of the journal in which the article was published (see e.g., Barbui, Cipriani, Malvini, and Tansella, 2006; Callaham, Wears, and Weber, 2002; Smith, 2008).

Citation analysis provides a quantitative method of determining the impact of a scholar, a journal, or a department on the field. It is based on the concept that "good work is work that others find useful and consequently cite in their own work" (Christenson and Sigelman 1985: 965). Citations have been used to measure the impact of a scholar and his or her work; if a work is highly cited, it suggests that colleagues in one's field find the work important and valuable. Similarly, citations are used to evaluate the impact of publications; a large number of citations to a given journal suggests that the journal enjoys high stature and prestige within the field. Although there is some debate as to whether citation counts accurately measure the quality of a work (e.g., Ferber 1986), they are commonly employed as a measure of the influence of that work on the field as a whole. It is important to realize that the distribution of citations of articles is highly skewed. Laband and Piette (1994) found that most of the scholarly articles published in economics journals were not cited, or were only cited rarely, and Hamilton (1990, 1991) concluded that this observation was true across a variety of scientific disciplines.

Another use of citations is in the area of "co-citation analysis", or the study of pairs of documents that are commonly cited together in a research paper (Mullens, Hargens, Hecht, and Kick, 1977). The assumption behind co-citation analysis is that the two co-cited works are related. Co-citation analysis is intended to locate related groups of works, where some might influence or inspire others.

Citation analysis has also been used to examine when an article becomes influential. For example, Glänzel and Garfield (2004) used citation analysis to conclude that delayed recognition of the importance of research publications in science is rare; almost all significant research is highly cited in the first three to five years after publication. Conversely, if a work is not highly cited during this time period, it is unlikely ever to be highly cited. However, this may not be true in criminology and criminal justice (see later).

Citation analysis is used in many different fields such as medicine (e.g., Logan and Shaw 1991; Lokker, McKibbon, McKinlay, Wilczynski, and Haynes, 2008), economics (e.g., Ferber 1986), biochemistry (e.g., Cano and Lind 1991), physics (e.g., Cole and Cole 1971), organizational science (e.g., Blackburn and Mitchell 1981), psychology (e.g., Bagby, Parker, and Bury 1990), entrepreneurship (Schildt, Zahra, and Sillanpää, 2006), English literature (Heinzkill, 2007), sociology (e.g., Bott and Hargens 1991), library and information science (e.g., LaBonte, 2005; Chikate and Patil, 2008), and of course criminology (e.g., Cohn, Farrington, and Wright, 1998). Chapter 2 briefly reviews the use of citation analysis in these other fields, while Chapter 3 reviews in more detail its use in criminology and criminal justice. Probably the best known example of citation analysis in criminology is the research by Wolfgang, Figlio, and Thornberry (1978), which employed citation analysis to determine the most-cited American books and articles from 1945 to 1972. The use of citation analysis is not limited to the United States; researchers around the world are employing it as a tool for evaluating influence. For example, a 1996 government report released in Australia listed citation analysis as one of the three main ways to measure the influence of scholarly journals (Murphy, 1996).

MEASURING INFLUENCE AND PRESTIGE

Unlike most measures of scholarly influence and prestige, such as peer rankings or professional awards, citation analysis provides an objective, transparent, replicable, and quantitative measure, which is not influenced by personal bias or special interest. Rushton (1984: 33) clearly explains the rationale for using citation counts as a measure of prestige: "If psychologist A's work has been cited 50 times in the world's literature that year, and psychologist B's only 5, A's work is assumed to have had more impact than B's, thereby making A the more eminent."

There is a substantial body of research that supports the strong relationship between citation counts and other measures of a scholar's influence, professional prestige, intellectual reputation, and scientific quality. Myers (1970) found that citation counts were highly correlated with peer ratings of professional eminence in psychology and with the receipt of scholarly prizes and appointments in psychology (such as the Distinguished Scientific

Contribution Award and the Presidency of the American Psychological Association). Rushton and Endler (1979) cited Garfield's (1977a, 1977b, 1977c) findings showing a clear relationship between citations and scholarly recognition (such as election to the National Academy of Sciences and/or the Royal Society of London). Cole and Cole (1971) discovered a significant relationship between citation counts and receiving a Nobel Prize in physics. Interestingly, in most cases scholars had high citation counts before they received Nobel Prizes rather than afterwards. Gordon and Vicari (1992) have demonstrated that citations are also highly correlated with scholarly productivity (i.e., publication rates). Both Hamermesh, Johnson, and Weisbrod (1982) and Diamond (1986) have shown that a scholar's citation frequency may significantly influence his or her salary.

A number of researchers (e.g., Roche and Smith 1978; Doerner, DeZee, and Lab 1982; Rushton, Littlefield, Russell, and Meltzer 1983) have found correlations between citation counts and ratings of the prestige of university departments. Rushton et al. (1983) found a significant relationship between departmental citation counts and the number of graduate students. Research into the prestige and eminence of doctoral programs (e.g., DeZee 1980) has also regularly found correlations between citations, peer rankings, and journal publications. For example, Endler, Rushton, and Roediger (1978) reported Pearson correlations of .60 or greater between peer rankings of psychology departments (in the United States, Canada, and the United Kingdom) and citation counts of departmental faculty members.

Rushton and Endler (1979) and Rushton (1984) discussed the reliability and validity of citation counts in some detail. Rushton (1984: 34) stated that "it is fair to say that citation measures meet all the psychometric criteria for reliability." For example, Myers (1970) reported a rank correlation of .91 between his citation index (based on all references in 14 prestigious psychology journals) and the number of citations in the Social Sciences Citation Index. Rushton and Endler (1977) demonstrated the year-to-year stability of citation counts in psychology, showing a correlation of .98 between the number of citations to the top 25 British psychologists in 1974 and in 1975. Similarly, based on the large body of evidence indicating that citation counts correlate strongly with a variety of other indicators, Rushton (1984: 34) stated that "citation counts are highly valid indices of quality."

More recently, Duy and Vaughan (2006) compared citation data with print and electronic journal usage as a measure of journal use. They found that electronic and print usage were significantly correlated, and that electronic journal usage also correlated significantly with local citation data. They concluded that "local citation is a valid measure of journal use..." (2006: 516)

There are several other measures of prestige and influence, but most of these are directly subject to some form of personal bias. One of the most common methods of measuring prestige is through peer review. For example, Fabianic (1979) ranked criminal justice Ph.D. programs based on a survey of members of the Academy of Criminal Justice Sciences and other criminal justice educators, and Mijares and Blackburn (1990) ranked four-year undergraduate criminal justice programs by surveying program directors to obtain their list of the top ten programs in the United States. These types of prestige surveys, which are admittedly subjective, have also been used frequently in criminology and criminal justice to rate academic journals (e.g., DeZee, 1980; Fabianic, 1980; Greene, Bynum, and Webb, 1985; McElrath, 1990; Parker and Goldfeder, 1979; Regoli, Poole, and Miracle, 1982; Shichor,

O'Brien, and Decker, 1981; Sorensen, Snell, and Rodriguez, 2006; Williams, McShane, and Wagoner, 1995).

The receipt of scholarly awards and/or prizes is effectively another form of peer ranking, as the recipients are generally chosen by prominent members of the particular field. These measures of prestige are clearly subjective, open to influence, and not truly quantitative. Regardless of one's desire to be objective, it is easy to be influenced by one's personal likes or dislikes of the individuals being reviewed, or one's knowledge (or lack of knowledge) of the individual, department, or scholarly work under consideration.

Another method of assessing prestige involves counts of journal publications by individuals or departmental faculty members. This may be enhanced by weighting the journals according to some system, so that articles published in more prestigious journals (those that are refereed, for example) are considered to be more significant than articles published in less important journals. However, while a publication count is a more objective and quantitative method than peer review, it is a measure of institutional and/or faculty activity or productivity and does not necessarily provide an indicator of the impact, influence, or significance of the published research in the field. Publishing an article does not ensure that it will be read or referred to, or that other scholars will consider it to be of significance. In addition, ranking or weighting journals is a subjective process. As Wolfgang, Figlio, and Thornberry (1978: 21) pointed out, "the explosion of scientific information inflates rates of publication, hence deflating the validity of publication rates as a measure of scientific productivity." Nevertheless, publication productivity is studied in Chapters 8 and 9.

It appears that, of these methods, only citation analysis provides a straightforward, objective, quantitative measure of scientific influence and prestige. While citation analysis has its shortcomings (see later), it appears to be more valid and more reliable than any other measure. The overwhelming body of evidence clearly supports the use of citation analysis as a measure of scholarly eminence, influence, and prestige, or as a way of determining "how many scientists are contributing through their published research to the movement of science" (Cole and Cole 1972: 369).

SOURCES OF CITATION DATA

There are several sources of citation data. One is the publications of Thomson Scientific, which include the Science Citation Index (SCI), Social Sciences Citation Index (SSCI), and the Arts and Humanities Citation Index (AHCI). The Institute for Scientific Information (ISI) was founded by Dr. Eugene Garfield, a pioneer in the field of citation indexing and analysis, in the 1950s. ISI published Current Contents, and developed and produced a number of citation indexes, including SCI, SSCI, and AHCI. These indexes included information on millions of citations in thousands of journals in hundreds of disciplines. These indexes made possible the systematic analysis of citations, both as a way of examining the influence and impact of a specific scholarly work and as a way of studying trends in a field. ISI is now owned and operated by Thomson Reuters, which has integrated the various indexes into a single online "Web of Science" that provides online access to journal articles and produces citation information and journal impact factors for a wide range of journals.

Thomson Reuters also operates Journal Citation Reports (JCR), which provides a variety of information, including impact factors, about science and social science journals, with statistics from 1997. The JCR Science Edition covers over 8,000 journals while the JCR Social Sciences Edition covers over 2,650 journals (Thomson Reuters, 2012d). The JCR provides journal level information; it is not a source of data on citations of individual scholars or articles. Within a specific year, the JCR can be searched for a specific journal, for all journals within a subject category, all journals published by a specific publisher, or all journals published in a specific country. For each journal/year, the JCR includes a considerable amount of information, including the total number of citations in the journal, the journal impact factor, the five year journal impact factor, the journal immediacy index (how frequently the average article from a journal is cited within the same year as publication), the journal cited half-life (the median age of its items cited in the current JCR year), and the journal citing half-life (the number of publication years from the current year that account for 50% of citations received by the journal), as well as several graphs and basic journal source data (Thomson Reuters, 2009).

Another way of obtaining citation data is to use online scientific archives such as Google Scholar and Elsevier's Scopus, both of which appeared in 2004 (Tenopir, 2007). Google Scholar provides free access to citation data from journals and conference proceedings. Scopus, also known as SciVerse Scopus, is a fee-based service providing abstract and citation data for peer reviewed literature and scientific web sources.

A third option is to examine reference lists of journals, scholarly books, textbooks, and the like in a given field and count the number of citations to a given scholar, work, or journal. This method, while somewhat time-consuming and tedious, avoids many of the problems inherent in the use of other data sources (see below) and it was developed successfully in our early research (e.g., Cohn and Farrington 1990, 1994a, 1994b, 1996; Wright and Cohn 1996).

There are several software options that scan articles, pull out references, and generate citation indexes. In general, these programs are designed to increase access to the academic literature. One example is CrossRef (www.crossref.org), a membership association with a mandate "to be the citation linking backbone for all scholarly information in electronic form" (CrossRef, 2012). While not an article database, CrossRef allows users to access the full-text content of a cited article directly from the reference citation. As Adam (2002) points out, once papers and references are interlinked, it would be possible to create citation indexes, impact factors, and so on. However, CrossRef currently is not doing this so it is not really a viable source for citation analysis data.

CiteSeer[X] (http://citeseer.ist.psu.edu/) is a digital library and search engine focusing mainly on the computer and information science literature. It does provide some citation statistics, but its narrow subject range means that its usefulness is limited. There are a number of other initiatives being developed, such as the Open Citation Project (opcit.eprints.org), which is designed to provide open access for published peer-reviewed articles. However, none of these provide coverage in as many disciplines as the ISI databases. Most are focused on the science literature, with little coverage of the social sciences. As a result, they are of limited use for scholars wishing to conduct citation analysis in criminology and criminal justice.

Multiple Citation Sources

Each source includes different citation data and therefore provides different results. Meho (2007: 34) suggests that "The rise in the use of Web-based databases and tools to access scientific literature has revealed how vital it is to use multiple citation sources to make accurate assessments of the impact and quality of scientists' work".

Take, for example, Terrie E. Moffitt's well known article on adolescence-limited and life-course-persistent behavior (Moffitt, 1993). According to the Web of Science on December 12, 2011, it had been cited a total of 2,581 times. However, on the same day Scopus said that this article had been cited 2,559 times since 1996, and Google Scholar said that it has been cited 4,260 times (probably since 1994). If only the Web of Science or Scopus had been used, many of the citations found through Google Scholar would have been missed. However, Web of Science and Scopus are more discriminating than Google Scholar in their standards for inclusion of material to be covered.

Using a sample of 25 highly published researchers in the field of information science, Meho and Yang (2007) compared the citation coverage of Web of Science, Google Scholar, and Scopus. They found that, compared with Web of Science, Scopus increased a scholar's citation count by an average of 35 percent, and Google Scholar increased it by an average of 160 percent. They also discovered that the magnitude of this increase varied by research area.

MEASURES OF SCHOLARLY IMPACT

Journal Impact Factor

The citation-based journal impact factor (JIF) is one of the most widely used measures of journal impact. It was originally developed by Dr. Eugene Garfield, the founder of the Institute for Scientific Information (ISI), for the purpose of evaluating the significance of a particular article and the immediate impact it had on the literature and thinking of the time. Originally it was designed to normalize citation data so that comparisons could be made between journals of different sizes (Garfield, 2003). It is now used not only for this purpose but also to rank journals and to evaluate scholars and institutions (Chew, Villanueva, and Van Der Weyden, 2007). Because the JIF is considered to be an objective way to judge the quality of research and research scholars, it is even being used nowadays to evaluate promotion applications and in the allocation of research funding (van Driel, Maier, and Maeseneer, 2007).

The JIF determines the average number of citations per article in a journal in the succeeding one to two years. So, for a given year T, the JIF for a specific journal is the average number of times articles published in that journal in the two previous years (T-1 and T-2) are cited in year T (Rahm and Thor, 2005). The impact factor is computed as follows:

$$JIF = \frac{\text{Number of citations received in year T by all documents published in J in years T-1 and T-2}}{\text{Number of citable documents published in J in years T-1 and T-2}}$$

where J is the journal under study in year T (Moed, 2005).

According to Garfield (2003: 366), "the two year period was chosen because in the fields that were of greatest interest to the readers of Current Contents, and later of the SCI, 25% of citations were accounted for in the year of publication plus the two previous years." He did state that users could calculate impact factors using longer time periods, using data available from ISI.

According to Adam (2002), the ISI specifically warns against using the JIF to compare journals in different disciplines (see also Garfield, 2003). This is because citation patterns, and the distribution of cited references, differ widely among fields. For example, Adam points out that, while mathematics researchers rarely cite more than one or two references, a typical paper in a field such as molecular biology contains dozens of references. Therefore, as noted by Seglen (1997), even comparable journals serving different disciplines may have widely varying impact factors. However, while the impact factors of journals in different disciplines cannot be compared, impact factors of journals within the same discipline can and have been compared and trends over time may be examined (Chew et al., 2007).

A survey of editors of top medical journals yielded information on a variety of factors that influence a journal's citation counts and impact factor. These include active recruitment of so-called high-impact articles (either by courting researchers or hiring editorial staff), improving various services to authors (such as speeding up review and "turn-around" time, fast-tracking potentially high-impact papers, and so on), finding market niches that attract scholars in that niche to publish in that journal, actively promoting journals to the popular media, and carefully selecting articles based on their quality (Chew, et al, 2007)

Nisonger (2004) has reviewed the advantages and problems of the impact factor. For example, it can be inflated by self-citations. Meho (2007) also discusses several weaknesses of the impact factor. It can be greatly influenced by a few highly cited articles or by many low or uncited articles. In addition, scholars and journals publishing review articles tend to have inflated citation counts and impact factors, because these types of articles tend to be highly cited. Impact factors also do not take into account articles that were used but not cited. In addition, because the impact factor uses only a one to two year time window, it does not capture the long-term impact of journals.

The one to two year time window seems much too short, at least in criminology and criminal justice. Imagine that an article X is published in a journal in month 1, and imagine that a scholar is writing an article Y that could cite article X. Imagine also that the scholar becomes aware of the existence of article X in month 1 and reads article X in month 1. (In practice, these assumptions are much too optimistic. It is more likely that the scholar will not become aware of, or read, article X until several months or even years after it is published.)

Now let us imagine that the scholar submits the finished article Y to a major journal in month 3. (In practice, this is also an optimistic assumption, because it may take much longer to bring an article to fruition.) The major journal may complete a review of article Y in month 6 and (at best) is almost certain to require revisions. Let us assume, optimistically, that the scholar resubmits the revised article Y in month 7 and that it is accepted by the journal after further reviews in month 8. (Of course, given the 90 percent rejection rate of many major journals, it is more likely that article Y will be rejected by the first journal and will have to be resubmitted to a second or even a third journal.)

There is then typically a delay of at least six months, and often 9-12 months, between the date of acceptance of an article and the date of its publication. Even making the most optimistic assumptions, an article X published in month 1 is unlikely to be cited in an article Y published before month 14. Therefore, it is almost impossible for an article published in year T-1 to be cited in year T in criminology and criminal justice unless special measures are taken.

Because of the reification of the journal impact factor, journals are taking special (and sometimes undesirable) measures to boost it. Electronic publication of articles months before the official publication date, journal notification of articles that are accepted and will be published, and electronic alerts of contents pages of journals, will all boost the JIF. Journals sometimes make special efforts to reduce the gap between acceptance and publication, for example by increasing their rejection rate for a short period. This also tends to boost the JIF, because articles in a journal tend to cite other articles published in the same journal. However, this variation in the rejection rate causes many good articles to be rejected.

In our view, it would be much better to base the journal impact factor for year T on articles published in the previous five years (T-1 to T-5). However, a number of highly cited articles are often not very highly cited in the first few years after publication. Consider, for example, the highly influential article by Moffitt (1993). Figure 1-1 shows the number of citations of this article in nine major criminology and criminal justice journals (see Chapters 5-6). There were no more than 4 citations of this article per year until 1997, then 9-10 in 1998-99, before increasing to 22 in 2000 and averaging about 20 per year in 2001-04. Clearly, this famous article did not become very highly cited in major journals until seven years after it was published.

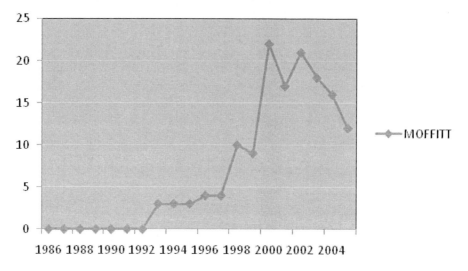

Figure 1-1. Citations of Moffitt (1993).

Van Driel, Maier, and De Maeseneer (2007) also have listed a number of concerns about whether the JIF is an appropriate, and equally important, a sufficient indicator of article quality. First, they point out that it is not always clear what makes an article "citeable," nor does Thomson ISI, the company that computes JIFs, provide much information on how they select the journals that are included in their database. Many journals are not included; Van Driel, Maier, and De Maeseneer (2007) pointed out that, of the 33,000+ biomedical journals indexed in Medline, only about 5,000 were included in the ISI's Journal Citation Reports database. In addition, there appears to be a regional bias that favors journals published in North America over those from other parts of the world. Essentially, according to Van Driel, Maier, and De Maeseneer (2007:401) "the journal impact factor is nothing more than an index of how often a specific journal has been cited in a selected group of journals."

In addition, Haddow (2008) pointed out that, while the JIF may be a key measure of journal quality, ISI indexes less than 50 percent of all peer reviewed journals that are published worldwide and that, of those indexed, less than one-third are in the humanities and social sciences. Seglin (1997) notes that about half of the citations to a specific journal come from about 15 percent of the articles published in that journal, and the most cited 50 percent of articles account for 90 percent of the citations. As a result, an average paper in a journal with a high JIF may not be more frequently cited than an average paper in a lower-ranking journal.

Download Counts

According to Meho (2007: 35), "The Web has enabled a number of alternative citation-based measures to be devised to get around some of the limitations of the citation-counting and impact-factor methods." One of these, which is only really possible because of the recent move to online full-text publication, is download counts. Download counts examine the number of times that an article has been downloaded from the Web. Unlike citation counts, which cannot be calculated until several years after an article is published, download counts are instantly recorded and therefore allow for real-time measurement.

Brody, Harnad, and Carr (2006) reported a significant positive correlation between download counts and citations for articles in mathematics and physics, suggesting that download counts reach their maximum predictive power after six months. They also found that download counts were positively correlated with impact factors. They suggested that download counts could serve as an "early-days estimate" of probable citation impact.

The Hirsch Index

The Hirsch index (or "h-index") was developed by physicist Jorge Hirsch (2005) and has been added to both the Web of Science and the Scopus Citation Tracker. It can also be calculated manually using Google Scholar. The h-index is designed to measure a scholar's productivity and the impact of his or her total scholarly output, but it can also be applied to the productivity and impact of a department or other research group.

The h-index is determined by ranking a scholar's articles by the number of times they are cited (in decreasing order), thus incorporating both the number of publications by a scholar and the number of citations per publication. A score of $h = 10$ would mean that the scholar has published 10 articles or papers, each of which was cited at least 10 times. Published articles with less than h citations do not count in the analysis. He argues that "two individuals with similar h s are comparable in terms of their overall scientific impact, even if their total number of papers or their total number of citations is very different. Conversely, comparing two individuals (of the same scientific age) with a similar number of total papers or of total citation count and very different h values, the one with the higher h is likely to be the more accomplished scientist" (Hirsch, 2005: 16569).

The h-index cannot be compared across disciplines because of differences in citation behavior but it has clear advantages over simply counting the total numbers of publications or citations. Hirsch found that, in physics, a moderately productive scholar has an h value similar to his or her number of years of service, while in biomedical fields, scholars tend to have much higher h values. The h-index tends to increase with the length of a scholar's academic career.

One of the main advantages of the h-index is that it incorporates both the magnitude of scholarly output and the impact of that output. As Meho (2007: 36) pointed out, because scientists with very few high-impact articles or with a lot of low-impact articles will have a low h-index, the statistic "helps distinguish between a 'one-hit wonder' and an enduring performer…"

However, the h-index does have some flaws as well (see e.g., Wendl, 2007). First, it is limited by the total number of publications; a scholar with only a small number of articles must have a small h-index, regardless of the influence and importance of those articles. Second, it fails to indicate the impact of a single extremely successful piece of scholarship. Third, the calculation of h is affected by the accuracy of the database used to compute the statistic. While h can be determined using a variety of online databases, the choice of database to use may affect the value of h, because each database has a different coverage. Fourth, the statistic includes self-citations, so a scholar could influence his or her own h-index through frequent self-citing. Fifth, the index does not consider the number of authors of a single work. Again, it would be possible for a group of scholars to increase their h values by agreeing to co-author all of their papers.

Meho (2007) also pointed out that the statistic did not take into consideration the purpose of a citation, so that negative citations identifying errors in a poorly-crafted piece of scholarship are counted equally with positive citations to seminal works.

The g-Index

Because of the limitations of the h-index, several alternatives have been developed. One of these is the g-index, which was developed by Leo Egghe, a Belgian scientist (see e.g., Egghe, 2006). The g-index is based on publication records and is designed to quantify the scientific productivity of scholars. Like the h-index, it is calculated by ranking articles in decreasing order of the number of citations received. The g-index is the largest number such that the top g articles together have at least g^2 citations. Therefore, a researcher with a g-index of 5 has published 5 articles that have together been cited at least 25 times. The g-index is obviously similar to the h-index but is designed to address some of the main drawbacks of the latter. The g-index sounds a little like measures of concentration or dispersion such as the Gini coefficient (see e.g Gastwirth, 1972).

The h-b-Index

The *h-b*-index, which was developed by Michael Banks, a Ph.D. student at the Max Planck Institute in Germany, extends the *h*-index (Dumé, 2006a). Instead of being based on an individual scholar, as is the *h*-index, the *h-b*-index is based on a topic search. Under the original *h*-index, a scholar with an *h*-index of 25 will have published at least 25 papers that have received at least 25 citations each. In the same way, if a topic has an *h-b*-index of 25, there are at least 25 papers on that topic that have each been cited at least 25 times. A second metric, *m*, normalizes the *h-b*-index, controlling for the number of years that papers on the topic have been published (because of course some topics have been studied for decades while others are much newer). The *m*-number indicates the current importance of a given topic. According to Banks, a topic with an *m* number greater than 3 is a "hot topic" while a topic that has both a large *m* and an *h-b*-index greater than 100 has had lasting popularity, both in the past and today. A topic with a large *h-b*-index but a small *m* is one that was popular in the past but is no longer a hot topic (Dumé, 2006a). There are several programs available on the Web that can calculate the *h-b*-index and *m* values.

The Creativity Index

Spanish scholar José Soler (Soler, 2007) developed a creativity index, C_a, that compares the number of references in a paper with the number of citations of that paper. An article with a lot of references but only a few citations has a low creativity level, while a highly-cited paper with a small number of references has a high creativity level. A scholar's C_a is calculated by adding up the total creativity for every paper written by that scholar. Dumé (2006b) pointed out that one advantage of this technique is that it controls for self-citations; scholars cannot increase their creativity indexes by citing their own works because the references and the citation counts will cancel each other out. In addition, review articles, which provide little new information but frequently are highly cited, will have a relatively low creativity index because they contain so many references. Other types of citation analysis do not take these issues into account.

PROBLEMS OF CITATION ANALYSIS

Citation analysis, as a method of measuring influence, is not perfect; it has a number of problems. Some of these are specific to the data source selected, while others are more general in nature.

Limitations of the Web of Science

Thomson Reuter's Web of Science (WoS) lists all bibliographic references made in an extremely large number of journals. It does not include citations *in* books and book chapters but does include citations *to* books and book chapters. As of January 2012, a total of 16,820 journals were included in the master journal list (Thomson Reuters, 2012a). The WoS is an extremely useful tool for bibliometric research; however, there are some key problems with its use as a source of data for citation analysis.

First of all, the WoS clearly does not include *all* published works. As of January 2012, SSCI obtained citations from 3,017 journals. This included 50 journals in criminology and penology, 139 sociology journals, 143 law journals, and over 730 psychology and psychiatry journals. Many of the important criminology and criminal justice journals are on the list, but some of the newer journals, such as *Criminology and Public Policy*, are not yet included, despite their influence in the field (Thomson Reuters, 2012b). Smith (1989: 5) pointed out that "Important results may be published, and cited, in journals not widely read outside a particular discipline, and therefore excluded from *SCI*". Also, Meho and Yang (2007) pointed out that the ISI databases primarily include titles from North America and Western Europe. Neuhaus and Daniel (2008) stated that the WoS has been criticized for the overrepresentation of titles in English, and the limited attention that is given to journals from Third World nations and countries that use other alphabets.

In addition, the WoS databases are mainly limited to journals, although certain highly-cited book series (such *Crime and Justice* from the University of Chicago Press) and some conference proceedings are also included. However, in general, citations from books, book chapters, technical reports, and so on are not counted. It is possible that this omission may produce a substantive bias. Cohn and Farrington (1994b) noted that the relative significance of books and journal articles varied among disciplines. Their research suggested that books were highly significant in criminology and criminal justice; the most-cited works of the most-cited authors were all books, rather than articles.

Thus, citation research using data from WoS is really only taking account of a small percentage of the research produced in the field. The coverage limitations may significantly impact a scholar's citation count. For example, Funkhouser's (1996) study of references in communications journals in 1990 looked at 13 journals covered by ISI and 14 not included in the database. He found that 27 of the most highly-cited authors received at least 25 percent of their citations from journals not in ISI. Nisonger (2004) conducted a study of his own citations and found that ISI captured less than 30 percent of his total lifetime citations. He suggested that rankings of the most-cited scholars or departments based on ISI data might change significantly if non-ISI data were also included, although he did not verify this suggestion empirically. Cronin, Snyder, and Atkins (1997: 260) looked at scholarly works in journals and monographs in sociology and found evidence to suggest that there may be "two populations of highly cited authors, one which is highly cited in monographs and one which is highly cited in journals." A study of citations in sociology based on data from the WoS might overlook, or at least underestimate, the true influence of scholars who are cited primarily outside the journal literature.

Second, the list of journals included in the WoS is not stable; it changes constantly as new journals are added or older journals are removed from the master journal list. The WoS website includes a list of "Journal Coverage Changes," which lists all journals whose status has changed over the past twelve months. In January 2012, that list ran to 20 single-spaced pages, with over 40 journals listed on each page (Thomson Reuters, 2012c). This makes any form of longitudinal research extremely difficult or impossible, as the database is not constant.

Third, WoS uses only the initials and surnames of cited authors, which may cause confusion when several individuals share the same surname and initial. This was a significant problem when the ISI databases were available in print form. Cohn and Farrington (1996) pointed out the difficulty, for example, of determining which of the many citations under the heading "J. Cohen" belonged to Jacqueline Cohen and which were to other individuals (such as Joseph Cohen or Jacob Cohen) with the same first initial and surname. Many years before, Garfield (1979) acknowledged that this was a significant concern; he found that the 137 works listed under "J. Cohen" in the 1974 SCI were written by eight different individuals. Other problems include the difficulties of distinguishing between the various R. Berks and P. Brantinghams. Endler, Rushton, and Roediger (1978) used an SSCI-based citation count to determine the top 100 psychologists and listed Milton Rosenberg as number 47. When Milton Rosenberg (1979) attempted to check this, he found that his citations had been combined with those of Morris Rosenberg, thus inflating his citation count.

Citations may also include or omit the author's middle initial or may use a "nickname" first initial. For example, Chapman (1989) found that his citations were distributed between A. Chapman, A.J. Chapman, and T. Chapman (the "T" presumably standing for "Tony", an abbreviation for Chapman's first name of Anthony). Similarly, although the first author of this book (Ellen G. Cohn) always uses her middle initial (to avoid confusion with another criminologist named Ellen S. Cohn), reference lists citing her articles often omit the middle initial. As a result, a search for citations of "E. Cohn" in the WoS will capture citations to works by both Ellen G. Cohn and Ellen S. Cohn, among others. Unfortunately, the move to an online database has not solved this problem. Searches of authors are still carried out using surnames and initials, rather than first names.

Chapman (1989) also pointed out that citation counts using the ISI databases may result in a bias against some married women as those counting may not know that the same person may be cited under more than one surname (e.g., Ilene Nagel, Ilene Bernstein, Ilene Nagel-Bernstein). Other individuals with hyphenated names, or who change their surnames, will create similar difficulties for the citation analyst.

A related problem, but one that does appears to have been solved with the move to an online database, is the first author issue. Originally, the ISI databases listed all citations to a work only under the name of the first author. This penalized junior authors in collaborative works, so that scholars who never had first authorship did not appear in the database (Long, McGinnis, and Allison 1980). Geis and Meier (1978) found that this practice penalized wives as well, because they were often second authors. It also favored scholars with surnames beginning with letters near the start of the alphabet, as there was some tendency for authors to be listed alphabetically (Lindsey 1980). However, the online WoS does access all authors to a given work when searching for cited references, so this bias has now been eliminated.

Another problem is that clerical or other errors in the original reference lists or bibliographies are repeated in the WoS. As Sweetland (1989: 292) pointed out, "whether one considers bibliographic references from the point of view of the author or the reader, the assumption is that the citations are accurate. Unfortunately, considerable evidence exists that suggests such an assumption is questionable". Misspellings in reference lists are fairly common. Farrington, for example, is frequently misspelled as Farington, Farringdon, or Faringdon, and Hirschi as Hirsch, Hirsh, or Hirshi. First initials may also be incorrect; Hirschi's citations have also been found under "P. Hirschi" and "L. Hirschi", as well as the correct "T. Hirschi" (Cohn and Farrington, 1996). Similarly, if a citation in the original reference list does not include all the authors of the references, but only lists the first few and subsumes the rest into the generic "et al.," those additional authors will not be included in WoS. There is a tendency in some fields (especially those related to medicine) to list only the first five authors of an article, followed by "et al."

Dates of articles are also frequently incorrect in the original bibliography, and thus are entered in SSCI/SCI under the incorrect year. Sweetland (1989) provided numerous examples of such errors, suggesting that about 7 percent of author errors were serious enough to make it difficult to locate a publication from the reference information. These errors have included misspelling the author's surname, incorrect author initials, omitting journal titles, and incorrect journal titles, page numbers, volume numbers, dates, and so forth. In a study of ten major American medical journals published in 1975, Goodrich and Roland (1977) found that, over all journals, an average of 29 percent of all citations contained errors. Similarly, Sweetland (1989) discovered author errors in 28 percent of cited articles. Other studies of citation accuracy have reached similar conclusions (e.g., Buchanan, 2006; DeLacey, Record, and Wade 1985; Lok, Chan, and Martinson 2001; Poyer 1979; Wyles 2004). It is important to note that these errors are not made by the WoS, but occur in the primary documents indexed by the WoS.

Another concern is that the WoS database includes self-citations. Self-citations are, of course, perfectly justifiable as authors commonly build on their own prior work. However, a study of citations as a measure of influence on others in a field should clearly omit self-citations.

Limitations of Google Scholar

Google Scholar (GS) was first released in 2004. It covers a wide variety of scholarly literature, including articles, books, abstracts, theses, preprints, technical reports, court opinions, and selected "scholarly" web pages. GS trawls full-text journal content and bibliographic databases. It has agreements with a number of publishers to allow it to index full-text content. One of the major advantages of GS is that it is a free service, available to anyone on the web. For individuals without the means to access fee-based databases such as ISI or Scopus, it is an extremely useful alternative (Vine, 2006).

According to Jascó (2008a), there are several positive features of GS, most of which relate to its content. The journal coverage has increased significantly, particularly after Elsevier and the American Chemical Society signed agreements to cooperate with Google and allow their digital collections to be indexed by GS. GS also includes book records, which frequently are not included in other databases. Bauer and Bakkalbasi (2005) considered that the inclusion of non-journal materials was a major strength of GS, when compared to WoS and Scopus. In addition, GS indexes documents in a wide variety of languages, including those that use other alphabets (e.g., Russian, Japanese, Korean, and Chinese). Neuhaus and Daniel (2006) also point out that the GS search interface is easy to use, although there appears to be a bias towards ranking older literature higher in the results list. Bauer and Bakkalbasi (2005) found that average citation counts obtained from GS tend to be higher than those obtained using WoS and they strongly recommend that researchers using WoS or Scopus should also consult GS.

However, Jascó (2008a, 2008b, 2009a, 2009b) also identified a number of problems with GS. One key concern is that GS does not provide any information about its coverage. There is no information as to which journals are trawled, which publishers have entered into trawling or indexing agreements with GS, or how often GS is updated, although the search can be limited to a particular time period. As Jascó (2008b: 440) pointed out, "From the launch of the service, it has been hopeless to derive any factual information from Google, Inc. regarding the dimension of the content of the database, its size, girth (width, length, and depth combined), or the sources included." As a result, there is no way to know which of the major publishers still refuse to cooperate with GS (as Elsevier did until 2007), which could significantly limit its coverage of the peer-reviewed journal literature. Bauer and Bakkalbasi (2005) echo this concern, arguing that, until GS clearly identifies what material is indexed, and how often the data are updated, "it cannot be considered a truly scholarly resource in the sense that Web of Science and Scopus are." The GS online "Help" page includes their answer to the question of what specific journals are covered, stating "Ahem, we index papers, not journals." (GoogleScholar, 2012).

Jascó has also identified some significant problems with the GS software that can greatly affect the accuracy of searches in general, and that limit the usefulness of GS as a source of data for citation analysis. First of all, GS cannot always distinguish author names from other parts of the text that is indexed. A test search by Jascó (2008a) discovered false names derived from section headings within articles, producing authors such as "P Population," "R Evaluation," "M Data," and so on. In addition, false names may be derived from options listed on the GS search menu, resulting in authors such as "P. Login" (from "Please Login) and P. Options (from "Payment Options"). In many cases, these false names replace those of the actual authors. As a result, the real authors are not only deprived of the credit for their work, but their publication and citation counts are erroneously reduced as well (Jascó, 2009a). Similarly, page numbers and phone numbers are often confused with publication years, and other software problems may produce duplicate records, artificially inflating the citation counts of a scholar. The unusual application of Boolean logic used by the GS software means that a search for "A OR B" may actually produce fewer results than a search for either "A" or "B" alone. Similarly, when searching within time ranges, GS was found to produce more hits as the time span was reduced (Jascó, 2009b).

Jascó (2008b, 438) stated that "The deficiencies in the GS software, from bibliometric and scientometric perspectives, dwarf the content limitations. The consequences are present in the entire GS universe for the simple reason that most of the problems are caused by the GS software... The problems are caused not merely by typos and other inaccuracies in the source data, nor by missing one or two highly cited articles and a dozen lowly cited papers..." He particularly points out the difficulties in computing an h-index based on unreliable GS data. Neuhaus and Daniel (2006) also have expressed their concern over using GS as a tool for citation analysis, because of the various shortcomings in the search process and source processing.

Limitations of Scopus

Scopus, a multidisciplinary abstract and citation database, was released by Elsevier in 2004. As of April 2011, it contained over 18,500 active titles from over 5,000 international publishers, including about 17,500 peer reviewed journals, about 1,800 of which are Open Access journals, 400 trade publications, 300 book series, and about 4.4 million conference papers from various proceedings and journals. This totals approximately 44.4 million records. Over 24 million patent records from five patent offices are also included, as are searches of about 315 million scientific web pages indexed via Elsevier's science-specific search engine, Scirus. Articles in press from over 3,750 journals are also included (Scopus, 2011).

While the majority of the journal titles come from the physical, life, and health sciences, there are almost 6,000 titles from the social sciences and over 2,700 titles in the arts and humanities. Unlike GS, however, Scopus is not free; it is necessary to purchase a subscription to Scopus to conduct searches. This may be a consideration for university libraries who already have a subscription to WoS; they must decide whether to retain WoS or switch to Scopus, or make the very expensive decision of subscribing to both.

Dess (2006) has identified several positive features of Scopus. It is extremely user friendly and very fast. The sort options are very functional, and the citation searching feature is an important tool. Each answer set also includes bibliometric summaries, which may be very useful to scholars.

However, Dess also pointed out a number of imitations of Scopus. One key issue is that the citation backfile only includes materials from 1996 onwards. This means that citation tracking is extremely limited. In addition, he found that the number of retrievals of web sources and patents varies greatly. For example, when Dess conducted the same search over a period of several days, he found that, while the Scopus retrievals remained constant, patent and web retrievals showed widely differing results (for example, patent retrievals ranged from a high of 470 hits to a low of only four). Another concern is that, when conducting a search, the number of hits may vary depending on the order in which the search terms are entered, particularly if the "search within" function is being used. Thus, searching for "delinquency" and then conducting a search within the results for "juvenile" may produce different results than if the two search terms were reversed.

Fingerman (2006) also points out that the natural sciences (life and health sciences, environmental, agricultural, and biological) are most heavily represented, followed by the "hard" sciences (chemistry, physics, math, engineering), while there is much more limited coverage of the social sciences. Jascó (2009c) also notes that, while the content coverage in the natural and applied sciences areas is excellent, Scopus is lacking in both the social sciences and the arts and humanities areas. Jascó particularly mentions the poor coverage of key journals in his field of Library and Information Sciences.

Jascó (2009c) also notes that over three million of the records in Scopus do not have any document type assigned. This makes it difficult to filter out certain types of documents. In addition, some of the document types are misleading. For example, book reviews from *Contemporary Psychology* (the American Psychological Association's former book review journal) may be designated either "review" or "article" (as there is no "book review" document type) or may have no document type assigned at all. He also found that, from 1975-2009, about one-third of the records in Scopus were lacking information on the country affiliation of the author or authors, and points out that Scopus only included the affiliations of all authors from 2003. Oddly enough, Jascó also found that approximately 656,000 records lacked an entry for the subject area, despite the fact that in many cases these were assigned at the journal level and could be determined quite easily.

General Limitations of Citation Analysis

In addition to the limitations discussed above, which may be specific to the use of particular online databases, there are also some more general problems of citation analysis. One of the most common objections to citation analysis is the claim that it is a crude and inaccurate measure of influence, focusing more on the quantity of citations than on the quality. However, as discussed above, citation counts correlate highly with almost all other measures of influence and scholarly prestige. It has also been suggested that high citation counts may indicate a past contribution to knowledge rather than a present or ongoing contribution (Travis 1987). However, in general, authors tend to cite more recent papers rather than older ones. Cohn and Farrington (1994a) suggested that the influence of a scholarly work decays rather like a radioactive substance. In the social sciences, Courtney, Kawchuk, and Spafford (1987) estimated that research works had a half-life of approximately six years, while Cole and Cole (1971) found that physics papers had a half-life of no more than five years.

Another issue is a possible bias against individuals working in a narrow specialty. As Chapman (1989: 340) stated, "researchers in sparsely-populated topic areas have relatively few colleagues who can cite them and few to cite. One consequence is likely to be that they are not frequently cited". Similarly, Cole and Cole (1971) pointed out that extremely influential research may not be recognized as such during the researcher's lifetime; it may be resisted or ignored (and not cited), thus depriving the researcher of proper recognition. However, they also feel that this problem may be decreasing with the increase of modern communication and evaluation systems. Garfield (1979) termed this the "Mendel syndrome", as he claimed that these critics of citation analysis inevitably point to the research of Gregor Mendel, whose research was ridiculed and ignored until well after his death, although he is now hailed as the founder of the modern science of genetics.

Smith (1989:5) claimed that "methods or recipe papers are particularly often cited and have spuriously heavy 'impact' ratings". Peritz (1983) found that methodological papers were more highly cited in sociology than theoretical or empirical articles. In psychology, Douglas (1992: 405) suggested that, if one wishes to write a highly cited article, "your best bet would be to devise or revise a paper-and-pencil test of personality or motivation, improve on a commonly used method, coin a snappy new word or phrase, or think of a new way to apply statistics". However, Garfield (1979: 363) pointed out that "methods papers do not inevitably draw a large number of references". Of the 100 most-cited works in chemistry, as compiled from SCI, he found that approximately 73 percent did not deal primarily with experimental methodology (Garfield 1977d). Similarly, Cohn and Farrington's (2007a, 2007b, 2008) research into the most-cited scholars in criminology and criminal justice journals did not find that authors of "recipe books" were among the most-cited scholars.

Another objection to citation analysis is that analysts typically do not distinguish between positive, neutral, and negative citations, or, as Chapman (1989: 341) puts it, "Citation does not necessarily denote approval". However, the evidence (e.g., Garfield 1979; Cohn and Farrington 1994a) suggests that the vast majority of citations are positive or neutral, rather than negative. Cole's (1975) analysis of 533 social deviance articles published from 1950 to 1973, specifically examining reactions to Merton's "Social structure and anomie" (1938) article, shows that the vast majority of citations to this article were positive or neutral; only 6 percent of citations were critical of Merton's work.

In any case, Cole and Cole (1971: 25) suggested that "these few pieces of research that stimulate wide criticism have, in fact, stimulated other research. Consequently, it must be considered mistaken but significant; it must be seen as work which has had an impact on future scientific research". Similarly, Cohn and Farrington (1994a: 530) pointed out that, if a scholar takes the trouble to formally criticize a work, "it is arguable that the work must have been of some substance and, hence, even its refutation has made some contribution to ... knowledge".

It also appears that citations of one work by a given author may be affected by the publication of another work. For example, Cole's (1975) study of Robert K. Merton's citations in four sociological journals found that citations of Merton (1938) were strongly affected by the publication of several other major studies which were inspired by Merton. Citations to Merton's article rose immediately following the publications of Cohen (1955) and Cloward and Ohlin (1960), but fell shortly after.

Another problem with citation analysis is that the number of citations a scholar receives may depend, at least in part, on the number of articles written by that scholar. Cohn and Farrington (see e.g., 2007a, 2007b, 2008; Cohn 2011a, 2011b) found that a scholar's high ranking could be a function either of a large number of citations of one or two major works (specialization) or of the large number of different works cited (versatility).

Chapman (1989: 341) also discussed the problem of "obliteration by incorporation"; the idea that individuals may be "so eminent and prolific in their fields that, although their names appear in the body of an article, they can elude the ordinary counting process because the writer neglects to list them in the references at the end of the text. In psychology, textual mentions of Freud, for example, are thus underrepresented in citation counts". Ferber (1986: 382) also suggested that "truly important work is no longer cited once everyone knows it". However, Garfield (1979: 365) felt that this was not a significant problem, as it only happened to works that had already made an extremely important, basic, and fundamental contribution to the field and "before the obliteration takes place, both the citation count and reputation of the scientist... usually reach a level that makes additional citation credits superfluous".

The selection of citations may be influenced by social factors such as personal likes and dislikes (e.g., Chapman 1989), attempts to please journal editors or editorial board members (e.g., Rushton 1984), a preference for citing same-sex authors (e.g., Ferber 1986), and so on. It is possible, for example, that faculty in a given university department may cite departmental colleagues as a way of boosting overall department citation counts, or may avoid citing faculty from a rival department to reduce that department's citation counts. Gilbert (1977) discussed some of the additional factors that may influence the selection of works to be cited, including the use of references as a means of persuading the scientific community of the importance and value of the work being discussed. Other factors that have been found to influence citation counts include the nationality of the authors (West and McIlwaine, 2002), the number of authors (Bornmann and Daniel, 2007), the number of pages (Bornmann and Daniel, 2007), and the methods used (Patsopoulos, Analatos, and Ioannidis, 2005). Even the name of a journal may have an effect; Smith (2008) found that changing the name of a journal appears to have a short-term negative effect on citation counts.

If citation analysis becomes a common way of evaluating academic productivity, analysts must guard against deliberate attempts to inflate citation counts. While it is probably true, as Garfield (1979) maintained, that it is difficult to use self-citations to inflate one's citation count without it becoming fairly obvious, it is also true that there are other, less obvious methods, such as the "you cite me, I'll cite you" approach. However, any such attempts would still require the scholars in question to have a reasonably high publication rate in journals that are visible and of at least of reasonably high quality.

The recent expansion of online full-text access to journals may have affected citation rates. Lawrence (2001) looked at articles in computer science and found a significant correlation between the probability that an article is freely available online and the number of times that article is cited, with articles available online receiving significantly more citations than those which were not available in e-format. The probability of an article being cited may depend on the cost and effort involved in reading it. Scholars, therefore, can inflate their citation counts by putting full-text versions of their works on their personal websites. Citations of books will inevitably decrease because obtaining them requires more cost and effort than obtaining articles electronically (although increasing publication of e-books may reverse this).

Henneken, Kurtz, Eichhorn, Accomazzi, Grant, Thompson, and Murray (2006) examined the effect of e-printing on citation rates in physics and astronomy. They focused on the impact of early access (when an article becomes available as an electronic pre-print, before it is published in a journal) and open access (when an article is available online freely and without restrictions). They found that papers available as e-prints were more likely to be read and cited than papers which did not appear as e-prints. They qualified their findings by noting that there may be a self-selection bias, so that the most important, and thus most citable, papers are more likely to be posted online. Eysenbach (2006) found similar results when examining citations of open access versus non-open access articles in biology.

Taylor (2007) looked at the impact of library access through "Big Deals" with publishers such as Elsevier, Springer, and Project Muse. A "Big Deal" is a licensing agreement that provides access to a publisher's e-journal content. These portfolio purchases provide libraries, and their users, access to journals that may not have previously been readily available. He found that citations of articles in these journals increased after a library obtained electronic access through a portfolio or Big Deal, particularly in the sciences and social sciences; only a small percentage of e-journals accessed were from the arts and humanities. Taylor (2007) did point out that articles from journals included in a portfolio had been accessible through interlibrary loan prior to the acquisition of the Big Deal and suggested that faculty were more willing to reference articles when they were easier to access.

Bugeja, Dimitrova, and Hong (2008) also found that the use of online sources varied by discipline. Their study of citations in history journals found that online citations of media history articles were rare, although they were common in other communication and journalism journals.

Finally, there are some clear ambiguities with citation analysis that Garfield (1979) has been at pains to mention. These include the fact that, while Nobel Prize winners and other similarly honored scholars have high citation rates, there are other scholars with equally high rates who have not received these types of peer recognition. In addition, some citation analysis research may not clearly differentiate between a scholar who receives a given number of citations over a short period and one who receives the same number of citations spread out over a much longer period of time.

CONCLUSIONS

We conclude that citation analysis is a valid and reliable measure of scholarly influence. Compared with other measures, such as peer rankings, awards, and election to prestigious posts or societies, citation analysis is more unbiased, objective, quantitative, transparent, and replicable. Nevertheless, citation counts are highly correlated with these other measures of scholarly prestige and influence.

There are some objections to citation analysis. First, the number of citations of a scholar depend to some extent on the number of publications of that scholar. However, publications are also a measure of scholarly influence, but somewhat less valid (since publishing a work does not guarantee that it will be read or that it will influence other scholars). Second, it is argued that citations can be highly critical. However, the evidence indicates that most citations are positive or neutral. Third, the number of citations depends on the number of scholars working on a particular topic or in a particular field. This is true. Fourth, citations can be influenced by personal likes or dislikes, attempts to curry favor with influential people such as journal editors, or explicit agreements among scholars to cite each other. While the importance of these problems (as a proportion of all citations, for example) may not be very great, more research is needed on them, and they are likely to increase as citation analysis becomes more widely used and important.

The largest source of citations used to be the citation indexes developed by the Institute for Scientific Information, including SSCI, SCI, and AHCI. In recent years, these have been integrated into a single online Web of Science, and citation data can also be obtained online from Google Scholar and Scopus, both of which first appeared in 2004. All of these citation indexes have serious problems.

A major problem is that they include self-citations, which should be excluded in any analysis of the influence of one scholar on another. A second major problem is that misspellings and mistakes in the original reference lists are carried over into the indexes, because there is no processing of the information to correct errors. A third major problem is that different people with the same names and initials may be amalgamated, just as the same person with different names is not amalgamated. A fourth major problem is changes in the coverage of indexes over time, which makes it impossible to carry out comparable longitudinal analyses to investigate, for example, changes in the most-cited scholars over time.

There are other problems that are specific to particular indexes. For example, Google Scholar is undiscriminating and sets no standards for inclusion of material, and it provides no information about its coverage or changes in coverage over time. If it includes all materials available on the Internet, a scholar could increase his or her citations by posting unpublished reports on the Internet containing numerous self-citations. In contrast, Web of Science and Scopus do specify their coverage and changes in coverage and do try to include only material that passes a minimum standard. The coverage of social science material (and international material) is greatest in Google Scholar and least in Scopus, which only includes material from 1996 onwards. Web of Science is largely limited to journals, while Scopus and Google Scholar include books.

As will be explained in Chapter 4, we have made big efforts to overcome these problems in our citation analyses. First, we have expended huge amounts of time to correct mistakes in reference lists, to distinguish different people with the same name and initials, and to amalgamate the same people with different names. We were only able to do this because we have analyzed a limited number of the most prestigious journals in criminology and criminal justice and because of our personal knowledge of many scholars. Second, we eliminated all self-citations. Third, we analyzed the same journals over time, so that we could carry out longitudinal analyses of changes in citations over a 20-year time period. We believe that our citation analyses, although relatively limited in scope, produce more valid results than any citation analyses based on any other source. And we believe that our citation analyses provide valid information about changes over time in scholarly influence in criminology and criminal justice.

Chapter 2

CITATION ANALYSIS IN DIFFERENT FIELDS

Citation analysis has been used in a variety of fields. In this chapter, some of the classic research in areas other than criminology and criminal justice will be briefly discussed. Table 2-1 summarizes the studies.

GENERAL STUDIES USING CITATION ANALYSIS

One of the earliest attempts to use citation analysis as a tool to evaluate journals was conducted by Garfield (1972), the founder of the Institute of Scientific Information (ISI) and the creator of SCI and SSCI. He conducted a systematic analysis of journal citation patterns in all journals covered by SCI in the last quarter of 1969 and found that the majority of references cited a relatively small number of journals, with only 25 journals (just over 1 percent of the journals covered by SCI) being cited in 24 percent of all references. Essentially, like Wolfgang, Figlio, and Sellin's (1972) well-known finding that a small number of "career criminals" commit a large number of crimes, Garfield found that a small number of "career cited" journals account for a large percentage of all citations to journals.

Garfield and Welljams-Dorof (1990) used the ISI database to study the different languages in which international research was conducted. They ranked the top 15 languages in the 1984 ISI database by the total number of source items. Not surprisingly, the most common language was English, with 85 percent of all source items written in that language. Similarly, the most common nationality of first authors (42 percent) was American. They also examined who wrote in which languages and who cited in which languages and found that English predominated as "the primary language of international research… also, most major scientific nations, regardless of their native language or languages, cite the English-language literature almost exclusively" (1990: 23-24).

Table 2-1. Studies Using Citation Analysis

Study	Field of study	Study focus	Citation source	Time period	Results
Garfield (1972)	General science and technology	Journal citation patterns	All journals in SCI	Last quarter of 1969	Average paper cited 1.7 times per year 25 journals (~1% of journals covered in SSCI) cited in 24% of all references
Garfield & Welljams-Dorof (1990)	General	Languages in which research conducted	ISI database	1984	85% of source items in ISI database written in English 42% of first authors American
Richards (1991)	General	Number of years in which members of Population Association of America in 1980 cited	SSCI	1981-1985	Bimodal distribution 22% of scholars cited in all 5 years 41% of scholars never cited
Richards (1991)	General	135 articles published in *J of Fertility and Sterility* in 1974	SSCI	1975-1984	Skewed distribution Total citations and number of years cited highly correlated
Buss (1976)	Psychology	Faculty of 32 Canadian psychology depts.	SSCI	1973-first half of 1975	More productive departments are more highly cited 4 depts accounted for over 50% of all citations
Endler (1977)	Psychology	Faculty of 35 Canadian psychology depts.	SSCI	1975	5 depts contributed over 55% of all citations Citation distributions skewed – disproportionately small number of psychologists had the major impact Full professors more likely to be cited Strong relationship between citations and publications
Rushton & Endler (1977)	Psychology	Faculty of 45 psychology depts in the UK	SSCI	1975	U of London and Oxford U accounted for almost 50% of all citations Citation distribution skewed Many faculty not cited
Rushton et al. (1983)	Psychology	Faculty of 39 psychology depts. in the UK	SSCI	1980-1981	Correlation between citations and production of first degrees and doctorates

Study	Field of study	Study focus	Citation source	Time period	Results
Bagby et al. (1990)	Psychology	Relative importance of attribution & cognitive dissonance theories	SSCI & SCI	1958-1987	Research activity on cognitive dissonance has declined Interest in attribution theory remained relatively constant
Gorenflo & McConnell (1991)	Psychology	Journal articles and scholars	24 introductory psychology textbooks	1985-1989	Only 12 of the most frequently cited articles were from the 1980s Median year of publication was 1968 Over 1/3 of the 79 most-cited articles were incorrectly cited in at least one textbook
Gordon & Vicari (1992)	Psychology	Scholars	Social psychology texts SSCI PsycINFO *J Experimental Social Psychology* *J Personality and Social Psychology* *Personality & Social Psychology Bulletin*	1987-1990 1987-1989 1980-1989 1980-1989	Most-cited authors in texts relatively stable Significant relationship between textbook & SSCI citation measures Significant relationship between scholarly productivity measures and SSCI citation measures No significant relationship between scholarly productivity measures and textbook citations
Pardeck et al. (1991)	Psychology; Social Work	Editorial board members in 1990 from 5 psychology and 5 social work journals	SSCI	1989	Mean citations for editorial boards in psychology higher than for those in social work
Roche & Smith (1978)	Sociology	Faculty in 24 graduate departments of sociology	SSCI	1974	Moderately strong correlations between citations and other subjective rankings and productivity measures Distinct relationship between journal reputation and its frequency of citation
Bott & Hargens (1991)	Sociology	Journal articles, books, book chapters published in 1974	SSCI	1974-1985	Positively skewed distribution of citations to journal articles Book chapters much less frequently cited than journal articles Majority of publications subsequently cited

Table 2-1. (Continued)

Study	Field of study	Study focus	Citation source	Time period	Results
Yoels (1973)	Sociology	Ph.D. dissertations	*American J of Sociology* *American Sociological Review*	1955-1969	Dissertations from 4 sociology programs accounted for over 50% of all citations to dissertations Most dissertations never cited
Hanson (1975)	Sociology	Ph.D. dissertations	Surveyed members of American Sociological Association re dissemination of their dissertations	Not stated	Dissertations likely to be cited in publications other than highly prestigious journals
Wright & Soma (1995)	Sociology	Ph.D. dissertations	*American J of Sociology* *American Sociological Review* *Social Forces*	1969-1973 1979-1983 1989-1993	Ph.D. dissertations are having a declining impact on sociological research Fewer dissertations cited over time
Wright (1995b)	Sociology	Introductory sociology textbooks	*American J of Sociology* *American Sociological Review* *Social Forces*	1960-1969; 1984-1993	Introductory textbooks highly cited in earlier period Seldom cited in recent journals
Ferber (1986)	Economics	Author vs. citer gender	*J of Economic Literature*	Sept 1982-June 1983	Researchers tend to cite a larger proportion of authors of their own sex Works by women more frequently cited in articles written by women Works by men more frequently cited in articles written by men
LaBand & Piette (1994)	Economics	Effect of type of peer review on citation count	Articles published in 28 economics journals	1984	Articles published in journals using blinded peer review cited significantly more than articles published in journals using nonblinded peer review
Smyth (1999)	Economics	Journals cited by Australian economists	*Australian Economic Papers* *Australian Economic Review* *Economic Papers* *Economic Record* *Economic Analysis & Policy*	1993-1997	Australian economists use a core of important journals Economics journals published in Australia are important to Australian economists but do not rank worldwide

Study	Field of study	Study focus	Citation source	Time period	Results
Schildt et al. (2006)	Entrepreneur-ship	Co-citation patterns in entrepreneurship related articles	SSCI	2000-2004	Entrepreneurship research highly fragmented Entrepreneurship research not highly cited outside the field
Reader & Watkins (2006)	Entrepreneur-ship	Co-citation patterns	SSCI	1972-2000	Clusters of authors exist Underlying themes characterizing and defining the field can be identified
Gregoire et al. (2006)	Entrepreneur-ship	Levels of convergence	*Frontiers of Entrepreneurship Research*	1981-2004	Convergence in entrepreneurship research exists Axes of convergence have evolved over time
Courtney et al. (1987)	Political science	Citations of articles in *Canadian J of Political Science*, 1968-1997	SSCI	Year of publication + 5 years	75% of articles cited at least once Articles more likely to be cited in non-Canadian publications Articles with Canadian content more likely to be cited English-language articles more likely to be cited
Blackburn & Mitchell (1981)	Organizational science	Citation analysis in organization sciences	*Academy of Management J* *Administrative Science Quarterly* *American J of Sociology* *American Sociological Review* *J of Applied Psychology* *Organization Behavior and Human Performance* *Personnel Psychology*	1957, 1967, 1977	Number of articles on study of organizations increased over time Relative importance of sample journals to study of organizations has increased over time
Cano & Lind (1991)	Medicine	Life cycles of "citation classics" vs. "ordinary" articles	SSCI	1957-1983	Journal articles exhibit two distinct citation life cycle patterns

Table 2-1. (Continued)

Study	Field of study	Study focus	Citation source	Time period	Results
Jones (2005)	Forensic science and legal medicine	Citations in six forensic science and legal medicine journals: *Amer J of Forensic Medicine and Pathology* *Forensic Science International* *International J of Legal Medicine* *J of Forensic Sciences* *Medicine, Science and the Law* *Science and Justice*	Thomson ISI	1981-2003	*International J of Legal Medicine* clearly dominated Two journals contained all ten of the most-cited papers published in the six journals The articles most-cited in the reference lists of the six journals all deal with aspects of forensic and population genetics
Smith (2008)	Occupational medicine	Citations in occupational medicine journals: *British J of Industrial Medicine* *J of Occupational and Environmental Medicine* *American J of Industrial Medicine* *Scandinavian J of Work* *International Archives of Occupational and Environmental Health*	Journal Citation Reports	1985-2006	Citations of all journals increased Two most highly-cited journals account for 45% of all citations of all journals
Hennekin et al. (2006)	Physics and astronomy	Impact of e-printing on citation rates of articles in four astronomy journals: *Astrophysical J* *Monthly Notices of the Royal Astronomical Society* *Astronomy & Astrophysics* *Proceedings of the Astronomical Society of the Pacific*	NASA-Smithsonian Astrophysics Data System	1985-1987 1997-1999	Articles that initially appear as arXiv e-prints more highly cited
Pancheshnikov (2007)	Library & information science	Citation patterns in faculty publications & masters theses	SCI Masters theses reference lists	2002-2004	Similarities exist in citation patterns of faculty and students Total number of citations in faculty publications over 40% higher than in student works Students cite more rarely-cited materials than faculty

Study	Field of study	Study focus	Citation source	Time period	Results
Sam & Tackie (2007)	Library & information science	Citation patterns in Ph.D. dissertations	Dissertation reference lists	1998-2004	Books and monographs more highly cited in dissertations than were journals Core group of 15 journals produced ~half of all journal citations
Chikate & Patil (2008)	Library & information science	Citation patterns in Ph.D. dissertations	Dissertation reference lists	1982-2005	42% of all citations in dissertations were to journals Over 72% of all cited articles were solo-authored Core group of 11 journals produced 1/3 of all citations of journal articles
Hutson (2002)	Archeology	Impact of gender on citation selection	American Antiquity	1977-first half of 1978; 1997 (1 issue); 1998-2000	Overall, women are cited less than would be expected by their rate of publication
			J of Field Archaeology	1989-1998	
			Ancient Mesoamerica	1990-1998	
			Southeastern Archaeology	1989-1998	
Heinzkill (2007)	Literature	Citations in English & American Literature	Articles in 42 English & American literary criticism journals mainly published in 2003	Mainly 2003	Over 75% of citations are of books rather than journal articles 55% of monographs cited are less than 20 years old Journal articles published within past 20 years most frequently cited Over 40% of cited monographs fall outside the core classifications for literature

Notes: SCI = Science Citation Index; SSCI = Social Science Citation Index; ISI = Institute of Scientific Information.

Richards (1991) proposed using the number of years in which a scholar is cited as an alternative measure of accomplishment and influence, circumventing many of the problems involved when using SSCI/SCI to obtain total citation counts. He compiled a list of the 271 scientists listed in the 1980 membership directory of the Population Association of America and determined whether each was cited in SSCI in each of the following five years, 1981 to 1985, taking care to minimize errors due to misattribution. Richards found a bimodal distribution, with 41 percent of the scholars never cited and 22 percent cited in all five years. As he noted, this skewed distribution is consistent with prior research into citation distribution.

Richards (1991) then examined 135 articles published in the *Journal of Fertility and Sterility* in 1974 and determined whether each article was cited in SSCI in the ten year period 1975-1984. He also noted articles that were cited two or more times in a given year and counted the total number of citations to each article over the ten-year period. Again, he found highly skewed distributions. He also found that the number of years cited and the total number of citations were highly correlated. Richards pointed out that years cited is easier to compute and less influenced by outliers, possibly making it a better measure of influence than total citations.

CITATION ANALYSIS IN PSYCHOLOGY

Rushton and Endler (1977) ranked 45 psychology departments in the United Kingdom based on the total number of citations each departmental faculty member received in the SSCI in 1975. They found that two of the 45 universities (the University of London and Oxford University) accounted for almost half of all citations of British psychologists. They also found that the distribution of citations across the members of the universities was significantly skewed, so that a very small number of "superstar" psychologists received a very large proportion of the citations while many faculty were not cited at all during the year. Earlier research into citations to faculty of Canadian psychology departments produced similar findings (Buss 1976; Endler 1977); Cohn, Farrington, and Sorenson (2000) would later find similar results when studying graduates of criminology and criminal justice programs (see Chapter 3). A follow-up to this research (Rushton et al., 1983) found a high correlation between total and mean citations to a university's psychology department and the number of first degrees and doctorates in psychology.

Bagby, Parker, and Bury (1990) used citation analysis to compare two key social psychological theories, attribution theory and cognitive dissonance theory, to determine whether the general consensus that cognitive dissonance theory is no longer an active area of research was true. They used one key book in each area as sources and tabulated citations to these books over the years 1958 to 1987, using SSCI and SCI, social psychology journals, and American Psychological Association journals (with the social psychology journals omitted). Based on citation counts, they confirmed their hypothesis that research into cognitive dissonance had declined while research into attribution theory had continued at a relatively constant rate.

Gorenflo and McConnell (1991) examined 24 introductory psychology textbooks published between 1985 and 1989 to determine the most-cited journal articles and scholars.

When looking at the most-cited articles, they found that three articles were cited in 22 of the 24 texts and 76 additional articles were cited in 10 or more textbooks. The median year of publication was 1968, almost 20 years before the publication of the oldest textbook examined. Of the 79 most frequently-cited articles, only 12 were published in the 1980s. Gorenflo and McConnell (1991: 10) concluded that "it typically takes 20 years or so before an article is perceived as being 'classic' by most authors of introductory psychology texts".

They also listed the most-cited authors in the textbooks, counting all citations, not just those to journal articles. They suggested that the differences between most frequently-cited authors and most frequently-cited articles was due to the fact that many of the most highly-cited authors published predominantly in book form. Gorenflo and McConnell also mentioned their concern about the large number of citation errors that they found in the textbooks.

Gordon and Vicari (1992) used citations in textbooks to study scientific eminence in social psychology. They examined eight social psychology textbooks published between 1987 and 1990, counted the total number of pages on which an author was cited in each textbook (not including bibliography pages), and summed across all eight texts. They corrected for self-citations (of the textbook author) by replacing the number of citations in the self-authored text with the mean number of citations of the author across the remaining seven textbooks. A total of 545 authors were found to have at least four citations in any one textbook or a total of ten or more citations overall. They compared their findings with citation data obtained from the 1987 to 1989 SSCI, with productivity data obtained from the PsycINFO database and from a count of publications in three key social psychology journals, and with findings from prior research into prestige in the field of social psychology. Overall, Gordon and Vicari found that the most-cited scholars in social psychology texts had remained fairly stable over the past 15 years. They reported a significant relationship between textbook citations and SSCI citations, and between citations in SSCI and scholarly productivity measures.

Pardeck et al. (1991) obtained lists of members of the editorial boards of five social work and five psychology journals during the year 1990 and counted the number of times each board member was cited in SSCI in 1989. They computed a "mean citation index" by dividing the total number of citations of all members of an editorial board by the total number of board members, and found that the mean citation indexes for editorial boards in psychology were generally higher than for those in social work. They suggested that "editorial boards of psychology journals are generally comprised of members who have higher levels of distinction and achievement within their discipline than editorial board members of social work journals" (1991: 527). However, as Cohn, Farrington, and Wright (1998) pointed out, this may not be a fair comparison. They suggested that a more accurate way to determine the distinction of editorial board members would be to compare their citation counts to those of non-board members in the same discipline, rather than comparing board members in different disciplines. It is possible that citation rates are higher overall in psychology than in social work, which could also account for the disparity noted by Pardeck et al. (1991).

CITATION ANALYSIS IN SOCIOLOGY

Roche and Smith (1978) used frequency of citations to rank departments of sociology, individual sociologists, and sociological journals. They found moderately strong correlations between citations and other subjective rankings and productivity measures, as well as a distinct relationship between the reputation of a journal and its frequency of citation.

Bott and Hargens (1991) looked at citations of journal articles, books, and edited book chapters in sociology published during 1974, using the five-year compilation volumes of SSCI. Using a random sample of 699 documents (553 journal articles, 113 sociological books, and 33 book chapters), they determined the number of citations received by each work between 1974 and 1985. They also searched around each work to check for errors in SSCI. They found a highly positively skewed distribution of citations to journal articles: the mean number of citations was 14.3, the median was 5, and the mode only 1. Less than 10 percent of the articles were never cited. Chapters in edited books were much less frequently cited than journal articles. The average book received about as many citations as an average paper in a top journal.

Overall, Bott and Hargens (1991: 155) found that "the great majority of sociological publications… are subsequently cited". This held true even when first-author self-citations were eliminated. However, the range of citation frequency was extremely large. They also found that journal-specific average citation levels were strongly correlated with other measures of journal prestige or status.

Yoels (1973) examined citations to sociology Ph.D. dissertations in articles appearing in two leading sociology journals, *American Journal of Sociology* and *American Sociological Review*, between 1955 and 1969. He found that dissertations completed by students in the most prestigious sociology departments were far more likely to be cited than dissertations completed by students in less prestigious departments and that dissertations usually were cited by the author (self-citations), the author's graduate-school professors, or the author's fellow graduate students. Yoels also found that citations to dissertations typically were made within six years of the completion of the dissertation, and that few dissertations were cited in the two journals (only 13.1 percent of the sociology dissertations completed from 1955 to 1969 were cited at least once).

On the other hand, Hanson (1975) found that, if citations in other types of publications, such as books, book chapters, monographs, research bulletins, presented papers, journal articles in less prestigious journals, and so on were included, a much larger percentage of dissertations are cited. He concluded that, "When one broadens the definition of dissemination…. a picture of more extensive transmission of dissertation results emerges" (1975: 238).

Extending this analysis from 1969 to 1993, Wright and Soma (1995) found that, over time, fewer journal articles and research notes cited sociology dissertations, fewer sociology dissertations were being cited in the journals, and the average age of cited dissertations increased markedly between the two time periods (from a mean age of 6.2 years from 1969 to 1973 to 11.2 years from 1989 to 1993). They concluded that sociology Ph.D. dissertations have had a declining impact on scholarship in sociology.

Wright (1995b) used citation analysis to add quantitative evidence to the long-standing debate in sociology over whether there ever was a "golden past" for introductory sociology textbooks, or a time when high-quality books were believed to have influenced the development of scholarship and thinking. He examined citations to introductory sociology textbooks in all articles and research notes published in three leading journals, *American Journal of Sociology*, *American Sociological Review*, and *Social Forces*, from 1960 to 1969 and from 1984 to 1993. He found that, although introductory textbooks were frequently cited during the earlier period, citations to these books all but disappeared from the journals during the later period. Wright concluded that, while introductory sociology textbooks once enjoyed a golden era, they had virtually no influence on modern sociological research.

CITATION ANALYSIS IN ECONOMICS

Ferber (1986) questioned whether researchers tended to cite members of their own gender more frequently than members of the opposite gender, hypothesizing that, in fields in which female scholars are in the minority, women are at a disadvantage in acquiring high citation counts. She obtained a sample of articles and research notes in the area of manpower, labor, and population, published between September 1982 and June 1983, and written by male authors only (MA), by female authors only (FA), or by a collaboration of at least one male and one female author (FMA). She then matched each FA and FMA article with an MA article with an identical classification from the *Journal of Economic Literature*. The references in these articles to FA, MA, and FMA publications were then counted. Self-citations were counted separately.

Ferber found that works by women were significantly more frequently cited in articles written by women than in those by men, and that the reverse was true for articles written by men. Citations in FMA articles fell somewhere in between. When articles dealing specifically with women or sex discrimination were examined separately, to test whether the results were a function of differences in subject matter, the gender differences in citation remained. She suggested several possible explanations for these findings, including the effects of networking (which may involve some segregation by gender) and the possibility that scholars tended to have a higher opinion of work by members of their own sex, and concluded by saying that "citations... should not be regarded as unbiased indicators of merit" (1986: 389).

LaBand and Piette (1994) used citation analysis to determine whether the type of peer review used in economics journals affected the citation count of articles published in those journals. In the blinded or double-blind peer review method, the identities of the authors and the reviewers are not disclosed. In the nonblinded or single-blind method, reviewers are aware of the identity of the authors of articles being reviewed, although authors do not know the identities of the reviewers. After controlling for factors such as article length and the relative quality of the publishing journal, LaBand and Piette found that articles published in journals that employed a double-blind peer review process received significantly more citations than articles published in journals using nonblinded peer review.

Smyth (1999) examined citations in articles published in five Australian economics journals to determine which journals Australian economists most commonly used in their research. As found in other disciplines, he reported that a large percentage of citations came from a small number of core journals. Smyth suggested that the results of this and similar studies could be used to assist libraries in making decisions regarding journal acquisition.

CITATION ANALYSIS IN ENTREPRENEURSHIP

Co-citation analysis has been used repeatedly in the field of entrepreneurship. Co-citations are the co-occurrence of references within articles. Authors who are frequently cited together, in the same articles or books, are considered to be related to each other. Co-citation analysis allows researchers to produce author co-citation maps, identifying authors who are frequently cited in the same papers, as well as helping to identify specialties or subfields of research through their association with a cluster of authors.

Schildt, Zahra, and Sillanpää (2006) analyzed co-citation patterns of articles related to entrepreneurship published between 2000 and 2004 to identify the dominant research streams in the field. Data on 733 articles with over 21,000 references were obtained from the SSCI. They found a total of 25 highly-cited groups of prior work on entrepreneurship, of which five were the most central. The data also allowed them to examine shifts in the importance and relative popularity of each group over time, by looking at the number of citations received by each group during the time period studied. Schildt et al. found that research in entrepreneurship was highly fragmented and that research findings were still fairly noncumulative, as shown by the limited number of citations of prior published works in the field. Even research conducted in core areas of entrepreneurship were not highly cited by scholars outside the field.

Reader and Watkins (2006) also used author co-citation analysis to examine the structure of the literature in entrepreneurship. They were able to identify nine clusters of authors whose work fell into similar areas as well as the underlying themes that defined and characterized the field.

Grégoire, Noël, Déry, and Béchard (2006) used co-citation analysis to determine levels of convergence in entrepreneurship research. Convergence refers to the idea that "as an intellectual field matures, it becomes increasingly characterized by a set of codified theories, models, methods, and/or measures – which are to direct ongoing research" (2006: 334). They examined over 20,000 references to all 960 full-length articles published in the *Frontiers of Entrepreneurship Research* series between 1981 and 2004 to analyze co-citation networks. They found a distinct evolution of the field over time. In addition, they reported that, while there has been convergence in entrepreneurship research over the past 25 years, overall levels of conceptual convergence were relatively low.

CITATION ANALYSIS IN POLITICAL SCIENCE

Courtney, Kawchuk, and Spafford (1987) looked at citations in all items (articles, review articles, notes, comments, and communications) published in the first ten volumes of the *Canadian Journal of Political Science/Revue canadienne de science politique* (*CJPS/Rcsp*) during the years 1968 to 1977. For each item, they obtained citation counts from the SSCI during its year of publication and for each of the next seven years. They found that approximately 73 percent of all items in the journal were cited at least once during the target period, with review articles being least likely to be cited. On average, English-language items were cited four times as often as those in French. Slightly more than half of all citations appeared in non-Canadian publications, while just over 25 percent were cited in *CJPS/Rcsp*.

CITATION ANALYSIS IN ORGANIZATIONAL SCIENCE

Blackburn and Mitchell (1981) examined citations in seven organizational science journals during the years 1957, 1967, and 1977. They developed four indices to summarize the citation information. The "self-feeding index" measured the frequency with which authors publishing in a given journal cited other articles published in that journal. The "producer-consumer index" measured the extent to which authors in one journal in the sample cited articles from the other journals in the sample. The "inside-outside index" examined the frequency with which authors cited articles from journals not in the sample. Finally, the "cross-pollination index" measured the exchange of knowledge among the three disciplines that made up organizational science (psychology, social psychology, and sociology).

CITATION ANALYSIS IN MEDICINE

Cano and Lind (1991) examined ten "citation classics", key articles in medicine and biochemistry with high citation counts, and compared them with ten "ordinary" articles, papers in the same fields with low-to-medium citation counts, all published between 1957 and 1960. Using SCI, they determined annual citation counts for each article during the period 1957 to 1983. They found two distinct life cycle patterns of articles. Type A consisted of a rapid accumulation of citations in the first four to seven years after publication, followed by a gradual decline. This pattern applied to some of the citation classics and all of the ordinary papers. Type B consisted of a moderate number of citations during the first six years, followed by a rapid increase. This pattern applied only to citation classics. This analysis is interesting in showing that it may take several years for an article to become highly cited (contrary to the ideas underlying the journal impact factor; see Chapter 1).

In what is the first in-depth study of citations in forensic science and legal medicine, Jones (2005) used citation analysis to identify the most highly cited articles, authors, and journals in forensic science and legal medicine between 1981 and 2003. He used data from Thomson's Institute for Scientific Information (ISI) to create a citation database for six leading journals in the field. An examination of the annual impact factors for each journal showed that the *International Journal of Legal Medicine* (IJLM) consistently dominated over the other journals. IJLM also had the highest citation impact, which was determined by dividing the number of total citations to the journal between 1997 and 2003 by the number of papers published in the journal during those years. Seven of the ten most highly-cited papers in the target journals appeared in IJLM, three were published in the *Journal of Forensic Sciences* (JFS), and none were from the other four journals. Jones also identified the articles that were most frequently cited in the reference lists of the target journals and found that they all dealt with aspects of forensic and population genetics, suggesting that citation analysis may be used to identify "hot topics" in a given field of study.

Smith (2008) conducted a citation analysis of five core journals in occupational medicine published between 1985 and 2006, using data obtained from Thomson Scientific's *Journal Citation Reports*. He found that citations of these journals increased greatly over the period of the study, rising from an average of about 5,400 per year in 1985 to almost 17,000 per year in 2006. However, the proportion of citations of each journal was not equally distributed; over the entire study period, two journals, the *Journal of Occupational and Environmental Medicine* and O*ccupational and Environmental Medicine*, accounted for approximately 45 percent of all citations of all journals. Smith also found that, in occupational medicine, there tended to be a long lag between publication and citation of an article.

Smith also determined impact factor scores for each journal in the study and found that, although the rank order of the journals varied from year to year, the impact factor score of each journal increased during the study period. He suggested that the significant increase in citations to journals in occupational medicine indicated that the field was attracting more attention in the scientific and medical community. He also discussed the applicability of citation analysis to occupational medicine, given the lag between publication and citation, and suggested that alternatives such as topic-based impact factors and journal rank indicators may be more appropriate. However, he stated that this does not mean that citation analysis is irrelevant to occupational medicine.

CITATION ANALYSIS IN PHYSICS AND ASTRONOMY

Hennekin et al. (2006) examined the impact of e-printing, or electronic preprinting, on citation rates in astronomy and physics. They found that papers available as arXiv e-prints (an archive for electronic preprints of scientific papers) were more highly cited than papers not available through these sources.

CITATION ANALYSIS IN LIBRARY AND INFORMATION SCIENCE

Pancheshnikov (2007) compared literature citations in faculty publications and masters theses in the Department of Biology of the University of Saskatchewan between 2002 and 2004. Her goal was to "assess the results of this as an indicator of literature use and as a background for collection management at a university library" (2007: 674-675). Pancheshnikov obtained data from the SCI and from the reference lists of the masters theses. Overall, she identified a number of similarities between the two sources, suggesting that patterns identified from either source could be used for basic collection management decisions. However, as faculty publications included references from significantly more sources than student theses, she concluded that faculty publications were a better and more comprehensive basis for library collection management, particularly of serial publications.

Sam and Tackie (2007) looked at over 2,000 citations in 67 dissertations accepted by the Department of Information Studies, University of Ghana, Legon, between 1998 and 2004, as a way of examining patterns in how various types of information formats (books, journals, conference proceedings, etc.) were used. They found that about 44 percent of all citations were to books and monographs and 25 percent were to journals. They also determined that, while 154 different journal titles were cited, a core group of 15 journals produced about half of all journal citations in the dissertations. Sam and Tackie pointed out that, based on their findings, libraries only have to subscribe to a small number of journals to meet the information needs of users.

Similarly, Chikate and Patil (2008) examined over 6,000 citations in 27 library and information science dissertations submitted to the University of Pune, India, between 1982 and 2005. Unlike Sam and Tackie (2007), they found much more reliance on journal articles than on books; approximately half of the citations in the dissertations studied were to journals. However, like the earlier study, they also found that a small core group of eleven journals produced about one-third of all citations of journal articles.

CITATION ANALYSIS IN ARCHEOLOGY

Hutson (2002) examined citation practices in four major archeology journals, looking at the impact of gender on citation selection. He grouped articles into four categories: articles by male authors only, articles by female authors only, mixed gender authorship articles with a male first author, and mixed gender authorship articles with a female first author. He found mixed results regarding equity issues for women scholars. In three of the journals, men were found to cite women at rates similar to those at which women cited women, although this was not always the case in all journals. In the fourth journal, the rate at which men cited women was significantly less than the rate at which women cited women. He also found that, overall, women were cited less than would be expected on the basis of their rate of publication.

Hutson also discussed a number of additional factors, other than the gender of the citing author, that could impact the rate of citation to women. These included gender segregation in research interests (both topical and regional specialization), the development of personal networks, the professional age of the citing author, the prestige of the citing author, and the total number of citations per paper. When these were examined, he found that, while specialization had some impact, the effects of author age and total number of citations were not significant.

CITATION ANALYSIS IN LITERATURE

Heinzkill (2007) looked at over 20,000 citations in 555 articles published in 42 English and American journals focusing on literary criticism. He found that about 76 percent of all citations were of books, while approximately 20 percent of citations were of journal articles. Heinzkill was also able to examine the characteristics of the works cited. The majority of cited books in both English and American literary scholarship were published within the past 20 years; journal articles published within that time frame were also most frequently cited. One unique finding of Heinzkill's study was that English and American literature was actually a very interdisciplinary field. The citations covered a very wide variety of subjects, many of which were well outside the expected literature topics, and nearly every general category in the Library of Congress subject classification system was represented.

CONCLUSIONS

Citation analysis is used widely in many different disciplines. Articles on citation analysis in different disciplines have yielded important insights into useful concepts and useful methods that could be applied to criminology and criminal justice.

Chapter 3

CITATION ANALYSIS IN CRIMINOLOGY AND CRIMINAL JUSTICE

As in other fields, the use of citation analysis in the field of criminology and criminal justice (CCJ) has become increasing popular. The technique has been widely used to evaluate the prestige and influence of scholars, journals, and university departments.

Wolfgang, Figlio, and Thornberry (1978) produced what is probably the most famous citation analysis study in criminology, and possibly the most in-depth study in any subject. They examined citations in a total of 3,690 scholarly works published between 1945 and 1972, including 556 American criminology books (excluding textbooks) and 3,134 journal articles. Using SCI (which was then only available in printed form), they counted the number of citations to each work. An examination of raw frequencies of citations revealed a characteristically skewed distribution, so that, rather than citations being evenly distributed over the source works, a small number of works were highly cited and the rest received few or no citations. About 0.5 percent of all scholarly works received about 25 percent of all citations, and about 2.2 percent of works received about 50 percent of all citations. Over 57 percent of all the source works were never cited. Their findings mirror those of Garfield (1972), again demonstrating that a small number of "career cited" works in criminology account for a large percentage of all citations.

MOST-CITED SCHOLARS

The Research of Ellen G. Cohn and David P. Farrington

In the first application of citation analysis to British criminology, Cohn and Farrington (1990) investigated the differences between British and American criminology, using one American journal (*Criminology*) and one British journal (*British Journal of Criminology*). They examined all articles published in each journal during 1984 to 1988 and counted all citations of articles published in the journals from 1974 to 1983. They found that articles published in the *British Journal of Criminology* were rarely cited in *Criminology*, and that the rate of citation of *British Journal of Criminology* in *Criminology* articles and in SSCI increased with the quantitativeness of the article.

Cohn and Farrington (1994a) next applied citation analysis to determine the most influential scholars in the English-speaking world. Table 3-1 summarizes CCJ citation analyses of scholars. They broadened their research to include not only England and the United States but also Canada (using the *Canadian Journal of Criminology*) and Australia and New Zealand (using the *Australian and New Zealand Journal of Criminology*). They determined the most-cited scholars in each journal during the five-year period 1986 to 1990 and calculated the correlations between rankings in the four journals. They found that, while those scholars who were highly-cited in *Criminology* tended also to be highly-cited in the other three journals, the reverse was not true. The correlations between the most highly-cited scholars in the *Australian and New Zealand Journal of Criminology* and in the other three journals were negative, suggesting that it was the most isolated journal. A combined measure of influence, which controlled for the number of citations in a journal and gave equal weight to citations in all journals, found that only four scholars, all Americans (Marvin E. Wolfgang, Alfred Blumstein, James Q. Wilson, and Michael J. Hindelang), were ranked among the top 50 in all four journals. Levi (1995) criticized this article and Cohn and Farrington (1995) replied to his criticisms.

Table 3-1. Citation Analyses of Scholars

Study	Unusual features	Journals investigated	Time period	Results – most cited scholars
Cohn & Farrington (1994a)		Australian & New Zealand J of Criminology British J of Criminology Canadian J of Criminology Criminology	1986-1990	Marvin E. Wolfgang Alfred Blumstein David P. Farrington James Q. Wilson Stanley Cohen
Cohn & Farrington (1998a)		Australian & New Zealand J of Criminology British J of Criminology Canadian J of Criminology Criminology	1991-1995	Travis Hirschi David P. Farrington Michael R. Gottfredson Alfred Blumstein John Braithwaite
Cohn & Farrington (2007a)		Australian & New Zealand J of Criminology British J of Criminology Canadian J of Criminology Criminology	1996-2000	John Braithwaite David Garland David P. Farrington Richard V. Ericson Ken Pease
Cohn (2011a)		Australian & New Zealand J of Criminology British J of Criminology Canadian J of Criminology Criminology	2001-2005	David P. Farrington Robert J. Sampson Travis HIrschi Michael R. Gottfredson Lawrence W. Sherman
Cohn & Farrington (1994b)		Criminal Justice and Behavior Criminology Justice Quarterly J of Criminal Justice J of Quantitative Criminology J of Research in Crime and Delinquency	1986-1990	Marvin E. Wolfgang Michael J. Hindelang Alfred Blumstein Travis Hirschi Michael R. Gottfredson

Study	Unusual features	Journals investigated	Time period	Results – most cited scholars
Cohn & Farrington (1998b)		Criminal Justice and Behavior Criminology Justice Quarterly J of Criminal Justice J of Quantitative Criminology J of Research in Crime and Delinquency	1991-1995	Travis Hirschi Michael R. Gottfredson Robert J. Sampson Alfred Blumstein Lawrence E. Cohen
Cohn & Farrington (2007b)		Criminal Justice and Behavior Criminology Justice Quarterly J of Criminal Justice J of Quantitative Criminology J of Research in Crime and Delinquency	1996-2000	Travis Hirschi Michael R. Gottfredson David P. Farrington Robert J. Sampson Delbert S. Elliott
Cohn (2011b)		Criminal Justice and Behavior Criminology Justice Quarterly J of Criminal Justice J of Quantitative Criminology J of Research in Crime and Delinquency	2001-2005	David P. Farrington Robert J. Sampson Travis Hirschi Francis T. Cullen Raymond Paternoster
Cohn, Farrington, & Wright (1998)		Australian & New Zealand J of Criminology British J of Criminology Canadian J of Criminology Criminal Justice and Behavior Criminology Justice Quarterly J of Criminal Justice J of Quantitative Criminology J of Research in Crime and Delinquency	1991-1995	Travis Hirschi Michael R. Gottfredson David P. Farrington Alfred Blumstein Marvin E. Wolfgang
Cohn & Farrington (1996)		Crime and Justice: A Review of Research	1979-1993	Michael J. Hindelang Alfred Blumstein Marvin E. Wolfgang Donald J. West Sheldon E. Glueck
Cohn, Farrington, & Wright (1998)		20 journals	1990	Marvin E. Wolfgang Travis Hirschi David P. Farrington Alfred Blumstein Michael R. Gottfredson
Cohn & Farrington (1999)		20 journals	1995	Lawrence W. Sherman Travis Hirschi Michael R. Gottfredson David P. Farrington
Cohn & Farrington (2008)		20 journals	2000	Robert J. Sampson David P. Farrington Francis T. Cullen Travis Hirschi

Table 3-1. (Continued)

Study	Unusual features	Journals investigated	Time period	Results – most cited scholars
Wright & Sheridan (1997)	Most cited scholars in women and crime issues	Women & Criminal Justice J of Criminal Justice Education Ten books on women & crime	1990-1994 1992 1990-1996	Meda Chesney-Lind Carol Smart Kathleen Daly Lynn E. Zimmer Rebecca E. Dobash Russell P. Dobash
Wright & Miller (1998)	Most cited scholars in police studies	American J of Police Criminology Justice Quarterly Police Forum Police Studies Policing & Society	1991-1995	Lawrence W. Sherman David H. Bayley Herman Goldstein James Q. Wilson Jerome H. Skolnick
Wright & Friedrichs (1998)	Most cited scholars in critical criminology	Crime, Law & Social Change J of Human Justice Social Justice 5 books	1991-1995 1980-1997	Jock Young Richard Quinney Brian D. MacLean John Lea Michel Foucault
Wright & Miller (1999)	Most cited scholars in corrections	Criminology J of Research in Crime & Delinquency J of Criminal Justice Justice Quarterly The Prison J	1992-1996	Francis T. Cullen Joan Petersilia Timothy J. Flanagan Bruce G. Link Nancy T. Wolfe
Wright, Bryant, & Miller (2001)	Most cited scholars in white-collar crime	Crime & Delinquency Criminology J of Research in Crime & Delinquency Justice Quarterly Law & Society Review 7 textbooks on white-collar crime	1990-1999	John Braithwaite Gilbert Geis Marshall B. Clinard Peter C. Yeager Stanton Wheeler
Shichor (1982)		20 introductory criminology textbooks	1976-1980	Edwin H. Sutherland Donald R. Cressey Marvin E. Wolfgang Richard Quinney
Wright (1995a)		23 introductory criminology textbooks	1989-1993	Travis Hirschi Edwin H. Sutherland Donald R. Cressey James Q. Wilson Marvin E. Wolfgang
Wright & Soma (1996)		53 introductory criminology textbooks	1963-1968; 1976-1980; 1989-1993	Little stability over time
Wright & Cohn (1996)		16 introductory criminal justice textbooks	1989-1993	James Q. Wilson Samuel Walker Lawrence W. Sherman Joan Petersilia George L. Kelling

Study	Unusual features	Journals investigated	Time period	Results – most cited scholars
Wright (2000)		22 introductory criminology textbooks	1994-1998	Travis Hirschi Edwin H. Sutherland Michael R. Gottfredson Marvin E. Wolfgang James Q. Wilson
Wright (2002)		23 introductory criminal justice textbooks	1994-1998	Samuel Walker Kathleen F. Maguire Joan Petersilia Lawrence W. Sherman Ann L. Pastore
Stack (2001)	Examined faculty in MA-level CCJ departments	SSCI	1988-2000	Steven Stack Richard Dembo John Laub Ann Witte Thomas Mieczkowski
Giblin & Schafer (2008)		12 reading lists for Ph.D. comprehensive examinations	2006	Robert J. Sampson Francis T. Cullen Travis Hirschi Raymond Paternoster John H. Laub
Rock (2005)		*British J of Delinquency* *British J of Criminology*	1951 1960, 1970, 1980, 1990, 2000	Hans Eysenck David Garland John Braithwaite

After collecting another five years of data, from 1991 to 1995, Cohn and Farrington (1998a; see also Cohn, Farrington, and Wright, 1998) again determined the most-cited scholars and looked at changes over time, comparing their results to those obtained from the earlier time period. The most-cited scholars on the combined measure of influence were Travis Hirschi, David P. Farrington, Michael R. Gottfredson, Alfred Blumstein, and John Braithwaite. Only two scholars (Farrington and Marvin Wolfgang, who was ranked 9th overall) were among the 50 most-cited scholars in all four journals, and only Wolfgang was among the 50 most-cited in all four journals in both time periods.

Cohn and Farrington (2007a) repeated the process again with data from 1996 to 2000, and again compared the results with the earlier waves of data. For 1996 to 2000, the most-cited scholars were John Braithwaite, David Garland, David P. Farrington, and Richard V. Ericson (who had not been among the most-cited scholars in either of the earlier studies). No scholar was among the most-cited in all four journals in this time period.

Finally, Cohn (2011a) collected a fourth wave of data for the years 2001 to 2005. The most-cited scholars in all four journals were David P. Farrington, Robert J. Sampson, Travis Hirschi, and Michael R. Gottfredson. Unlike the prior time period, in which no scholar was among the most-cited in all four journals, in this study the top four scholars all were among the most-cited scholars in all four journals, and the next two (Lawrence W. Sherman and

Terrie E. Moffitt) were among the most-cited in three journals. Some of these results are presented in Chapter 5.

In addition to analyzing international journals, Cohn and Farrington (1994b) also examined citations in six major American criminology and criminal justice journals in 1986 to 1990 and found that the most-cited authors in these journals were Marvin E. Wolfgang, Michael J. Hindelang, and Alfred Blumstein. Cohn and Farrington also studied the most-cited works by these authors to determine in what areas and topics their influence lay during that time period. It was determined that "their influence was linked to the perceived importance of criminal career research and the longitudinal method, measuring crime and delinquency, and the prestigious National Academy of Science Reports" (1994b: 532).

Cohn and Farrington (1998b; see also Cohn, Farrington, and Wright, 2008) extended this research to encompass the next five years of data (1991 to 1995) and found that the most-cited scholars in the six American journals were Travis Hirschi, Michael R. Gottfredson, Robert J. Sampson, and Alfred Blumstein. Hirschi was the only scholar who was ranked in the top five in both categories of criminology and criminal justice journals. When they compared the results to the previous time period, they found that 28 of the top 50 most-cited scholars in 1991-95 were also ranked in the top 50 in 1986-90. The most-cited works of the most-cited scholars were primarily theoretical, or devoted to longitudinal or criminal career research.

Cohn and Farrington (2007b) continued this longitudinal analysis, examining the next five-year period, 1996 to 2000. The most-cited scholars in the six journals during this time period were Travis Hirschi, Michael R. Gottfredson, David P. Farrington, Robert J. Sampson, and Delbert S. Elliott. Hirschi also was ranked among the ten most-cited scholars in each of the six individual journals studied. In most cases, the most-cited works of these scholars were books rather than journal articles.

Cohn (2011b) again extended this analysis, using a fourth wave of data for the years 2001 to 2005. The most-cited scholars in all six journals in this time period were David P. Farrington, Robert J. Sampson, Travis Hirschi, Raymond Paternoster, and Michael R. Gottfredson. Some of these results are presented in Chapter 5.

Cohn, Farrington, and Wright (1998) compared their lists of the most-cited scholars in nine leading American and international journals between 1991 and 1995 with lists developed from Wolfgang, Figlio and Thornberry's (1978) analysis of scholarly articles and books published between 1945 and 1972, Wright and Soma's (1996) study of introductory criminology textbooks published between 1963 and 1968, and Wright's (1995a) and Wright and Cohn's (1996) analysis of introductory criminology textbooks published between 1989 and 1993. This produced a longitudinal study of the most-cited scholars in criminology and criminal justice from 1945 to 1995. While they did find some similarity between the most-cited scholars in earlier and recent textbooks, there was almost no agreement between the most-cited scholars in earlier and recent academic publications. They concluded that, "In general, we found more change than continuity over time when considering the most-cited scholars in criminology and criminal justice" (Cohn, Farrington, and Wright, 1998: 86).

Cohn and Farrington's (1996) next research project focused specifically on articles published in *Crime and Justice: A Review of Research*, a serial publication, between 1979 and 1993. All 12 general volumes were examined, looking separately at the six issues published in 1979 to 1985 and the six issues published in 1986 to 1993. They found that the most-cited scholars in both time periods combined were again Hindelang, Blumstein, and Wolfgang.

When citation rankings in *Crime and Justice* during the 1986 to 1993 time period were compared with the 1986 to 1990 data from their prior research using journals, Cohn and Farrington found significant positive correlations between scores in *Crime and Justice* and scores in American criminology journals, American criminal justice journals, and international criminology journals. However, citation rankings from 1979 to 1985 in *Crime and Justice* were negatively correlated with the 1986 to 1993 data, and uncorrelated with scores in the journals, suggesting that there were changes in influence between the two time periods.

Cohn and Farrington (1996) also examined SSCI to determine the most-cited works in criminology and criminal justice. They searched SSCI for citations of over 350 CCJ books and articles that were considered to be important and that they expected to be highly cited, and listed the most-cited works during 1979 to 1985 and 1986 to 1993. One interesting finding was that the most-cited works tended to be books rather than journal articles. Cohn and Farrington also attempted to develop some basic mathematical models of citation careers of works, along the lines of age-crime research (see Farrington, 1986). They showed citation careers of specific works, distinguishing between careers that were increasing, those that were decreasing, those that were curvilinear (increasing to a peak number of citations per year and then decreasing), and those that were stable. Quantitatively-oriented research monographs were relatively more highly cited in *Crime and Justice*, while more general, qualitative, non-technical, or theoretical works were relatively more highly cited in SSCI.

One criticism that was leveled against much of the research conducted by Cohn and Farrington was that it was based on a relatively small number of mainstream journals, and that there might be a bias against scholars in more specialized areas. In response to this, Cohn, Farrington, and Wright (1998) expanded the range of their research to include citations in 20 journals published in 1990. They examined citations from five American criminology journals, five American criminal justice journals, five international criminology journals, and five international criminal justice journals. As in their earlier research, they used a combined measure of influence to control for journal size and to ensure that citations in all journals were given equal weight. The most-cited scholars in all 20 journals were Marvin E. Wolfgang, Travis Hirschi, David P. Farrington, Alfred Blumstein, and Michael R. Gottfredson.

Cohn and Farrington (1999) continued this study, collecting data from the same 20 journals for the year 1995 and comparing the results with those obtained from the earlier study. The most-cited scholars in all 20 journals in 1995 were Lawrence W. Sherman, Travis Hirschi, Michael R. Gottfredson, and David P. Farrington. Surprisingly, Marvin E. Wolfgang, the most-cited scholar in 1990, did not even appear in the table of most-cited scholars in 1995. Cohn and Farrington also noted that citation counts were correlated with other indicators of scholarly prestige; for example, many of the most-cited scholars had received awards from or served as president of the American Society of Criminology. They also compared the results of this study to the most-cited scholars in the nine American and international journals that they had studied before and found a considerable overlap in the most-cited scholars. Ten of the twenty most-cited scholars in twenty journals in 1995 were also among the twenty most-cited scholars in nine journals in 1991-1995, and twelve of the twenty most-cited scholars in twenty journals in 1990 were among the 21 most-cited scholars in nine journals in 1986-1990.

Cohn and Farrington (2008) collected a third wave of citation data, for the year 2000, and compared the results with the earlier findings. The most-cited scholars in the twenty journals in 2000 were Robert J. Sampson, David P. Farrington, Francis T. Cullen, and Travis Hirschi. A comparison of the citation rankings over the three waves of data clearly shows the advance of younger scholars, such as Sampson, and the decline of older (and in some cases, deceased) scholars such as Marvin E. Wolfgang. Eight of the ten most-cited scholars in 2000 had been among the top forty in 1995. When the results were compared with the most-cited scholars in the nine American and international journals for the years 1996-2000, Cohn and Farrington again found considerable overlap. Eight of the twenty most-cited scholars in the twenty journals in 2000 were also among the twenty most-cited scholars in the nine journals. Chapter 7 extends this series of analyses of citations in twenty journals to 2005.

Cohn, Farrington, and Wright (2008) combined citation and publication analysis when they rated journal prestige based on an analysis of where scholars publish, using what they termed the "luminaries technique". They compiled a master list of the most-cited scholars in CCJ, using results from Cohn and Farrington (1994b), Wright (1995a), and Wright and Cohn (1996). A list of 85 scholarly journals with a continuous publication record from 1990 to 1994 that primarily published articles and research notes in CCJ was compiled using two bibliographies of journals (Vaughn and del Carmen, 1992; Wright and Rogers, 1996).

Cohn et al. (2008) determined the authors of all articles and research notes in these journals during the years of the study and ranked the journals based both on an unweighted system that did not consider the number of co-authors as well as a weighted system that considered the fraction of authorship attributed to the most-cited scholars (or luminaries). Journals were standardized based on the number of articles and research notes published. Approximately 58 percent of the journals contained at least one article or research note authored or co-authored by a luminary. When the rankings obtained by the luminary analysis were compared to other journal rankings obtained using reputational (Williams, McShane, and Wagoner, 1995), citation (Stack, 1987), and composite (Sorensen, Patterson, and Widmayer, 1992) methods, all rank order correlations were statistically significant. They concluded that the luminaries procedure "appears to be a promising new way to evaluate periodicals" (Cohn, Farrington, and Wright, 1998: 99).

The Research of Richard A. Wright

Richard A. Wright and colleagues conducted a series of studies examining the most-cited scholars and works in specific sub-fields of criminology. One notable difference in Wright's subject-specific studies is that, instead of including self-citations (as Wright did in some of his citation analyses of textbooks; see below) or deliberately excluding them (as Cohn and Farrington did in their research), Wright developed a formula to adjust for self-citations that projected the average number of citations a scholar receives in works that s/he did not write into works that s/he did write (see, e.g., Wright and Friedrichs, 1998 for a detailed explanation of his approach towards self-citations).

Noting that few women, or scholars researching women and crime issues, appeared in the lists of most-cited scholars in citation studies of CCJ, Wright and Sheridan (1997) looked at the most-cited scholars and works in women and crime publications, including books, edited books, and journal articles. Their findings are noticeably different from those obtained by Cohn and Farrington's research using leading journals or Wright and colleagues' research examining introductory textbooks, suggesting that "women scholars and women and crime scholarship are neglected in the leading criminology and criminal justice journals and textbooks" (Wright and Sheridan, 1997: 50). In addition, their list of the 29 most-cited works in women and crime publications bears little resemblance to the 29 most-cited works identified by Cohn and Farrington's (1996) analysis of publications listed in the SSCI; it appears that books and articles that are considered important in scholarships on women and crime are not those generally recognized as influential in the broader field of CCJ.

Wright and Miller (1998) examined the most-cited scholars and works in police studies, analyzing articles and research notes in the area of police studies that were published in two general criminology and criminal justice journals, *Criminology* and *Justice Quarterly*, as well as all articles and research notes in four journals specifically devoted to policing from 1991 to 1995, to compile a list of the 50 most-cited scholars in police studies. Wright and Miller compared their list to those obtained in other citation analysis research, including Cohn and Farrington's (1994b) list of most-cited scholars in six leading American criminology and criminal justice journals, Cohn and Farrington's (1996) list of most-cited scholars in *Crime and Justice*, Wright's (1995a) list of most-cited scholars in 23 recent introductory criminology textbooks, and Wright and Cohn's (1996) list of most-cited scholars in 16 recent introductory criminal justice textbooks. There was little overlap with any of these other studies, suggesting that scholarly works considered important in police studies are overlooked in more general citation studies.

Wright and Friedrichs (1998) pointed out that most citation research in criminology and criminal justice, particularly studies that focus on citations in academic journals, examined works by mainstream scholars, which may inadvertently marginalize critical criminologists. They used citation analysis to study critical criminology, examining 18 books published between 1980 to 1997 (nine of which were edited volumes) and three journals devoted primarily to critical criminological issues (published from 1991 to 1995) to determine the most-cited scholars in critical criminology and the most-cited works. Overall, they found that Jock Young was by far the most prominent figure in the field. Interestingly, all of the most-cited works were books; no articles, book chapters, or other types of publications appeared on the list of the most-cited works in critical criminology. When Wright and Friedrichs (1998) compared their findings to those of studies of highly-cited scholars in mainstream CCJ journals and textbooks, they found that their results were highly divergent and that few critical criminologists appeared on general lists of most-cited scholars in CCJ.

Wright and Miller (1999) then examined journal articles and research notes in the area of corrections that were published between 1992 and 1996 to determine the most-cited scholars and works in that field. As in Wright's other topic-specific research, a comparison of the results to those of general citation studies in CCJ showed little similarity in the lists of highly-cited scholars.

Wright, Bryant, and Miller (2001) next turned their attention to the area of white-collar crime, examining articles and textbooks published in that area between 1990 and 1999. Again, there was little convergence between their lists of most-cited scholars and those of researchers conducing general citation studies in CCJ textbooks and journals.

Shichor (1982) examined citations in 20 introductory criminology textbooks published between 1976 and early 1980 to determine the most influential scholars in the field. Following a procedure used in earlier citation analyses of sociology textbooks (Bain 1962; Oromaner 1968), Shichor first compiled a list of all scholars who received at least five citations in at least 40 percent (eight or more) of the textbooks, and then counted the total number of citations received by each of these scholars. Using this rather arbitrary technique, the four most-cited scholars were Edwin H. Sutherland, Donald R. Cressey, Marvin E. Wolfgang, and Richard Quinney. Shichor found that, with one exception (James Q. Wilson), the 19 most-cited scholars in the textbooks were all sociologists; however, he also noted that almost all the texts analyzed were written by sociologists.

Allen (1983) criticized Shichor's (1982) work, discussing the process of textbook review and publication, and suggesting that citations in textbooks may be affected by editorial policy and production factors. He suggested that "one of the latent factors in citations may be the insistence by reviewers and editors that more citations be made to major criminologists, those with substantial reputations, with recognized prominence in the field, or with substantial numbers of former students who might adopt the proposed work" (1983: 177). In reply, Shichor (1983: 197) accepted Allen's comments, but argued that the most highly-cited scholars in the textbooks may still be considered to be the most influential, "since their works are being communicated to the largest audience and will be used by the students".

Richard A. Wright and his associates conducted a series of studies that extended the analysis of the most-cited scholars to later introductory CCJ textbooks. Using the same technique as Shichor (1982), Wright (1995a) compiled a list of the 47 most-cited scholars in 23 introductory criminology textbooks published from 1989 to 1993. Comparing these findings to those of Shichor (1982) and Cohn and Farrington (1994b), Wright (1995a) found higher correlations between the most-cited scholars in earlier and later criminology textbooks than between the most-cited scholars in recent criminology textbooks and recent journals. He noted that scholars who were extensively cited in recent textbooks but not in journals tended to be criminological theorists whose publications appeared decades ago (e.g. Emile Durkheim, Edwin H. Sutherland, and George B. Vold); scholars who were extensively cited in recent journals but not textbooks were largely quantitative researchers whose work appeared recently (within the previous 15 years; e.g., Suzanne S. Ageton, Richard A. Berk, Jacqueline Cohen, Marvin D. Krohn, and Robert J. Sampson).

Again using the same technique as Shichor (1982), Wright and Soma (1996) compiled a list of the 65 most-cited scholars in 53 introductory criminology textbooks published during three five-year periods, 1963 to 1968, 1976 to 1980, and 1989 to 1993. They found little stability among the most-cited scholars over time; only seven names (10.8 percent) appeared among the most-cited scholars in all three time periods (Albert K. Cohen, Marshall B. Clinard, Donald R. Cressey, Thorsten Sellin, Edwin H. Sutherland, Gresham M. Sykes, and Marvin E. Wolfgang). They concluded that prominence was ephemeral for most scholars in criminology, although they linked several career factors to the likelihood of enduring fame, including longevity, perseverance, and breadth of scholarship (i.e., making important theoretical and empirical contributions, while conducting research in several different areas).

Once again using the same technique, Wright and Cohn (1996) identified the 22 most-cited scholars in 16 introductory criminal justice textbooks published from 1989 to 1993. Comparing these findings to those of Wright (1995a) and Cohn and Farrington (1994b), they found fairly low correlations between the most-cited scholars in recent criminal justice journals and textbooks. While the most-cited scholars in introductory criminal justice textbooks were primarily applied (or practitioner/policy-oriented) researchers, and the most-cited scholars in introductory criminology textbooks were mostly academic researchers (especially criminological theorists), those who were extensively cited in criminal justice journals included a mixture of applied and academic researchers.

In two closely related articles, Wright (1996, 1997) used citation analysis to estimate the match between what journals report and what textbooks discuss. By comparing the most-cited scholars in recent leading journals (see Cohn and Farrington 1994b) to the most-cited scholars in recent textbooks (Wright, 1995a; Wright and Cohn, 1996), Wright ranked 39 textbooks in criminology (1996) and criminal justice (1997) by how extensively they cited the same scholars who were heavily cited in the journals. Wright (1997: 84) interpreted these rankings as "empirical estimates of the extent to which particular textbooks prominently discussed the same influential scholars and studies that were featured in the leading journals," but stressed that they were not intended to serve as an indicator or assessment of textbook quality.

Two studies have demonstrated the declining influence of criminology textbooks (Wright and Carroll, 1994) and criminology textbook authors (Wright, 1998) on recent scholarship. Wright and Carroll (1994) compared citations to 45 textbooks published from 1918 to 1965 and 49 textbooks published from 1976 to 1985 in seven leading criminology, criminal justice, and sociology journals appearing from 1966 to 1972 and from 1986 to 1992. They found that the earlier textbooks were cited far more often in the journals than were the newer texts, suggesting that criminology textbooks, like introductory sociology textbooks (Wright, 1995b), once enjoyed a golden era during which they substantially impacted scholarship. In a related study, Wright (1998) showed that the authors of criminology textbooks years ago were better known scholars than were the more recent authors. When 23 authors and coauthors of criminology textbooks appearing from 1936 to 1965 were compared to 55 authors and coauthors of criminology textbooks appearing from 1984 to 1993, a far larger percentage of the former were rated among the most-cited scholars of their time. Over time, the writers of CCJ textbooks have generally become more specialized and published less in scholarly journals.

Wright (2000) looked at the most-cited scholars in 22 introductory criminology textbooks published between 1994 and 1998, the five-year period immediately following his prior study of introductory criminology textbooks (Wright, 1995a). This allowed him to analyze changes in citation patterns in these textbooks over time; he also compared his findings to several other studies of citations in criminology textbooks (Shichor, 1982; Wright and Soma, 1996) as well as to citation studies of the most-cited scholars in leading American criminology journals (Cohn and Farrington, 1994b, 1998b). Wright (2000: 123) found that, in general, "there is more agreement between the most-cited scholars in leading criminology journals over time and in criminology textbooks over time than between the most-cited scholars in journals and in textbooks over time or at the same time". He also found an apparent lag effect, suggesting that textbooks lag several years behind journals in reporting the research of well-known and highly-cited scholars.

Finally, Wright (2002) compiled a list of influential scholars, using data from previous citation studies of introductory CCJ textbooks, to determine citation counts of these scholars in 23 introductory criminal justice textbooks published between 1994 and 1998, to investigate changes in citation patterns over time. He compared his rankings with those obtained in previous studies of introductory textbooks (Wright 1995a, 2000; Wright and Cohn 1996) and with those obtained by Cohn and Farrington (1994b, 1998b) in their studies of the most-cited scholars in leading CCJ journals. As Wright (2000) found in his earlier study of criminology textbooks, he discovered that there was more agreement between the most-cited scholars over time in the same type of publication (either journals or textbooks), than between the two types of publications.

Cohn, Farrington, and Wright (1998) applied citation analysis to the question of the degree of convergence or divergence between the two academic disciplines of criminology and criminal justice, as well as considering the possibility of a third paradigm, that of complementarity. They reanalyzed data from two previous citation studies of textbooks (Wright, 1995a; Wright and Cohn, 1996) as well as two previous citation studies of journals (Cohn and Farrington 1994b; Cohn, Farrington, and Wright, 1998) in CCJ. From these studies, they compiled lists of the most-cited scholars in criminology *or* criminal justice publications (to consider divergence or complementarity) and in criminology *and* criminal justice publications (to consider convergence). Cohn et al. (1998) found only a weak association between the most cited scholars in criminology and criminal justice textbooks, which appeared to contradict the convergence perspective.

Further support for either the divergence or complementarity approach came when they examined the specific areas of expertise of the most-cited scholars. They concluded that those scholars who were highly cited in only criminology textbooks were known for contributions to the etiology of crime, while those who were highly cited in only criminal justice textbooks were well known for studying criminal justice institutions or subsystems. Many of the scholars who were highly cited in both groups of textbooks had made contributions to both areas, so the textbooks could be citing and discussing different areas of their expertise. For example, Gresham M. Sykes was known for both neutralization theory (Sykes and Matza, 1957) and for his classic study of prisons (Sykes, 1958). Cohn et al. (1998) suggested that the criminology texts were citing and discussing Sykes' etiological work while the criminal justice texts were citing and discussing his prison studies.

An examination of citations in journals continued to provide support for the divergence or complementarity perspectives, as the relationship between the most-cited scholars in the two sets of journals was also fairly weak. Overall, Cohn et al. (1998) found clear evidence that publications in criminology cited different prominent scholars than those who were cited in publications in criminal justice. They concluded, however, by suggesting that, rather than criminology and criminal justice being two separate disciplines, they may be two parts of one discipline, supporting each other in a complementary relationship.

Other Research on Most-Cited Scholars

Stack (2001) examined the impact on scholarly productivity in criminal justice of the field of terminal degree, looking at faculty in master's-level criminal justice departments. While he focused primarily on publication productivity (see Chapter 8), he also examined citations. The study was restricted to criminal justice departments that offered a master's degree but not a Ph.D. in criminal justice, housed in large universities (with a student enrollment of at least 20,000 students) that offered Ph.D. degrees in other fields and that were located in large cities (at least 250,000 people). A total of ten programs were identified and data on citations received to articles published by the faculty in these programs were obtained from SSCI for the years 1988 through 2000. Overall, Stack found that the most-cited authors in these departments were Steven Stack, Richard Dembo, John Laub, Ann Witte, and Thomas Mieczkowski.

More recently, Giblin and Schafer (2008) extended the concept of citation analysis by examining an unpublished source of citations: reading lists provided to students in CCJ doctoral programs to assist them in preparing for comprehensive examinations. They found a considerable amount of agreement between the most-cited scholars on these reading lists and the most-cited scholars identified in other studies using textbooks and/or journals, which "reinforces the scholars that have and continue to influence criminological thought" (2008: 88).

EVALUATING UNIVERSITY PROGRAMS

DeZee (1980) identified three main methods that could be used to rank CCJ programs: peer ratings of program prestige, journal publications by program faculty, and citation analysis. In the past 30 years, the use of both publication and citation analysis to evaluate and/or rank criminology programs at various universities has increased greatly. Most of the studies concentrate on American CCJ programs, although a few also include Canadian departments as well. The majority of the studies are limited to programs that offer the Ph.D. degree. Analyses of publication productivity will be discussed in Chapter 8.

Table 3-2. Citation Analyses of Departments

Study	Journals investigated	Time period	Results – 5 most cited departments
DeZee (1980)	5 introductory criminology and criminal justice textbooks	1970-1978	U of Pennsylvania U at Albany Florida State U John Jay College Portland State U
Thomas & Bronick (1984)	SSCI	1979-1980	Vanderbilt U Yale U U of Pennsylvania U of California-Berkeley New York U
Sorensen, Patterson & Widmayer (1992)	Introductory criminology textbooks	1986-1991	U of California-Berkeley Bowling Green U U of Pennsylvania Rutgers U U of Tennessee-Knoxville
Sorensen, Patterson & Widmayer (1992)	Introductory criminal justice textbooks	1986-1991	U of California-Berkeley Rutgers U U of Maryland American U Arizona State U
Cohn & Farrington (1998c)	Criminal Justice and Behavior Criminology J of Criminal Justice J of Quantitative Criminology J of Research in Crime and Delinquency Justice Quarterly	1991-1995	U of Maryland U of Cincinnati Rutgers U U at Albany U of California-Irvine

DeZee (1980) focused on citations to faculty in five introductory CCJ textbooks and found that citations in texts correlated highly with peer rankings and journal publications. He found that the most-cited departments (those with faculty members cited a minimum of 20 times in the five textbooks) were the University of Pennsylvania, the University at Albany (formerly SUNY-Albany), Florida State University, John Jay College, Portland State University, and the University of Maryland (see Table 3-2). DeZee argued that citation analysis provided information about both current and future trends in the discipline.

Thomas and Bronick (1984) identified a sample of 36 doctoral programs in CCJ. Of these, six awarded doctoral degrees in criminology and/or criminal justice and 30 were sociology departments which employed a minimum of three or four faculty specializing in criminology. Using SSCI to obtain citation counts over a two-year period (1979 to 1980), Thomas and Bronick employed five different citation-based measures: total number of citations, number of citations per faculty member, number of citations per experience year, number of citations per experience year per faculty member, and overall university ranking (an average of the first four measures). According to the overall average university ranking, the top five programs were Vanderbilt University, Yale University, the University of Pennsylvania, the University of California-Berkeley, and New York University. None of the most-cited departments were independent programs of criminology or criminal justice; the highest-ranked independent program was the University at Albany, with an overall ranking of 13.

However, Thomas and Bronick's work was severely criticized by Travis (1987) and Sorensen, Patterson, and Widmayer (1992). In addition to the concern about the use of citations as a measure of departmental quality, Travis (1987) warned against the problem of reductionism, suggesting that, although Thomas and Bronick (1984) controlled for various factors (length of faculty career, faculty size, etc.), they used "only a single measure of quality of doctoral programs – the number of citations of the work of program faculty that appeared in the Social Science Citation Index" (Travis 1987: 160). Both Travis and Sorensen, Patterson, and Widmayer (1992) expressed concern over the method of sample selection; Sorensen, Patterson and Widmayer (1992: 9) felt that "Thomas and Bronick biased it in favor of sociology programs by selecting some sociology programs with three faculty members specializing in criminology and by excluding more than half of the independent criminal justice/criminology programs without sufficient rationale".

In replying to Travis' critique, Thomas (1987: 169) argued that "virtually every single development of any consequence to criminology… this century has come from the work of people with backgrounds in sociology". While admitting that the focus on citations as a single measure of quality was a cause for concern, he stated that the strong correlation between citation frequency and many other prestige-related variables had been so clearly and frequently demonstrated that "citation-based measures have far more utility than they might appear to have initially" (Thomas 1987: 168).

Sorensen, Patterson, and Widmayer (1992) measured the quality of 23 CCJ doctoral programs. However, they were unwilling to rely on SSCI as a source of citations, as Thomas and Bronick (1984) did, fearing that this would bias the results in favor of those departments "whose faculty members publish and cite others in traditional sociological journals" (Sorensen, Patterson, and Widmayer 1992: 21). Instead, they followed the lead of DeZee (1980) and focused on citations in 43 introductory textbooks, examining citations in criminology and criminal justice textbooks separately. Their citation measure consisted of the number of pages on which a faculty member's name or work appeared, as opposed to the number of citations per text.

When the programs were ranked by the average number of citations per faculty member, the five most-cited programs in introductory criminology texts were the University of

California-Berkeley, Bowling Green University, the University of Pennsylvania, Rutgers University, and the University of Tennessee-Knoxville. The five most-cited programs in introductory criminal justice texts were the University of California-Berkeley, Rutgers University, the University of Maryland, American University, and Arizona State University. Interestingly, Sorensen, Patterson, and Widmayer (1992: 23) also ranked the departments by the raw number of citations (without standardizing for the number of faculty) and found that "departments with large faculties often lose rank when the average number of publications is considered".

Marenin (1993) criticized the Sorensen, Patterson, and Widmayer (1992) research, pointing out that, in the case of Washington State University (WSU), where he was the director of the criminal justice program, they had erred in estimating the number of faculty at the university. However, even a brief glance at the raw data (Sorensen, Patterson, and Widmayer 1992: 26-27) makes it clear that WSU had no citations in criminal justice texts and only two citations in criminology texts during the period in question, so this clearly was a minor issue. Marenin (1993: 190) also criticized Sorensen, Patterson, and Widmayer's productivity measures (number of journal publications, number of pages published, etc.) as being "biased toward single-minded disciplines". However, as Sorensen, Patterson, and Widmayer (1993) pointed out, the data for these measures were obtained from a variety of social science indices, including SSCI, which covers journals in a wide variety of fields. Marenin considered that the citation measures were narrow as well; he thought that the focus on introductory textbooks limited the field to traditional criminology and criminal justice research and thus biased the results against more multidisciplinary Ph.D. programs, such as WSU. Sorensen, Patterson, and Widmayer (1993) replied that the University of California-Berkeley, with a Ph.D. in jurisprudence and social policy (clearly multidisciplinary in nature), ranked first on average citations per faculty member in both types of textbooks, as well as ranking highly on the raw citation counts.

Cohn and Farrington (1998c) assessed the quality of 20 American doctoral programs in criminology and criminal justice, based on the citation counts of the faculty in those programs. Like many of the earlier studies, such as Sorensen, Patterson, and Widmayer (1992), Cohn and Farrington chose not to rely on SSCI as the source of the citation counts. However, rather than follow their lead and use textbooks, Cohn and Farrington based their study on citations in six major American criminology and criminal justice journals during the years 1991 to 1995. Using citations per faculty member per journal, the top four programs were the University of Maryland, the University of Cincinnati, Rutgers University, and the University at Albany.

Because of their concern that the presence of a small number of highly-cited individuals might significantly affect the overall average citation rate, Cohn and Farrington (1998c) also ranked the programs according to the percentage of faculty members with at least one citation. Again, the University of Maryland was ranked first, as every faculty member in that program was cited in at least one of the six source journals.

EVALUATING JOURNALS

Poole and Regoli (1981: 473) defined journal eminence or prestige by "the relative frequency with which a particular periodical is cited in the criminological literature". Using *Criminology* as the source journal, they used the frequency of citations in *Criminology* during the five year period May 1975 to November 1979 to rank 43 criminology and criminal justice journals (see Table 3-3). Poole and Regoli's citation-based rankings were found to be highly correlated with subjective peer rankings of the same journals (obtained by Shichor, O'Brien, and Decker, 1981), so that there was "an overall similarity between the rank order of the subjective ratings and the rank order of citation counts for the journals" (1981: 475).

Stack (1987) pointed out that, like much of the other prior research which ranked journals, Poole and Regoli's (1981) study used only one source journal (*Criminology*) and failed to adjust for the age of each ranked journal or the number of articles published in it. In his research, Stack (1987) employed a large number of source journals, using citation analysis to consider the relative impact and importance of 26 CCJ journals. Citation counts were obtained from SSCI for the years 1984 and 1985. Stack first obtained a raw citation count (the number of citations of articles in a given journal) from articles published in source journals in 1984 or 1985. Realizing that this method biases the results in favor of older journals, he removed the bias by computing an age-adjusted citation count, counting the number of citations in 1985 source journals of articles published in the 26 journals in 1983 and 1984. Stack found a correlation of $r = .80$ between the ratings using raw citation counts and age-standardized counts.

Finally, to control for both age and the number of articles published by each journal, Stack (1987) computed an impact factor by dividing the age-adjusted citation count by the number of articles published in the given journal in 1983 and 1984. He considered this factor to be a measure of the quality of a journal and its impact on the field. Correlations between the impact factor and the other measures were still significant (age-adjusted vs. impact factor $r = .72$, $p < .05$; raw count vs. impact factor $r = .54$, $p < .05$). Stack also compared his rankings with those of Shichor, O'Brien, and Decker's (1981) subjective rankings and Poole and Regoli's (1981) citation counts. He found that his impact factor score was significantly correlated with Shichor, O'Brien, and Decker's subjective scores but not with the Poole and Regoli raw impact score (although the correlation coefficient was nearly significant).

Sorensen (2009) conducted an impact assessment of CCJ journals, using citations obtained from ten top tier journals. He calculated three citation measures: the total number of citations attributed to any of 67 target journals (which included citations in editorials and notes, as well as self-citations), an adjusted citation count that included only citations from articles published in 2003 through the current issue in 2007 (and omitted self-citations), and the impact factor (which was computed by dividing the number of citations during 2007 to articles published in 2006 and 2005 by the number of articles published in each target journal during those two years). Sorensen found that the impact measures were very consistent, with significant overall correlations between them.

Table 3-3. Additional Studies using Citation Analysis

Study	Study focus	Citation source	Time period	Results
Wolfgang et al. (1978)	Citations in scholarly works	SCI	1945-1972	Skewed distribution - small number of works highly cited; over 57% never cited
Poole & Regoli (1981)	Journal prestige	*Criminology*	1975-1979	Overall similarity between citation rankings and subjective peer rankings
Stack (1987)	Journal prestige	SSCI	1984-1985	Overall moderate association between journal impact factor and subjective prestige ratings
Sorensen (2009)	Journal impact of 67 target journals	*Crime & Delinquency Crime & Public Policy Criminal Justice & Behavior Criminology J of Criminal Justice J of Experimental Criminology J of Quantitative Criminology J of Research in Crime & Delinquency Justice Quarterly Theoretical Criminology*	2007	Top journals fairly consistent across three measures (total citations, adjusted citation count, impact factor) but not locked into specific ranks Peer ratings highly correlated with all impact measures
Jennings, Higgins, & Khey (2009)	Journal prestige	JCR	1997-2007	Rankings relatively stable at high end of rakings Variability in rankings over time and in titles making the top 20 list each year
Gabbidon & Greene (2001)	African American scholarship	40 American CCJ textbooks	1918-1960	Almost 63% of textbooks cited African American scholars Claims of exclusion may be overstated
Rock (2005)	Age distribution of citations	*British J of Criminology*	1960, 1970, 1980, 1990, 2000	Citation dates followed distinct J-shaped curve with most citations dated within 20 years of journal publication
		British J of Delinquency	1951	
Telep (2009)	Randomized experiments in CCJ	SSCI Google Scholar	Up to Sept/Oct 2007	Articles published in non-criminology journals tend to be more highly-cited Experiments focusing on areas that have relevance outside of CCJ as well as within the field tend to be more highly-cited GS citation counts tend to be higher for recent publications; SSCI more effective at capturing citations of older studies

Notes: JCR = Journal Citation Reports; SCI = Science Citation Index; SSCI = Social Science Citation Index; CCJ = Criminology and Criminal Justice; GS = Google Scholar.

The top journals were fairly consistent across the three measures, but except for *Criminology* (which ranked top in all three measures), they were not "locked in" to a specific rank, so that the choice of measure would affect which journal was ranked second, third, and so on. For example, the *Journal of Research in Crime and Delinquency* was ranked second using total citations, *Justice Quarterly* was ranked second using the adjusted citation count, and *Criminology and Public Policy* was ranked second using the impact factor. Sorensen (2009) also compared these rankings to those obtained from his earlier study of journal prestige using peer rankings (Sorensen, Snell, and Rodriguez, 2006) and found peer ratings were highly correlated with all the impact measures. Sorensen concluded that no single measure was truly able to determine journal prestige or impact and warned scholars against using a rating scale based on only one dimension of journal quality.

Jennings, Higgins, and Khey (2009) examined the impact factors and rankings of CCJ journals that had been ranked in the top twenty over the previous ten years to determine if the consistency between the two measures was stable over time. They obtained information on each of the journals ranked by the Journal Citation Reports (JCR) as the top twenty journals in the "Criminology and Penology" subject area each year (1997-2007). A total of 29 journals were studied, as there was some variability in the list of top twenty journals over the ten years of the study. The rankings obtained from JCR were also compared with those from other studies of journal quality and prestige (Poole and Regoli, 1981; Shichor et al., 1981; Sorensen et al., 2006; Stack, 1987; Williams et al., 1995). Overall, they found that, at the high end of the rankings, the rankings were relatively stable, with *Criminology* and *Journal of Research in Crime and Delinquency* being ranked as the top journals. However, they also found considerable variability in the journal rankings over time and in the titles in the top twenty list each year.

OTHER APPLICATIONS OF CITATION ANALYSIS

Gabbidon and Greene (2001) examined the extent to which African American scholarship was cited in 40 American criminology textbooks published between 1918 and 1960. They found that African American scholars were cited in nearly 63 percent of the textbooks, and almost 48 percent of the texts contained multiple references to African American scholarship. Four of the five most-cited African American scholars were affiliated with the University of Chicago, which was expected in light of the Chicago School's influence during that period. Overall, they concluded that claims of the exclusion of African American scholarship from CCJ textbooks may be overstated, although many important themes found in the early writings of African American scholars were excluded from the texts.

Rock (2005) used citation analysis to study "chronocentrism" in British criminology. Early research into the age distribution of citations (Nicholas, Ritchie, and Ritchie, 1978) reported a pattern that resembled a J-shaped curve, although this study did not examine criminological research. Rock (2005) examined the dates of all citations in Volume 1 of the *British Journal of Criminology*, published in 1960, and for additional volumes at ten-year intervals through the year 2000. He also charted citations in the first (1951) volume of *The British Journal of Delinquency*, the forerunner to the BJC. In every volume, he found that the citation dates followed a distinct J-shaped curve, with the vast majority of citations dated no more than twenty years before the volume's date of publication. Overall, he found that scholars tend to cite recent works and ignore older studies, even those that had been highly cited in previous decades.

Telep (2009) used citation analysis to identify the most-cited randomized experiments in criminology and criminal justice, as a way of determining those that have had the most influence on the field. After compiling a list of 184 experiments between 1957 and 2005 in six subfields (policing, courts, corrections, community, schools, and early prevention), Telep obtained citation counts from both SSCI and Google Scholar (GS) and ranked the studies on the number of citations per year from each source. Overall, he found that articles published in non-criminology journals, especially medical journals, tended to be more highly cited, although some studies that were published in criminology and sociology journals, particularly the Minneapolis Domestic Violence Experiment (Sherman and Berk, 1984), which was published in *American Sociological Review,* and the Omaha Police Experiment (Dunford, Huizinga, and Elliott, 1990), which was published in *Criminology*, were fairly widely cited as well.

Additionally, he found that those experiments that focused on areas that have relevance outside criminal justice, as well as within the field, tended to be cited more frequently (e.g., the experiments on domestic violence were of key importance to feminist and women's studies scholars as well as to criminal justice researchers). When comparing SSCI and GS, Telep (2009) found that citation counts obtained from GS tended to be higher for recent publications but were clearly lower for older publications, while SSCI was more effective at capturing citations of older studies. However, SSCI was limited by its failure to include as wide a range of CCJ journals as GS.

CONCLUSIONS

Despite various problems, citation analysis is an extremely useful technique for assessing the prestige and influence of journals, scholars and university departments in criminology and criminal justice, and it is being used increasingly. We hope that Chapters 5-7, which describe our own citation analyses, will demonstrate this clearly. They focus on citations of scholars in major criminology and criminal justice journals.

Chapter 4

METHODS USED IN CITATION ANALYSES

Chapters 1 through 3 discussed the various sources of data for citation analysis in different fields. While each method has a variety of advantages and disadvantages, we have chosen to examine the reference lists of major journals in the field of criminology and criminal justice (CCJ). While it is both tedious and time-consuming, this method yields accurate results and avoids many of the problems (described in Chapter 1) that are inherent in the other methods, most of which involve online sources of data. Our method of citation analysis is objective, quantitative, transparent, and replicable, and the raw data are available to any researcher who has access to the reference lists of the chosen journals.

SELECTING JOURNALS

The first step in the data collection process was to select the specific journals to be studied. Because we are interested in both American and international journals, we had a wide range of choices. Our selection of journals was made in the late 1980s, when we originally began this line of research, and the journals were chosen to meet the needs of the specific research projects being conducted at the time.

Obviously, we were limited to only those journals which were being published in 1986. Newer journals, such as the *Journal of Experimental Criminology*, *Criminology and Public Policy*, and the *European Journal of Criminology,* were not in print in 1986 and therefore were not possible sources of citation data at that time. Because we are carrying out a longitudinal study, it is not possible to change the journals being examined and still compare our results to those obtained in earlier time periods. In addition, because of language limitations, we limited ourselves to journals published primarily in English.

Obviously, our selection of journals was at least partly dependent upon how one defines criminology and criminal justice (CCJ). Even in the 1980s, there were a large number of journals that addressed crime-related topics. Criminology has been defined as "An interdisciplinary profession built around the scientific study of crime and criminal behavior, including their manifestations, causes, legal aspects, and control" (Schmalleger, 2012: 11), while criminal justice is the scientific study of the criminal law and the criminal justice system, including the police, the courts, corrections, and the juvenile justice system.

Articles on CCJ are published in a wide variety of journals that are centrally concerned with other disciplines, such as sociology (e.g., *Social Forces, Deviant Behavior, American Sociological Review*, and *Social Problems*), child and adolescent psychology and psychopathology (e.g., *Development and Psychopathology, Journal of Adolescence*, and the *Journal of Youth and Adolescence*), legal/social issues (e.g., *Law and Human Behavior, Law and Social Inquiry, Behavioral Sciences and the Law*, and *Law and Society Review*), and so on (see Vaughn, del Carmen, Perfecto, and Charand, 2004, for an extremely useful annotated list of 326 journals relating to CCJ). However, many of these journals are not *centrally* concerned with CCJ, and so we did not include them in our analysis. Many scholars who conduct research in CCJ, but who were initially trained in some other discipline, may prefer to publish some or all of their research in the mainstream journals of their original discipline, rather than in mainstream CCJ journals.

In addition, there are a large number of more specialized journals that publish only on very specific topics. Examples of specialized journals that publish articles relating to CCJ include *Homicide Studies, Journal of Threat Assessment, Juvenile and Family Court Journal, Policing: An International Journal of Police Strategies and Management, Child Maltreatment*, and the *American Journal of Drug and Alcohol Abuse*. While specialist journals publish many extremely important works, we chose not to include them in our analyses because their focus is very narrow and it does not encompass the entire field of CCJ.

Our original research (Cohn and Farrington, 1990) used citations to examine differences between British and American criminology. To do this, we compared citations in two journals, *Criminology* (CRIM) and the *British Journal of Criminology* (BJC), which we argued were the most prestigious criminology journals in the two countries. CRIM is the official journal of the American Society of Criminology and is sent to all members, giving it an extremely wide circulation and increasing the likelihood that articles in this journal will be noticed and read by American criminologists more than articles in other American criminology journals. BJC is published by Oxford University Press and is unambiguously the leading criminological journal in the United Kingdom.

We later expanded our analyses to include the leading peer-reviewed criminology journals in other English-speaking countries – specifically Canada, Australia, and New Zealand (Cohn and Farrington 1994a). The leading criminological journal in Canada is the *Canadian Journal of Criminology and Criminal Justice* (CJC), formerly the *Canadian Journal of Criminology*. While this journal is published partly in French, many articles are in English and those that are not in English include an English abstract. The primary journal in Australia and New Zealand is the *Australian and New Zealand Journal of Criminology* (ANZ).

Our next project was to examine citations in major CCJ journals published in the United States (Cohn and Farrington 1994b). We focused specifically on American journals, which we defined as those with American editors and publishers. For this study, international journals, and journals with a significant international content, such as *Crime, Law, and Social Change*, the *International Journal of Comparative and Applied Criminal Justice*, and the *International Journal of Offender Therapy and Comparative Criminology*, were explicitly excluded from the analysis.

We selected three journals that we considered to be centrally concerned with criminology and three that were centrally concerned with criminal justice. The three criminology journals we chose were CRIM, the *Journal of Quantitative Criminology* (JQC), and the *Journal of*

Research in Crime and Delinquency (JRCD). The three criminal justice journals we selected were *Justice Quarterly* (JQ), the *Journal of Criminal Justice* (JCJ), and *Criminal Justice and Behavior* (CJB).

These journals were not chosen arbitrarily; there was empirical evidence to support our selection of these six journals as major journals in the field in the 1980s (and today). Shichor, O'Brien, and Decker (1981) surveyed a sample of over 150 American criminologists, asking them to rate 42 American and non-American journals that contained articles on CCJ (not all the journals were centrally concerned with CCJ). The *Journal of Criminal Law and Criminology* (JCLC) had the highest average rating, followed by CRIM and JRCD. JCJ was ranked fifth in the survey, after *Crime and Delinquency* (CD). The next most-highly ranked American CCJ journals were *Criminal Justice Review* (CJR), *Federal Probation* (FP), and CJB.

In a much larger survey of over 1,000 American criminologists, Regoli, Poole, and Miracle (1982) found that the most highly-ranked and prestigious CCJ journals were CRIM, JRCD, JCLC, CD, JCJ, and CJB. Fabianic's (1980) survey of criminal justice professionals obtained similar results, finding that the most highly-ranked journals were JCLC, JCJ, CRIM, and JRCD. Similarly, in Parker and Goldfeder's (1979) survey of heads of graduate programs, the most highly-ranked CCJ journals were JCLC, CRIM, CD, JCJ, FP, JRCD, and CJB.

Poole and Regoli (1981) studied the frequency of journal citations in CRIM between 1975 and 1979 and found an extremely high rank correlation of 0.75 between their citation-based rankings of journals and the subjective ratings of importance by Shichor et al. (1981). Based on citations, the most highly-ranked journal was JCLC, followed by CRIM, CD, JRCD, and FP. Similarly, Cohn and Farrington (1990) examined the journals cited in CRIM between 1984 and 1988 and, after controlling for the number of articles available for citation, found that the most-cited American CCJ journals were CRIM, JCLC, JRCD, CD, JCJ, and CJB. Stack (1987) studied citations of journals using the Social Science Citation Index (SSCI). After controlling for the number of articles that could be cited, he found that the most-cited American CCJ journals were CRIM, JRCD, CD, JCLC, CJB, and JCJ.

Although existing research suggested that JCLC, CD, and FP were among the most important American CCJ journals, we did not use these in our research. In the 1980s, JCLC's legal style of footnoting excluded the initials of the authors cited, making it almost impossible to distinguish between different authors with the same surname. JCLC still uses footnotes today, although the first name or initials of authors are now included. However, the footnote style still makes it difficult to easily access the information needed for citation analysis. First, it would be necessary to search through each article for footnotes containing references and then individually copy those references to a separate file. Second, the references begin with first rather than last names, so each reference would have to be individually edited to reverse the first and last names so that references could be sorted by a scholar's last name. Finally, many footnotes contain other material in addition to references; all this extraneous material would have to be identified and deleted. In addition to the problems involved in obtaining citation data for JCLC, a large percentage of their articles are on topics relating to criminal law, rather than to criminology and criminal justice (Sorensen, 2009).

FP was not included among the major American CCJ journals because it is a specialist journal, focusing on probation, rather than a more general CCJ journal. CD was not included because almost half of its issues were special issues on particular topics, involving solicited articles on specific subjects rather than unsolicited articles on general CCJ topics.

JQ and JQC were not included in the early research on journal prestige because they did not exist when much of the research was conducted. JQ began publication in 1984 and JQC in 1985. However, at the time of our original research, we felt that these two journals, and indeed all of those in our final group of six journals, were more prestigious than *Criminal Justice Review* and other American CCJ journals (e.g., *Journal of Crime and Justice*).

At this point, we had a total of nine journals: three American criminology journals (CRIM, JQC, and JRCD), three American criminal justice journals (JQ, JCJ, and CJB), and three international journals (ANZ, BJC, and CJC). Citations in these journals are analyzed in Chapters 5 and 6. In addition, we had examined citations in a tenth serial publication, *Crime and Justice: A Review of Research* (Cohn and Farrington 1996), bringing the total number of publications studied to ten. While these are all well-known, high-quality, peer reviewed publications, our analyses were clearly vulnerable to the criticism that the limited number of journals studied could create a bias against scholars who publish in less mainstream or slightly lower-tier journals. It could be argued that the most-cited scholars are, at least in part, specific to particular journals, so that the results might differ if different journals were analyzed.

To avoid this type of criticism, we decided to investigate the most-cited scholars in a much larger number of American and international CCJ journals (Cohn, Farrington, and Wright, 1998). After some deliberation, we decided to add ten additional important and mainstream CCJ journals, doubling the number of journals examined from ten to twenty. Our goal was to compare American and international journals, and to compare criminology and criminal justice journals, so we chose to examine five journals in each of the four possible categories: American criminology journals, American criminal justice journals, international criminology journals, and international criminal justice journals. However, selecting ten additional journals was not an easy task.

We first added eight additional CCJ journals: CD, *Criminal Justice Review* (CJR), FP, *Criminologie* (CRGE), *Contemporary Crises* (now renamed *Crime, Law and Social Change:* CLSC), the *International Journal of Comparative and Applied Criminal Justice* (IJCA), the *International Journal of Offender Therapy and Comparative Criminology* (IJOT), and *Social Justice (*SJ). Then we added two additional journals, *Journal of Interpersonal Violence* (JIV) and *Violence and Victims* (VAV).

This selection was not made lightly or arbitrarily; we considered and rejected a variety of other academic journals (although we did not consider non-academic publications such as *The Police Chief*). Some journals, such as the *Journal of Crime and Justice* and the *Howard Journal of Criminal Justice*, simply had too few citations to analyze. Others were on very specific aspects of CCJ, such as the *Journal of Police Science and Administration*, *Police Studies*, *Policing*, *The Prison Journal*, *Criminal Justice History*, *Victimology*, and *Juvenile and Family Court Journal*. Others, as noted above, included articles on CCJ but were primarily focused on disciplines bordering on CCJ, such as the sociology of deviance, socio-legal studies, legal psychology, and child and adolescent psychopathology. In addition, we did not consider more mainstream journals in cognate disciplines such as sociology, psychology, psychiatry, economics, statistics, or drug and alcohol studies. Overall, we concluded that the twenty journals we ultimately selected would be widely viewed as mainstream CCJ journals by scholars working in CCJ. Citations in these journals are analyzed in Chapter 7.

The classification of journals as international versus American was determined using data from 1990. Four of the international criminology journals (ANZ, BJC, CJC, and CRGE) were published outside the United States and contained very few American authors. The fifth, CLSC, was originally subtitled "An International Journal", is published in The Netherlands, contained only 18 percent American authors in 2005, and included fourteen non-Americans out of twenty-seven editors, senior editors, and associate editors in 2005.

Of the five international criminal justice journals, one, IJCA, is the official journal of the American Society of Criminology's Division of International Criminology and is explicitly international in its focus. IJOT, "a journal of international cooperation", is also explicitly international in its focus, and included twenty-nine non-Americans out of fifty-six consulting and associate editors in 2005. SJ, a project of "Global Options", included an international editorial advisory board drawn from thirteen countries in addition to the United States in 2005. CJB, the official publication of the International Association for Correctional and Forensic Psychology, is subtitled "An International Journal," and the journal information clearly states that "articles... are welcomed from throughout the world". CAJ, according to its promotional material, "since 1979 has presented a review of the latest international research". Its editor, Michael H. Tonry, was located in the United Kingdom in 1999-2004.

OBTAINING THE CITATION DATA

Once we had selected our journals, the next step was to obtain the citations to be analyzed. Citations were obtained from the reference lists of all articles in each selected journal. "Articles" included not only research articles, but also research notes, comments, and rejoinders. However, book reviews, book review articles, editorials, introductions to special issues, letters, and obituaries were excluded.

For each journal, the reference pages for every article had to be entered into the computer. Originally, this was done by photocopying the reference lists, scanning these printed copies with an optical scanner, and then editing the resulting text to correct scanner-created typographical errors. However, with the advent of full-text online journals, it became increasingly possible to download the references from online copies of the journals into a word processing program for editing. This has significantly reduced both the time and cost of the data entry process, and has helped reduce errors. In addition, we printed out the table of contents for each issue and, for each article, printed out the title page and reference pages for cross-checking. This helped us to ensure that no references were omitted during the data editing and analysis stages of the research.

Once the reference lists were scanned or downloaded into the computer, we edited them to convert them into a format suitable for analysis. This was an extremely labor-intensive task. When a reference had multiple authors, duplicate listings were made of the reference, with each co-author listed first. This allowed all authors to receive credit for the citation, not just the first author (as was the norm in SSCI until recently). In addition, self-citations were identified and marked for later exclusion. Institutional authors (e.g., National Institute of Justice, Home Office) were not included; when these appeared, the listings were deleted from the data set.

While the reference list formats of most journals require all authors to be listed, some journals (such as CJB) allow the use of "et al." in the reference list. For all references that specified "et al." instead of listing every author of the work, the original work or an online source were checked so that, whenever possible, the names of all co-authors were obtained and included in the data set.

Every cited author was included, not just first authors. We did not inversely weight citation counts according to the number of co-authors, as is often done in studies of publication productivity (see e.g., Rice, Cohn, and Farrington, 2005; Steiner and Schwartz, 2006; Shutt and Barnes, 2008). In addition, it was not practicable to restrict the study to only published works, so unpublished works, conference papers, and so on were included if they were cited.

All self-citations were excluded. However, after some debate, we decided to note but not exclude co-author citations (Cohn and Farrington, 1996). A co-author citation occurs when the author of an article cites a work he or she has co-authored with colleagues. For example, if Jacqueline Cohen publishes an article in which she cites a work by Alfred Blumstein and Jacqueline Cohen, Blumstein is a co-author citation. As such, Blumstein was given credit for the citation but not Cohen, because of the exclusion of self-citations.

Extensive checking was carried out to ensure that no references were omitted, to make certain that all self-citations were identified, to minimize typographical errors, and to detect mistakes in the original reference lists (which were distressingly common). The photocopied versions of the reference lists were used for cross-checking. Each page was examined, the number of cited authors counted, and any self-citations and co-author citations were identified. After the reference list for an article was edited, the number of authors in the computer file was compared with the count obtained from the printed version and any discrepancies were identified and corrected.

During the editing process, we maintained careful records of the total number of authors cited in each article, the number of self-citations, the number of co-author citations, and the number of "eligible" citations (which was computed by subtracting the number of self-citations from the total number of authors cited). We also recorded the number of authors of each article and the nationality of each author. Nationality was defined not by citizenship but by the country of the academic, governmental, or other institution with which the author was affiliated. If an author was affiliated with multiple institutions in different countries (e.g., David Weisburd, who was affiliated simultaneously with the University of Maryland in the United States and Hebrew University-Jerusalem in Israel), the first-listed institution was used. For those authors who were not affiliated with any institution, their geographic location was used.

For the nine journals that we originally studied, citations were obtained annually, and combined in periods of five years. For our study of twenty journals, only one year of data was obtained. This was done out of necessity, because of the extensive amount of labor involved in obtained and editing five years worth of data for all twenty journals.

COUNTING CITATIONS

Once all the references for a specific journal were entered into the computer and edited appropriately, the data were sorted into alphabetical order and the resulting list was examined to determine the number of times each name occurred. At this point, the previously-identified self-citations were noted but were not included in a scholar's total citation count.

The process of counting citations was extremely time-consuming, as it was not as simple as just counting the number of times a given scholar was cited. Many journals use only last names and initials, not full names, in their reference lists. This makes the process more difficult, particularly in those cases where there are multiple scholars with the same last name and initials. Where references did not include first names and/or middle initials, a considerable amount of time was spent checking them against the original source publications to distinguish between, for example, the various D. Smiths (David A, David E., David J., Douglas A., etc.), the various J. Cohens (Jacqueline, Jacob, Joseph, etc.) and the two P. Brantinghams (Paul J. and Patricia L.). In addition, when there were two scholars with the same name (such as David Brown, Richard Sparks, Richard Wright, and Patrick O'Malley), it was necessary to examine the complete citation listings carefully to distinguish between them. Citations to scholars with multiple names (e.g., Kimberly Kempf/Leonard) also had to be amalgamated, when they were known.

In addition, it was necessary to spend a great deal of time checking and correcting a depressingly large number and variety of errors that were found in the original reference lists. For example, it was not uncommon to see a reference to a "T. Hirsch" or "T. Hirshi" instead of "T. Hirschi," or one to "J. Sampson" instead of "R.J. Sampson." This task required a detailed knowledge of criminologists and works, so as to maximize the accuracy of the data. While we were frequently able to determine quite easily from the title of the article or the article's co-authors that a citation to "L. E. Cohn" really referred to L. E. Cohen, or that one to "R. A. Sampson" really referred to "R. J. Sampson", someone who was less familiar with the literature would be less likely to recognize these types of errors, which are bound to occur in more mechanical counts of citations. While it is unlikely that we were able to correct every error in every reference list, it is likely that the vast majority of them were corrected, especially those involving the most-cited authors in each journal.

One important advantage of citation analysis for the researcher, apart from the fact that it is quantitative and objective, is that the raw data are readily available to anyone who wishes to try to replicate this research. However, it is important to realize that one year of citations in a journal such as CRIM may include over 4,000 cited authors, who all need checking. It is possible that another researcher may not replicate our results exactly, because of mistakes in the spelling of authors' names in reference lists that may not have been detected, either by us or by the other researcher, difficulties in distinguishing between individuals with the same initial and surname, possible inconsistencies in what is defined as an 'article,' or simply because of minor and infrequent clerical errors that, despite careful checking, may have crept into the computerization of such a large number of citations. However, we are confident that our main conclusions would hold up with only marginal changes in any replication.

CAREER CONCEPTS

Cohn and Farrington (1996) argued that certain concepts originally developed in criminal career research could be used insightfully to enhance research into citation analysis. Specifically, they focused on the distinction between the prevalence and frequency of citations. One problem that arises from using the total number of citations as a measure of scholarly influence is that there are two ways in which a scholar might obtain a large number of citations. First, the scholar might have a high prevalence; in other words, the scholar is cited in many different articles. This might involve repeated citations of only a few works by the scholar or it might occur because many different works by that scholar are cited. Second, the scholar might have a high frequency; he or she is cited many times in a few articles. This situation can only occur if many different works by the scholar are being cited, as each individual work will only appear once in the reference list of each article in which the scholar is cited. A high prevalence may be a better measure of the scholar's influence on many others in the field than a high frequency, which may reflect a significant influence on only a few other researchers.

In addition, Cohn and Farrington (1996) drew a distinction between specialization and versatility. Highly-cited authors who have one or two works frequently cited are specialized. Often, these highly-cited works are books, and often they present a major theory. Highly-cited authors who have many different works cited, with no single work standing out as particularly highly cited, are considered to be versatile. These authors tend to have written a large number of articles rather than a single seminal book, although some specialized authors may also have many different works cited. Logically, a high frequency of citation must be associated with versatility, while a high prevalence may be associated with specialization, although it could also be associated with versatility, if a number of different works by a scholar were cited in many different articles. This would also indicate that the scholar's works were influencing a large number of other researchers.

These concepts were applied to the analysis of the citation data once the counting process was completed and checked. The fifty most-cited scholars in each journal were identified and ranked, with the most-cited scholar receiving a rank of 1. Where two or more scholars had the same number of citations in a journal, they were given the same average ranking. For the most-cited scholars, the number of different works cited and the number of different articles in which they were cited were also determined, as a way of measuring prevalence, frequency, versatility, and specialization. These rankings also were compared to rankings obtained during earlier waves of the research, to provide information about the rise and fall of the influence of individual scholars.

COMBINED MEASURES OF INFLUENCE

While ranking scholars by the number of citations received was a valid way of measuring influence in a single journal, we could not simply add together a scholar's citations in several journals to measure his or her influence. If we had done this, then authors who were highly cited in journals with a relatively high number of citations, such as CRIM or JQ, would have dominated, while those scholars who were highly cited in journals with fewer citations per article would have been eliminated from consideration.

In order to produce a combined measure of influence based on multiple journals with an equal weight given to each journal, each cited scholar was given a score of 51 minus his or her rank on citations in each individual journal. Thus, the most-cited author in each journal had a score of 50 ($51 - 1$), and all authors whose ranking in a journal was outside the top 50 received a score of zero. When examining, for example, the three American criminology journals (CRIM, JQC, and JRCD), each scholar's scores on all three journals were added together, to produce a total score out of a theoretical maximum of 150.

This process allowed us to examine various groupings of journals which had vastly different numbers of citations per article, and still give each journal equal weighting in the analysis.

CONCLUSIONS

Our analyses of nine major journals originally covered the years 1986-90 (Cohn and Farrington, 1994a, 1994b). These analyses were then extended to cover 1991-95 (Cohn and Farrington, 1998a, 1998b) and 1996-2000 (Cohn and Farrington, 2007a, 2007b). In this book, we present results for 2001-2005, and analyze longitudinal trends in scholarly influence over time.

Our analyses of twenty major journals originally covered the year 1990 (Cohn et al., 2008) and were then extended to 1995 (Cohn and Farrington, 1999) and 2000 (Cohn and Farrington, 2008). In this book, we present results for 2005, and analyze longitudinal trends in scholarly influence over time.

Citation analyses of this type have certain limitations. First, the research is based on citations in a relatively small number of mainstream CCJ journals. Because of this, it may underestimate the influence of those scholars who publish mainly in other journals, either journals based in other disciplines (e.g., psychology or sociology) or journals that are more specialized (e.g., *Homicide Studies*, *Journal of Elder Abuse and Neglect*, *Sexual Abuse*), focusing on a very narrow area within the broader field of CCJ.

Second, the longitudinal nature of these citation analyses limits the study to those journals that were being published in 1986 (for the study of American and international journals) or 1990 (for the expanded study of twenty journals). Therefore, newer journals that were not being published at the time this research began (e.g., *Criminology and Public Policy*, *Journal of Experimental Criminology*, *European Journal of Criminology*) cannot be added to the study.

Third, the research cannot be adapted to take advantage of new sources of citation data, such as Scopus, Google Scholar, or the Web of Science. With a longitudinal design, the method of data collection developed at the start of the study must be used throughout.

Fourth, methods of data analysis cannot be changed. For example, while self-citations have been eliminated from the data, co-author citations have not. Although it would be interesting to examine the impact of co-author citations, it is not possible to begin eliminating them at this point.

Despite the limitations that it creates, one of the main strengths of this research is the longitudinal design. This research is based on the collection of comparable citation data from major CCJ journals over a twenty-year period. Electronic sources of data, such as Scopus, Google Scholar, or the Web of Science, did not exist in their current form at the start of this research, so it would not be possible to carry out a twenty-year longitudinal study based on them. Additionally, these sources are continually changing the journals from which citations are drawn, making it impossible to obtain comparable longitudinal data on citations from them.

Another strength of this research is the extensive checking, informed by a breadth and depth of knowledge about criminology and criminal justice, that was carried out in an effort to minimize errors. This focused careful checking of the data was designed to correct the many errors that appear in reference lists and that are automatically included when conducting more mechanical analyses (e.g., through the use of online sources of citation data), as explained above. Journal reference lists contain a surprising number of errors of various types. For example, authors' names are frequently misspelled, middle initials may be omitted or be incorrect, first and middle initials may be reversed or may be attached to the surname of a co-author, and dates of references may be incorrect. These errors are carried over intact by online sources of citation data, which do not check citations for accuracy. The painstaking examination that we conducted, which required an extensive and in-depth knowledge of scholars and the CCJ literature, may not have corrected every error but it clearly corrected many that would have been missed if a more mechanical analysis had been used.

Another strength of this research is that self-citations were excluded. None of the web-based sources of citation data exclude self-citations, nor are they clearly identified for manual extraction by a researcher.

While the limited number of journals examined in this research is perhaps a limitation, it is also in some ways a strength of the research. The journals that have been selected are all prestigious CCJ journals. If a broader, more generic source of citation data had been used, citations from a wide variety of journals and trade publications that are either much less prestigious or are only peripherally associated with CCJ would also have been included. This would have diluted the focus on scholarly prestige and influence.

Chapter 5

MOST-CITED SCHOLARS IN GROUPS OF JOURNALS

In this chapter, we analyze citations in three major American criminology journals, three major American criminal justice journals, and three major international criminology and criminal justice (CCJ) journals. Our analyses are carried out for the 2001-05 time period and compared with our previous results for 1986-90, 1991-95, and 1996-2000, using exactly the same methodology. We establish the most-cited scholars in 2001-05 and compare citation trends over time. (Part of the information in this chapter has been published in Cohn 2011a, 2011b).

AMERICAN CRIMINOLOGY JOURNALS

As described in Chapter 4, we selected for analysis three journals that we considered to be centrally concerned with criminology: *Criminology* (CRIM), *Journal of Quantitative Criminology* (JQC), and *Journal of Research in Crime and Delinquency* (JRCD). Citations in each of these three journals were examined for the period 2001-05 and the results compared with findings from our earlier research.

Criminology (CRIM)

A total of 184 articles were published in CRIM between 2001-05, by a total of 417 individual authors, 90 percent of whom (376) were American. The majority of the non-American authors were from Canada (10), the Netherlands (10), or the United Kingdom (9). These articles included a total of 21,005 cited authors, of which 1,069 were self-citations and 911 were coauthor citations. After removing self-citations, there were a total of 19,936 eligible cited authors, an average of 108 cited authors per article. The number of cited authors has been increasing noticeably over time: in the 1996-00 time period there were 15,583 cited authors (91 per article), in 1991-95 there were 10,650 (81 per article), and in 1986-90 there were 11,405 (68 per article). Overall, the number of cited authors per article in CRIM has increased by 59 percent since the first wave of this research. However, the number of published articles increased by only 10 percent, up from 167 in 1986-90.

Table 5-1 shows the 49 most-cited scholars in CRIM in 2001-05. The most-cited scholar was Robert J. Sampson, who was cited 320 times. Overall, 62 different works by Sampson were cited in 103 different articles in CRIM; he was cited in 56 percent of all the articles published in CRIM during 2001-05. His most-cited work, *Crime in the Making* (Sampson and Laub, 1993), was cited 38 times. Thus, Sampson had both a high prevalence and a high frequency of citations, and his citations showed both specialization, as he had one very highly cited work, and versatility, as he had 62 different works cited.

Table 5-1 also shows the comparable rankings of the most-cited scholars in CRIM in the three earlier time periods we have examined: 1996-2000, 1991-1995, and 1986-1990. From this, it may be seen that Sampson was also the most-cited scholar in 1996-00 and his most-cited work during that time period was also *Crime in the Making*. His advancement in the rankings has been fairly rapid; he rose from 26 in 1986-90 to 7 in 1991-95 and first in 1996-00 and 2001-05. The increase in his citation career parallels his increasing influence in the field of criminology; he was appointed to a professorship at Harvard University in 2003.

In the two earlier time periods, 1991-95 and 1986-90, the most cited scholar was Travis Hirschi. His most-cited works were *A General Theory of Crime* (Gottfredson and Hirschi, 1990) in 1991-95 and *Causes of Delinquency* (Hirschi, 1969) in 1986-90. Like Sampson, Hirschi was clearly a specialized author.

Of the scholars appearing in Table 5-1, 33 of them (67 percent) had been ranked in the top 50 in 1996-00, 24 (49 percent) had been ranked in the top 50 in 1991-95, and 18 (37 percent) had been ranked in the top 50 in 1986-90. All but four of the top 20 scholars in 2001-05 were also in the top 25 in 1996-00.

The highest new entrants in the top 50 in 2001-05 were Alex R. Piquero, Avshalom Caspi, and Paul Mazerolle. Other scholars who advanced considerably in the rankings include John H. Laub, who went from rank 23.5 in 1991-95 to 12 in 1996-00 and third in 2001-05. Terrie E. Moffitt, the highest ranked female scholar in CRIM, is also noticeable for her advancement. She did not even appear in the list of the most-cited scholars in 1986-90 or 1991-95 but was ranked 20 in 1996-00 and in 2001-05 was ranked second. Other notable advances between 1996-00 and 2001-05 were made by Stephen W. Raudenbush, who rose from 37.5 to 10, and Raymond Paternoster, who rose from 27 to 4. Paternoster was the editor of CRIM from 2004 to 2005. The editors of journals between 2001 and 2005 are listed because it has been argued (e.g. Rushton, 1984) that scholars sometimes attempt to improve their probability of publication by citing journal editors or editorial board members.

Scholars who moved down in ranking between 1996-00 and 2001-05 include Travis Hirschi (from 2 to 6), Michael J. Gottfredson (from 3 to 11), Robert J. Bursik (from 4 to 13), Harold G. Grasmick (from 6.5 to 21) Delbert S. Elliott (from 6.5 to 22), John L. Hagan (from 8 to 23.5), David Huizinga (from 10 to 36.5) and Charles R. Tittle (from 9 to 41). Marvin E. Wolfgang, who died in 1998, was once a very highly cited scholar but no longer appears in the table.

All except one of the top 20 scholars in 1996-00 were in the top 50 in 2001-05. The only one who did not appear was Douglas A. Smith (16.5) who died in 2005.

Table 5-1. Most-Cited Scholars in *Criminology*

Rank	Rank in 1996-00	Rank in 1991-95	Rank in 1986-90	Name	Cites
1	1	7	26	Robert J. Sampson	320
2	20	---	---	Terrie E. Moffitt	146
3	12	23.5	---	John H. Laub	144
4	27	9.5	---	Raymond Paternoster[3]	136
5	11	20	---	Daniel S. Nagin	130
6	2	1	1	Travis Hirschi	117
7	---	---	---	Alex R. Piquero	107
8	5	3	2.5	David P. Farrington	105
9	14.5	---	42	Darrell J. Steffensmeier	98
10	37.5	---	---	Stephen W. Raudenbush	96
11	3	2	9	Michael R. Gottfredson	94
12	20	5	6	Alfred Blumstein	93
13	4	16.5	---	Robert J. Bursik[2]	90
14	---	---	---	Avshalom Caspi	84
15	18	34.5	---	Kenneth C. Land	83
16	28	---	---	Robert Agnew	80
17	24.5	45	---	William J. Wilson	79
18	---	---	---	Paul Mazerolle	74
19.5	33	23.5	32.5	Rolf Loeber	73
19.5	13	---	27	Steven F. Messner	73
21	6.5	13	---	Harold G. Grasmick	70
22	6.5	4	4	Delbert S. Elliott	67
24	---	45	---	Francis T. Cullen	64
24	8	11.5	7	John L. Hagan	64
24	---	---	---	John H. Kramer	64
26	16.5	14	22	Lawrence E. Cohen	62
27	34.5	---	---	Allen E. Liska	59
28	24.5	48.5	38.5	Donald J. Black	58
30	---	---	---	Robert Brame	57
30	---	---	---	Janet L. Lauritsen	57
30	---	---	---	D. Wayne Osgood	57
32	14.5	---	---	Terence P. Thornberry	55
34	---	---	---	Richard Rosenfeld	52
34	---	---	---	Jeffrey T. Ulmer	52
34	46	---	---	Mark Warr	52
36.5	10	9.5	21	David Huizinga	50
36.5	---	---	---	Patricia L. McCall	50
38	22	30	24	Albert J. Reiss	49
41	32	6	8	Jacqueline Cohen	48
41	24.5	20	14	Marvin D. Krohn	48
41	40	---	---	Phil A. Silva	48
41	---	---	---	Magda Stouthamer-Loeber	48
41	9	8	20	Charles R. Tittle[1]	48
44	43	---	---	Terance D. Miethe	47
46	---	---	---	Elijah Anderson	46
46	---	---	---	Ruth D. Peterson	46
46	---	---	---	Cassia Spohn	46
48	---	---	---	Felton Earls	45
49	20	15	15.5	Ronald L. Akers	44

[1] Editor, 1992-97; [2] Editor, 1996-2003; [3] Editor, 2004-05.

Journal of Quantitative Criminology (JQC)

A total of 90 articles were published in JQC between 2001-2005, by 213 individual authors, 89% of whom (190) were American. The majority of the non-American authors were from the United Kingdom (7), Canada (5), and the Netherlands (5). These articles contained a total of 7,559 cited authors, of which 582 were self-citations and 541 were coauthor citations; after self-citations were removed, there were a total of 6,977 eligible cited authors, or an average of 77.5 cited authors per article.

The number of cited authors in JQC clearly has been increasing over time. In the 1996-00 time period there were 7,395 cited authors (79 per article), in 1991-95 there were 5,839 (69 per article), and in 1986-90 there were 4,708 (47 per article). Overall, the number of cited authors per article in JQC has increased by about two-thirds since 1986, although it did not increase at all between the two most recent waves of this research.

Table 5-2 shows the 52 most-cited scholars in JQC in 2001 to 2005 (up to a rank of 50). The most-cited scholar, Daniel S. Nagin, was cited 103 times. He was a very versatile author, with 34 different works cited in 31 different articles. His most-cited works, each with seven citations, were all journal articles: "A comparison of Poisson, negative binomial, and semiparametric mixed Poisson regression models with empirical applications to criminal careers research," (Land, McCall, and Nagin, 1996), "Age, criminal careers, and population heterogeneity," (Nagin and Land, 1993), and "Trajectories of change in criminal offending," (Laub, Nagin, and Sampson (1998). As no single work stood out as being highly-cited, Nagin was not a specialized author.

Table 5-2 also shows the comparable rankings of the most-cited scholars in JQC in the three previous time periods. David P Farrington was the most-cited scholar in 1996-00; his most-cited work was "The stability of criminal potential from childhood to adulthood" (Nagin and Farrington, 1992). Travis Hirschi was the most-cited scholar in 1991-95; his most-cited work then was *Causes of Delinquency* (Hirschi, 1969). Marvin E. Wolfgang was the most-cited scholar in 1986-90; his most-cited work then was *Delinquency in a Birth Cohort* (Wolfgang, Figlio, and Sellin, 1972).

Of the scholars appearing in Table 5-2, thirty of them (58 percent) had been ranked in the top 50 in 1996-00, 24 (46 percent) had been ranked in the top 50 in 1991-05, and 16 (31 percent) had been ranked in the top 50 in 1986-90. The highest ranked female scholar in JQC in 2001-05, as in CRIM, was Terrie E. Moffit, who was ranked 9.

A number of scholars showed noticeable advancement in the rankings between 1996-00 and 2001-05. Raymond Paternoster advanced from rank 44.5 in 1991-95 to rank 40 in 1996-00 and 8 in 2001-05. David Cantor also advanced considerably, from 46.5 in 1996-00 to 12 in 2001-05, as did Robert Agnew (from 22.5 to 14), Darrell J. Steffensmeier (from 36 to 18) and J. David Hawkins (from 40 to 20.5). Kenneth C. Land has also been moving steadily upward in the rankings, from 49 in 1986-90 to 21 in 1991-95, 7.5 in 1996-00, and 4 in 2000-05. The highest new entrants in the top 50 were Terrie E. Moffitt (9), Alex R. Piquero (13), and Avshalom Caspi (16). Scholars who have moved downward in the rankings included Jacqueline Cohen (from 5.5 in 1986-90 to 33.5 in 2001-05), Michael J. Hindelang (from 5.5 in 1986-90 to 27 in 2001-05), and Lawrence E. Cohen (from 3 in 1986-90 to 41.5 in 2001-05).

Table 5-2. Most-Cited Scholars in Journal of Quantitative Criminology

Rank	Rank in 1996-00	Rank in 1991-95	Rank in 1986-90	Name	Cites
1	4.5	12.5	---	Daniel S. Nagin	103
2.5	4.5	1	8	Travis Hirschi	67
2.5	3	6	---	Robert J. Sampson	67
4	7.5	21	49	Kenneth C. Land	52
5	7.5	5	4	Michael R. Gottfredson	51
6	1	2	9.5	David P. Farrington	44
7	2	3	2	Alfred Blumstein	42
8	40	44.5	---	Raymond Paternoster	41
9	---	---	---	Terrie E. Moffitt	37
10.5	14	7	25	Delbert S. Elliott	36
10.5	12	18	---	John H. Laub[1]	36
12	46.5	---	22.5	David Cantor	34
13	---	---	---	Alex R. Piquero	30
14	22.5	---	---	Robert Agnew	29
15	9	28.5	---	Rolf Loeber	28
16	---	---	---	Avshalom Caspi	27
18	13	9	31.5	David Huizinga	26
18	17.5	21	---	Marvin D. Krohn	26
18	36	18	---	Darrell J. Steffensmeier	26
20.5	40	---	---	J. David Hawkins	25
20.5	---	---	---	Stephen W. Raudenbush	25
22.5	---	---	---	Francis T. Cullen	24
22.5	11	39	19.5	John L. Hagan	24
24.5	24.5	10	16.5	David F. Greenberg	23
24.5	---	---	---	Paul Mazerolle	23
27	---	---	---	Robert J. Bursik	22
27	20	18	5.5	Michael J. Hindelang	22
27	27.5	15.5	---	Terence P. Thornberry	22
30	---	---	---	Gary Kleck	21
30	---	---	---	Donald B. Rubin	21
30	27.5	25.5	43	Wesley G. Skogan	21
33.5	---	---	---	Robert Brame	20
33.5	6	4	5.5	Jacqueline Cohen	20
33.5	27.5	35	---	Lawrence W. Sherman	20
33.5	---	---	---	Phil A. Silva	20
37.5	31.5	---	15	Peter M. Bentler	19
37.5	---	---	---	John H. Kramer	19
37.5	---	---	---	D. Wayne Osgood	19
37.5		---	---	Richard E. Tremblay	19
41.5	16	12.5	3	Lawrence E. Cohen	18
41.5	---	---	---	James P. Lynch	18
41.5	---	---	---	Patricia L. McCall	18
41.5	36	39	43	James Q. Wilson	18
45.5	22.5	32	---	Ronald L. Akers	17
45.5	---	---	---	Bruce J. Arneklev	17
45.5	50.5	---	---	Terance D. Miethe	17
45.5	---	---	---	Susan F. Turner	17
50	---	---	---	Albert D. Biderman	16
50	43	---	---	Albert J. Reiss	16
50	---	---	---	Cassia Spohn	16
50	---	---	---	Charles R. Tittle	16
50	---	---	---	Kirk R. Williams	16

[1] Editor, 1992-96.

The top nine scholars in 1996-00 all survived to be in the top 34 in 2001-05. The highest-ranked scholars in 1991-95 who did not remain in the top 50 in 2001-05 were Christy A. Visher (10) and Douglas A. Smith (15).

Journal of Research in Crime and Delinquency (JRCD)

A total of 83 articles were published in JRCD in 2001-05 by 197 authors, 94 percent of whom (186) were American. The majority of the non-American authors were from the Netherlands (4), Canada (2), and Australia (2). These articles contained a total of 9,495 cited authors, of which 551 were self-citations and 455 were coauthor citations. After self-citations were removed, a total of 8,944 cited authors (an average of 108 per article) remained. This may be compared with 8,590 cited authors (94 per article) in 1996-00, 7,121 (68 per article) in 1991-95, and 5,422 (67 per article) in 1986-90. Overall, the number of cited authors per article in JRCD increased by about 60 percent over this time period.

Table 5-3 shows the 51 most-cited scholars in JRCD during the years 2001 to 2005. The most-cited author, Robert J. Sampson, was cited 115 times. His most-cited work in JRCD, as in CRIM, was *Crime in the Making* (Sampson and Laub, 1993), which was cited 15 times. In total, Sampson had 47 different works cited in 42 different articles in JRCD. Thus, as in CRIM, Sampson again shows both a high prevalence and a high frequency of citations. He also shows versatility, with 47 different works cited, but less specialization than was found in CRIM.

Table 5-3 also shows the comparable rankings of the most-cited scholars in JRCD in 1996-00, 1991-95, and 1986-90. As in CRIM, Robert J. Sampson was also the most-cited scholar in 1996-00 and his most-cited work was again *Crime in the Making*. Travis Hirschi was the most-cited scholar in the two earlier time periods, 1991-95 and 1986-90, and his most-cited work in both time periods was *Causes of Delinquency* (Hirschi, 1969), although this was closely followed by *A General Theory of Crime* (Gottfredson and Hirschi, 1990) in 1991-95. Of the most-cited scholars appearing in Table 5.3, 30 of them (59 percent) had been ranked in the top 50 in 1996-00, 24 (47 percent) had been ranked in the top 50 in 1991-95, and 15 (29 percent) had been ranked in the top 50 in 1986-90.

The highest new entrants in the top 50 in 2001-05 were Ralph B. Taylor (16), Stephen W. Raudenbush (19), Bruce J. Arneklev (21), and William J. Wilson (21). Terrie E. Moffitt, the highest-ranked female scholar in JRCD, was also noticeable for her advancement. Although she did not appear on the lists of most-cited scholars in either 1986-90 or 1991-95, she was ranked 24.5 in 1996-00 and 5 in 2001-05. Other scholars who showed considerable advancement include Francis T. Cullen, who went from rank 49.5 in 1996-00 to 9 in 2001-05, Daniel S. Nagin (from 24.5 to 9), Rolf Loeber (28.5 to 13), and Charles R. Tittle (from 28.5 to 14). Scholars who moved downwards in rank between 1996-00 and 2001-05 include Lawrence E. Cohen (from 4 to 36), Michael J. Hindelang (from 2 to 44), and John L. Hagan (from 3 to 48.5).

All of the top 14 scholars in 1996-00 survived to be in the top 50 in 2001-05. The highest-ranked scholars in 1996-00 who were not in the top 50 in 2001-05, and thus do not appear in the table, were Douglas A. Smith (15.5) and Marcus Felson (17).

Table 5-3. Most-Cited Scholars in Journal of Research in Crime and Delinquency

Rank	Rank in 1996-00	Rank in 1991-95	Rank in 1986-90	Name	Cites
1	1	6	20.5	Robert J. Sampson	115
2	2	1	1	Travis Hirschi	79
3	3	4	6	Michael R. Gottfredson	57
4	8	5	---	David P. Farrington	55
5	24.5	---	---	Terrie E. Moffitt	54
6	14	7	14	Raymond Paternoster	53
7	13	9	---	Robert J. Bursik	48
9	49.5	35	---	Francis T. Cullen	46
9	5.5	2	11.5	Delbert S. Elliott	46
9	24.5	35	---	Daniel S. Nagin	46
11	5.5	---	---	Robert Agnew	44
12	12	---	---	John H. Laub	43
13	28.5	39	---	Rolf Loeber	42
14	28.5	15	8	Charles R. Tittle	41
15	18	19	34.5	Harold G. Grasmick	39
16	---	---	---	Ralph B. Taylor	37
17.5	7	3	---	David Huizinga	34
17.5	28.5	---	---	Gerald R. Patterson	34
19	---	---	---	Stephen W. Raudenbush	32
21	---	---	---	Bruce J. Arneklev	31
21	28.5	31	---	Kenneth C. Land	31
21	---	---	---	William J. Wilson	31
23.5	24.5	15	18	Alfred Blumstein	30
23.5	10	20.5	11.5	Marvin D. Krohn	30
26	---	---	---	Velmer S. Burton	28
26	19	45.5	---	Steven F. Messner	28
26	36.5	---	---	Wesley G. Skogan	28
28.5	40	22.5	---	Lawrence W. Sherman	27
28.5	---	---	---	Phil A. Silva	27
30.5	---	---	---	Avshalom Caspi	26
30.5	---	---	---	Alex R. Piquero	26
32	4	---	---	Terence P. Thornberry	24
33	---	---	---	T. David Evans	23
36	---	---	---	Robert Brame	22
36	20	8	4	Lawrence E. Cohen	22
36	---	---	---	R. Gregory Dunaway	22
36	---	---	---	Richard Rosenfeld	22
36	---	---	---	Magda Stouthamer-Loeber	22
40.5	---	---	---	Scott H. Decker	21
40.5	---	---	---	George L. Kelling	21
40.5	---	---	---	Paul Mazerolle	21
40.5	---	---	---	Darrell J. Steffensmeier	21
44	10	13	29.5	Ronald L. Akers	20
44	15.5	24	2	Michael J. Hindelang	20
44	---	---	---	D. Wayne Osgood	20
48.5	---	---	---	Peter M. Bentler	19
48.5	40	27	29.5	Jacqueline Cohen	19
48.5	10	15	3	John L. Hagan	19
48.5	24.5	---	---	Terance D. Miethe	19
48.5	---	---	---	Cathy S. Widom	19
48.5	---	27	15.5	James Q. Wilson	19

Three Criminology Journals Combined

It is clear that there is a considerable amount of agreement among the three criminology journals as to the most-cited scholars in 2001-05. In all three journals, Robert J. Sampson, Travis Hirschi, and David P. Farrington were among the eight most-cited scholars in both 2001-05 and 1996-00. Terrie E. Moffitt, John H. Laub, Raymond Paternoster, Daniel S. Nagin, and Michael R. Gottfredson were among the top 12 scholars in all three journals in 2001-05. However, the rankings in each journal were affected by the differing focuses of the journals. For example, JQC focuses more on methodology than JRCD and scholars who are better known for their methodological contributions, such as Daniel S. Nagin, Kenneth C. Land, and Alfred Blumstein, tended to be more highly cited in JQC than in JRCD.

As described in Chapter 4, a combined measure of influence based on all three criminology journals was computed, with each cited author given a score of 51 minus his or her rank on citations in each individual journal. The scores on all three journals were added for each cited author, yielding a total score out of a theoretical maximum of 150 and ensuring that equal weight was given to each of the three journals.

Table 5-4 shows the 30 most-cited scholars in the three American criminology journals in 2001-05, using this combined measure. All of these scholars were ranked in the top 50 in at least two of the three journals, and the top 22 scholars were ranked in the top 50 in all three journals. Of the 30 most-cited scholars, only three (Harold G. Grasmick, William J. Wilson, and Steven F. Messner) were not among the most-cited scholars in all three journals.

The most-cited scholar in the three American criminology journals was Robert J. Sampson. His most-cited work, *Crime in the Making* (Sampson and Laub, 1993), was cited 44 times. Travis Hirschi was the second most-cited scholar and his most-cited work was *A General Theory of Crime* (Gottfredson and Hirschi, 1990), which was cited 91 times. The most-cited female scholar was Terrie E. Moffitt, who was ranked fourth. Her most-cited work was the article "Adolescence-limited and life-course persistent antisocial behavior" (Moffitt, 1993), which was cited 51 times. All three are clearly specialists, with one or two highly-cited works. However, the third most-cited scholar, Daniel Nagin, was a versatile author; his most highly-cited work, "Enduring individual differences and rational choice theories of crime" (Nagin and Paternoster, 1993), was cited only 23 times. Similarly, David P. Farrington, who was the fifth most-cited scholar in the three American criminology journals and the most highly-cited non-American scholar, was also a versatile author. His most highly-cited work, "Age and crime" (Farrington, 1986), was cited only 17 times. Overall, in 2001-05, as in earlier time periods, the most-cited works of the most highly-cited scholars tended to be on longitudinal/criminal career research and/or criminological theories. However, unlike in earlier time periods, the most-cited works during 2001-05 were equally likely to be articles as books.

Table 5-4 also shows the comparable rankings of the most-cited scholars in 1996-00, 1991-95, and 1986-90. Of the 30 most-cited scholars in 2001-05, 21 (70 percent) were also in the top 30 in 1996-00, 17 (57 percent) were in the top 30 in 1991-95, and 10 (33 percent) were in the top 30 in 1986-90. Six of the top ten scholars in 1996-00, four of the top ten scholars in 1991-95, and three of the top ten scholars in 1986-00 remained in the top ten in 2001-05. Travis Hirschi, David P. Farrington, and Michael R. Gottfredson were among the ten most-cited scholars in all four time periods. Robert J. Sampson advanced from 21 in 1986-90 to 5 in 1991-95 and first in 1996-00 and 2001-05. There is a considerable amount of stability as the top 14 scholars in this table were also among the most-cited scholars in these three journals in 1996-00. The highest new entrants in 2001-05 were Stephen W. Raudenbush (15), Alex R. Piquero (16), and Francis T. Cullen (17).

Scholars who advanced noticeably between 1996-00 and 2001-05 include Terrie E. Moffitt, who moved from a rank of 28 to 4, Raymond Paternoster (from 24 to 5.5), and Kenneth C. Land (from 16 to 9). Moving down the table from the earliest period, 1986-90, to the current period, 2001-05, were John L. Hagan (from 7 to 26), Alfred Blumstein (from 5 to 12), and Lawrence E. Cohen (from 6 to 30). The highest-ranked scholars in 1996-00 who did not appear in the top 30 in 2001-05 were Douglas A. Smith (12 in 1996-00), Ronald L. Akers (14.5), Christy A. Visher (18), and Michael J. Hindelang (19). Hindelang fell from 2.5 in 1986-90 to 12 in 1991-95, 19 in 1996-00, and 41 in 2001-05. His most-cited work in 2001-05 was *Measuring Delinquency* (Hindelang, Hirschi, and Weis, 1981), which was cited 27 times. It is clear that Hindelang's influence extended well beyond his death in 1982.

Table 5-4. Most-Cited Scholars in Three American Criminology Journals

Rank	Rank in 1996-00	Rank in 1991-95	Rank in 1986-90	Name	CRIM	JQC	JRCD	TOTAL
1	1	5	21	Robert J. Sampson	50	48.5	50	148.5
2	2	1	1	Travis Hirschi	45	48.5	49	142.5
3	9	17	--	Daniel S. Nagin	46	50	42	138
4	28	--	--	Terrie E. Moffitt	49	42	46	137
5.5	4	2	10	David P. Farrington	43	45	47	135
5.5	24	14	30	Raymond Paternoster	47	43	45	135
7	3	3	4	Michael R. Gottfredson	40	46	48	134
8	8	28	--	John H. Laub	48	40.5	39	127.5
9	16	23	--	Kenneth C. Land	36	47	30	113
10	17	--	--	Robert Agnew	35	37	40	112
11	5	4	8	Delbert S. Elliott	29	40.5	42	111.5
12	11	7	5	Alfred Blumstein	39	44	27.5	110.5
13	20	20	--	Robert J. Bursik	38	24	44	106
14	21	26	--	Rolf Loeber	31.5	36	38	105.5
15	--	--	--	Stephen W. Raudenbush	41	30.5	32	103.5
16	--	--	--	Alex R. Piquero	44	38	20.5	102.5
17	--	--	--	Francis T. Cullen	27	28.5	42	97.5
18	--	--	--	Avshalom Caspi	37	35	20.5	92.5
19	--	--	--	Darrell J. Steffensmeier	42	33	10.5	85.5
20	7	6	--	David Huizinga	14.5	33	33.5	81
21	13	15	14	Marvin D. Krohn	10	33	27.5	70.5
22	--	--	--	Paul Mazerolle	33	26.5	10.5	70
23	22	21.5	--	Harold G. Grasmick	30	0	36	66
24	--	--	--	William J. Wilson	34	0	30	64
25	10	--	--	Terence P. Thornberry	19	24	19	62
26	6	16	7	John L. Hagan	27	28.5	2.5	58
27	25	--	--	Steven F. Messner	31.5	0	25	56.5
28	--	--	--	Robert Brame	21	17.5	15	53.5
29	--	--	--	Phil A. Silva	10	17.5	22.5	50
30	14.5	8	6	Lawrence E. Cohen	25	9.5	15	49.5

Table 5-5. Most-Cited Scholars in *Justice Quarterly*

Rank	Rank in 1996-00	Rank in 1991-95	Rank in 1986-90	Name	Cites
1	2	12.5	---	Robert J. Sampson	175
2	8.5	4.5	3	Travis Hirschi	97
3	3	3	1	Francis T. Cullen[1]	86
4	23	---	---	John H. Laub	80
5	14.5	6	7.5	Michael R. Gottfredson	77
6	4	45	28	Raymond Paternoster	75
7	20.5	---	---	Harold G. Grasmick	65
8	8.5	---	---	Robert J. Bursik	61
9	---	---	---	Alex R. Piquero	59
10.5	29.5	19.5	28	David P. Farrington	57
10.5	17	1	18	Lawrence W. Sherman	57
12	---	---	---	Stephen W. Raudenbush	55
13	---	---	---	Daniel S. Nagin	53
14	---	---	---	Mark Warr	52
15	40	---	---	Terence P. Thornberry	47
16	11.5	8.5	---	David Huizinga	44
18	1	2	9.5	John L. Hagan	43
18	---	---	---	Janet L. Lauritsen	43
18	34.5	45	---	Darrell J. Steffensmeier	43
21	17	---	---	Theodore G. Chiricos	42
21	8.5	15	5	Wesley G. Skogan	42
21	46.5	---	---	Charles R. Tittle	42
23.5	20.5	8.5	---	Delbert S. Elliott	40
23.5	46.5	38	---	Marvin D. Krohn	40
25	20.5	4.5	2	James Q. Wilson	39
26.5	---	---	---	Allen E. Liska	38
26.5	25.5	---	---	William J. Wilson	38
28	---	27.5	---	Jeffrey A. Fagan	37
30	5	---	---	Robert Agnew	36
30	---	---	---	Steven F. Messner	36
30	17	32.5	33	Albert J. Reiss	36
32	---	---	---	John Braithwaite	35
34	---	38	---	Rolf Loeber	34
34	40	---	---	Terrie E. Moffitt	34
34	---	---	---	Robert E. Worden	34
36	---	19	15	Ronald L. Akers	33
37	40	12.5	33	Lawrence E. Cohen	31
39	24	---	---	Scott H. Decker	30
39	---	---	---	Kathleen F. Ferraro	30
39	---	---	---	D. Wayne Osgood	30
41.5	---	---	---	George L. Kelling	29
41.5	---	---	---	Paul Mazerolle	29
44	46.5	---	---	Donald J. Black	28
44	---	---	---	Robert Brame	28
44	34.5	---	28	Samuel Walker	28
47.5	46.5	19.5	4	Alfred Blumstein	27
47.5	---	---	---	Kenneth C. Land	27
47.5	---	---	---	David L. Weisburd	27
47.5	---	27.5	5	Marvin E. Wolfgang	27
50.5	---	32.5	11	Michael J. Hindelang	26
50.5	---	---	28	Alan J. Lizotte	26

[1] Editor, 1987-89.

AMERICAN CRIMINAL JUSTICE JOURNALS

As described in Chapter 4, we selected for analysis three journals that we considered to be centrally concerned with criminal justice: *Justice Quarterly* (JQ), *Journal of Criminal Justice* (JCJ), and *Criminal Justice and Behavior* (CJB).

Justice Quarterly (JQ)

Between 2001 and 2005, a total of 144 articles were published in JQ by 324 individual authors, almost all of whom (314 or 97 percent) were American. These articles contained 15,878 cited authors, of which 781 were self-citations and 547 were coauthor citations. After self-citations were removed, there were a total of 15,097 eligible cited authors, an average of 105 per article. This can be compared with 12,636 eligible cited authors in 1996-00 (84 per article), 9,188 in 1991-95 (67 per article) and 9,393 in 1986-90 (68 per article). Overall, the number of cited authors per article has increased by over 50 percent.

Table 5-5 shows the most-cited scholars in JQ in 2001-05. The most-cited scholar, Robert J. Sampson, was cited 175 times. Sampson's most-cited work, *Crime in the Making* (Sampson and Laub, 1993) was cited 22 times and a total of 45 different works by Sampson were cited in 65 different articles. Thus, Sampson had both a high prevalence and frequency of citations, and his citations showed both specialization, with one highly-cited work, and versatility, with 45 different works cited.

Table 5-5 also shows the comparable rankings of these scholars in JQ in the three previous time periods, 1996-00, 1991-95 and 1986-90. John L. Hagan was the most-cited scholar in 1996-00, although his most-cited work during that time period, "Changing conceptions of race" (Peterson and Hagan, 1984), was only cited seven times. Thus, Hagan was a versatile scholar, as his large number of citations was mainly a function of the large number of his different works that were cited. Lawrence W. Sherman was the most-cited scholar in 1991-95. His most-cited during that time period was "Hot spots of predatory crime" (Sherman, Gartin, and Buerger, 1989). Like Hagan, Sherman's high rank was due to his versatility and his large number of different works cited. Francis T. Cullen was the most-cited scholar in 1986-90. His most-cited work then was *Reaffirming Rehabilitation* (Cullen and Gilbert, 1982) and he also was a versatile author. The highest ranked female scholar in JQ in 2001-05 was Janet L. Lauritsen (18). Only Hirschi and Cullen were among the ten most-cited scholars in all four time periods studied. A total of twenty-nine of the most-cited scholars in JQ (57 percent) had been ranked in the top 50 in 1996-00, 22 (43 percent) had been ranked in the top 50 in 1991-95, and 17 (33 percent) had been ranked in the top 50 in 1986-90.

The highest new entrant in the top 10 in 2001-00 was Alex R. Piquero (9). Other scholars who advanced in the rankings included Robert J. Sampson, who went from rank 12.5 in 1991-95 to second in 1996-00 and first in 2001-05. Sampson was not among the 50 most-cited scholars in 1986-90. Harold G. Grasmick also moved up from 20.5 in 1996-00 to 7 in 2001-05, as did David P. Farrington (from 28 in 1986-90 to 19.5 in 1991-95, 29.5 in 1996-00 and 10.5 in 2001-05). Scholars who moved downwards in the rankings included James Q. Wilson (from 2 to 25), John L. Hagan (from 9.5 to 18), Wesley G. Skogan (from 5 to 21), and Alfred Blumstein (from 4 to 47.5). Eight of the top 10 scholars from 1996-00 remained in the top 50 (actually, in the top 31) in 2001-05. The only two who did not appear in the most-cited list in 2001-05 were Peter K. Manning (ranked 6 in 1996-00) and Douglas A. Smith (ranked 8.5 in 1996-00).

Journal of Criminal Justice (JCJ)

A total of 242 articles were published in JCJ between 2001-2005 by 591 authors, of whom 472 (91 percent) were American. The non-American authors were most commonly from Canada (18), the United Kingdom (7), Australia (5), and China (5). These articles contained a total of 20,083 cited authors, of which 809 were self-citations and 713 were coauthor citations, resulting in 19,274 eligible citations, or an average of 80 cited authors per article. This is a significant increase over prior time periods. In 1996-00 there were 12,744 cited authors (65 per article), in 1991-95 there were 9,716 (50 per article), and in 1986-90 there were 7,234 cited authors (40 per article). Overall, the number of cited authors per article has doubled since the start of this research.

Table 5-6 shows the most-cited scholars in JCJ in 2001 to 2005. The most-cited scholar, Francis T. Cullen, was cited 150 times. Cullen was an extremely versatile author, with 71 different works cited in 62 different articles. Essentially, Cullen was cited at least once in 26 percent of all articles in JCJ. His most-cited work was an article, "The social dimensions of correctional officer stress" (Cullen, Link, Wolfe, and Frank, 1985), which was cited only nine times.

Cullen was also the most cited scholar in 1996-00, with the same most-cited work (Cullen et al, 1985), and a similarly high versatility. John L. Hagan was the most-cited scholar in 1991-95. His most-cited work then was "Extra-legal attributes and criminal sentencing" (Hagan, 1974), and he also was a versatile author, with a large number of different works cited. Robert M. Regoli was the most-cited scholar in 1986-90. His most-cited work then was "Police cynicism and professionalism" (Lotz and Regoli, 1977), and he too was a versatile author. The highest ranked female scholar in JCJ in 2001-05 was Terrie E. Moffitt, who was ranked 6.

Of the scholars appearing in Table 5-6, 25 of them (47 percent) had been ranked in the top 50 in 1996-00, 24 (45 percent) had been ranked in the top 50 in 1991-95, and ten (19 percent) had been ranked in the top 50 in 1986-90. There was considerably more variability in JCJ than in the four journals discussed above. There was no scholar who appeared in the top ten most-cited scholars in all four time periods, although three scholars (Francis T. Cullen, Wesley G. Skogan, and Alfred Blumstein) appeared in the top twenty most-cited scholars in all four time periods.

The highest new entrants in the top 50 were Raymond Paternoster (4) Terrie E. Moffitt (6), Robert J. Bursik (7), and Daniel S. Nagin (8). Robert J. Sampson advanced from rank 23 in 1991-95 and 27.5 in 1996-00 to 2 in 2001-05. James Frank advanced considerably, from 38.5 in 1996-00 to 16.5 in 2001-05, as did Doris L. MacKenzie, who rose from 35 in 1996-00 to 16.5 in 2001-05. Scholars who moved downward in rank from 1986-90 to 2001-05 included Alfred Blumstein (from 4.5 to 20), John L. Hagan (from 7 to 24.5), Lawrence W. Sherman (from 3 to 29.5), and Robert M. Regoli (from 1 to 41.5). Eleven of the top 15 scholars in 1996-00 remained in the top 50 (actually the top 35) in 2001-05. The four that did not appear in the table were Marvin E. Wolfgang (ranked 5.5 in 1996-00), Ronald L. Akers (9), Eric D. Poole (9) and Michael H. Tonry (13.5).

Table 5-6. Most-Cited Scholars in *Journal of Criminal Justice*

Rank	Rank in 1996-00	Rank in 1991-95	Rank in 1986-90	Name	Cites
1	1	2	17.5	Francis T. Cullen	150
2	27.5	23	---	Robert J. Sampson	122
3	4	34	---	David P. Farrington	108
4	---	---	---	Raymond Paternoster	80
5	2	3.5	---	Travis Hirschi	74
6	---	---	---	Terrie E. Moffitt	71
7	---	---	---	Robert J. Bursik	66
8	---	---	---	Daniel S. Nagin	62
9.5	3	9	31	Michael R. Gottfredson	61
9.5	---	---	---	Harold G. Grasmick	61
11	---	---	---	Robert E. Worden	59
12	13.5	23	17.5	Wesley G. Skogan	56
13	---	28	---	Geoffrey P. Alpert	55
14	---	---	---	John H. Laub	54
15	---	---	---	Alex R. Piquero	51
16.5	38.5	---	---	James Frank	50
16.5	35	---	---	Doris L. MacKenzie	50
18	---	---	---	Rolf Loeber	48
20	7.5	14.5	4.5	Alfred Blumstein	47
20	---	---	---	Robert Brame	47
20	---	---	---	Paul Mazerolle	47
22.5	11	6	22.5	Joan Petersilia	46
22.5	18.5	28	---	Samuel Walker	46
24.5	31	48	---	David H. Bayley	45
24.5	13.5	1	7	John L. Hagan	45
26.5	---	---	---	Stephen D. Mastrofski	44
26.5	7.5	5	11.5	James Q. Wilson	44
28	13.5	---	---	Robert Agnew	43
29.5	5.5	7.5	3	Lawrence W. Sherman	42
29.5	22	14.5	---	Douglas A. Smith	42
32	---	---	---	Velmer S. Burton	38
32	---	---	---	Steven F. Messner	38
32	---	---	---	Stephen W. Raudenbush	38
34	---	---	---	Roger B. Parks	37
35	5.5	3.5	4.5	Marvin E. Wolfgang	36
36.5	24.5	48	31	Albert J. Reiss	35
36.5	---	---	---	Ralph B. Taylor	35
39	46.5	---	22.5	Jerome H. Skolnick	34
39	---	---	---	Mark Warr	34
39	---	---	---	Kevin N. Wright	34
41.5	---	10.5	---	Lawrence E. Cohen	32
41.5	16.5	7.5	1	Robert M. Regoli	32
45	38.5	---	---	Scott H. Decker	31
45	18.5	34	---	Nancy C. Jurik	31
45	---	---	---	Michael D. Reisig	31
45	---	---	---	Stephen G. Tibbetts	31
45	---	23	---	Susan F. Turner	31
50.5	---	---	---	John R. Hepburn	30
50.5	---	---	---	Victor E. Kappeler	30
50.5	---	48	---	Kenneth C. Land	30
50.5	---	---	---	Phil A. Silva	30
50.5	46.5	48	---	Charles R. Tittle	30
50.5	46.5	12.5	---	John T. Whitehead	30

Criminal Justice and Behavior (CJB)

In CJB in 2001 to 2005, a total of 155 articles were published by 431 authors, only 69% of whom (229) were American, making CJB clearly the most international of the six American journals. A large number of authors (90) were Canadian; in addition, there were 15 authors from the United Kingdom and 14 from the Netherlands. These articles contained a total of 16,011 cited authors, of which 1,098 were self-citations and 950 were coauthor citations, resulting in 14,913 eligible cited authors (an average of 96 per article). When this figure is compared with 10,400 eligible cited authors in 1996-00 (76 per article), 7,442 in 1991-95 (55 per article) and 6,267 in 1986-90 (46 per article), it becomes clear that the number of cited authors per article in CJB more than doubled over this time period.

Table 5-7 shows the most-cited scholars in CJB in 2001-05. The most-cited scholar, Don A. Andrews, was cited 150 times. His most-cited work in CJB were the three editions of his book, *The Psychology of Criminal Conduct* (Andrews and Bonta, 1994), which were cited a total of 25 times (the 1994 first edition was cited 9 times, the 1998 second edition was cited 13 times, and the 2003 third edition was cited 3 times). Andrews was clearly a versatile author, with 42 different works cited in 41 different articles. The comparable rankings in earlier time periods are also presented, showing that Andrews also was the most-cited scholar in 1996-00, with the same most-cited work. Andrews was the second most-cited scholar in 1991-95, which is particularly impressive because he was not ranked at all in 1986-90.

The most-cited scholar in 1991-95 was William L. Marshall, whose most-cited works then were "The long-term evaluation of a behavioral treatment program for child molesters" (Marshall and Barbaree, 1988) and "Erectile responses among heterosexual child molesters, father-daughter incest offenders and matched nonoffenders" (Barbaree and Marshall, 1989). Marshall's large number of citations was primarily a function of the large number of his different works that were cited, which may be related to the fact that in 1991-95 CJB published a number of articles focusing on sex offenders. Edwin I. Megargee, the most-cited scholar in 1986-90, was a specialized author whose most-cited work then was *Classifying Criminal Offenders* (Megargee and Bohn, 1979). Of the top 14 scholars in Table 5-7, ten of them (all except John T. Monahan, Henry J. Steadman, Edward P. Mulvey, and Francis T. Cullen) were Canadian researchers well-known for their research on the effectiveness of correctional treatment, psychopathy, and/or risk assessment.

Twenty-nine of the scholars appearing in Table 5-7 (59 percent) had been ranked in the top 50 in 1996-00, 17 (35 percent) had been ranked in the top 50 in 1991-95, and only 10 (20 percent) had been ranked in the top 50 in 1986-90, clearly illustrating how the focus of the research published in CJB has been changing over time. Only Robert D. Hare and John T. Monahan were among the 20 most-cited scholars in all four time periods.

Eleven of the most-cited scholars in CJB were women; the highest-ranked female scholar in CJB in 2001-05 was Marnie E. Rice, who was ranked 4. Scholars who made big advances between 1996-00 and 2001-05 include John T. Monahan (from 16.5 to 7), Henry J. Steadman (23.5 to 10), and Thomas Grisso (30.5 to 15). The highest-ranking scholars who appeared in the table for the first time were Edward P. Mulvey (12), R. Karl Hanson (13.5), and Loren H. Roth (16). Scholars who moved down in rank between 1986-90 and 2001-05 included Edwin I. Megargee (from 1 to 48.5) and Robert R. Ross (from 5 to 46). Of the top 18 scholars in 1996-00, only Travis Hirschi did not remain in the top 50 in 2001-05.

Table 5-7. Most-Cited Scholars in *Criminal Justice and Behavior*

Rank	Rank in 1996-00	Rank in 1991-95	Rank in 1986-90	Name	Cites
1	1	2	---	Don A. Andrews	150
2	2	8	---	James L. Bonta	145
3	3	15	6	Robert D. Hare	127
4	4	19	---	Marnie E. Rice	110
5	5	15	---	Grant T. Harris	106
6	6	3	28.5	Vernon L. Quinsey	105
7	16.5	10.5	7.5	John T. Monahan	100
8	8	---	---	Stephen D. Hart	87
9	7	38	3	Paul Gendreau	76
10	23.5	---	10	Henry J. Steadman	67
11	16.5	---	---	Christopher D. Webster	64
12	---	---	---	Edward P. Mulvey	58
13.5	11.5	27.5	16.5	Francis T. Cullen	56
13.5	---	---	---	R. Karl Hanson	56
15	30.5	---	---	Thomas Grisso	52
16	---	---	---	Loren H. Roth	47
17	30.5	---	---	Catherine A. Cormier	46
18	30.5	---	---	Rolf Loeber	45
19	13	---	---	Robert D. Hoge	43
20	---	---	---	David J. Simourd	41
22	11.5	4	---	Howard E. Barbaree	40
22	---	---	---	Kevin S. Douglas	40
22	---	9.5	---	Robert D. Rogers	40
24.5	---	---	---	Paul S. Appelbaum	38
24.5	25.5	---	---	Adele E. Forth	38
26.5	18	47	---	David P. Farrington	37
26.5	---	---	---	Eric Silver	37
28	30.5	---	---	Claire E. Goggin	36
30	---	---	---	Kirk Heilbrun	33
30	14	19	---	Lawrence L. Motiuk	33
30	37.5	---	---	Ralph C. Serin	33
32	---	---	---	Stephen Wong	32
34	---	---	---	David Eaves	31
34	---	---	---	Paul E. Meehl	31
34	---	---	---	Pamela C. Robbins	31
36	---	---	---	Randall T. Salekin	30
37.5	9.5	---	---	Terrie E. Moffitt	29
37.5	---	---	---	Kenneth W. Sewell	29
39	19.5	15	---	J. Stephen Wormith	27
41	21.5	---	---	M. Douglas Anglin	25
41	---	---	---	Steven Banks	25
41	45.5	---	---	Doris L. MacKenzie	25
43.5	---	---	---	George De Leon	24
43.5	---	---	---	James R. P. Ogloff	24
46	---	---	---	David J. Cooke	23
46	50.5	1	40.5	William L. Marshall	23
46	15	---	5	Robert R. Ross	23
48.5	30.5	19	1	Edwin I. Megargee	22
48.5	---	29.5	33.5	David D. Robinson	22

Three Criminal Justice Journals Combined

A combined measure of influence based on all three criminal justice journals was computed; Table 5-8 shows the 30 most-cited scholars on this combined measure. There appears to be considerably less agreement as to the most-cited scholars in the criminal justice journals than among the criminology journals. Of the scholars appearing in Table 5-8, only Francis T. Cullen (1), David P. Farrington (2), and Terrie E. Moffitt (13) were among the top 50 scholars in all three journals. A number of the scholars that appeared from rank 20 onwards were ranked in the top 50 in only one of the three journals.

Table 5-8. Most-Cited Scholars in Three American Criminal Justice Journals

Rank	Rank in 1996-00	Rank in 1991-95	Rank in 1986-90	Name	JQ	JCJ	CJB	TOTAL
1	1	1	4	Francis T. Cullen	48	50	37.5	135.5
2	4	17	--	David P. Farrington	40.5	48	24.5	113
3	12	11	--	Robert J. Sampson	50	49	0	99
4	2	3	16	Travis Hirschi	49	46	0	95
5	24.5	--	--	Raymond Paternoster	45	47	0	92
6	3	6	12	Michael R. Gottfredson	46	41.5	0	87.5
7	--	--	--	Robert J. Bursik	43	44	0	87
8	--	--	--	Harold G. Grasmick	44	41.5	0	85.5
9	--	--	--	John H. Laub	47	37	0	84
10	--	--	--	Rolf Loeber	17	33	33	83
11	--	--	--	Daniel S. Nagin	38	43	0	81
12	--	--	--	Alex R. Piquero	42	36	0	78
13	17	--	--	Terrie E. Moffitt	17	45	13.5	75.5
14	8.5	13.5	14	Wesley G. Skogan	30	39	0	69
15	8.5	4	13	Lawrence W. Sherman	40.5	21.5	0	62
16	5	2	10	John L. Hagan	33	26.5	0	59.5
17	--	--	--	Stephen W. Raudenbush	39	19	0	58
18	--	--	--	Robert E. Worden	17	40	0	57
19	11	5	7.5	James Q. Wilson	26	24.5	0	50.5
20	19	18	--	Don A. Andrews	0	0	50	50
21.5	20.5	--	--	James L. Bonta	0	0	49	49
21.5	--	--	--	Mark Warr	37	12	0	49
23	22.5	--	--	Robert D. Hare	0	0	48	48
24	24.5	--	--	Marnie E. Rice	0	0	47	47
25	26	--	--	Grant T. Harris	0	0	46	46
26	28.5	23	--	Vernon L. Quinsey	0	0	45	45
27	--	--	--	Doris L. MacKenzie	0	34.5	10	44.5
28.5	7	--	--	Robert Agnew	21	23	0	44
28.5	--	--	--	John T. Monahan	0	0	44	44
30	--	--	--	Stephen D. Hart	0	0	43	43

The most-cited scholar in the three American criminal justice journals was Francis T. Cullen, whose most-cited work, "Does correctional treatment work? A clinically relevant and psychologically informed meta-analysis" (Andrews et al., 1990), was cited 21 times. Cullen was also the most-cited scholar in these three journals in 1996-00 and in 1991-05, moving up from a rank of 4 in 1986-90. The second most-cited scholar was David P. Farrington, whose most-cited work, "Life-course trajectories of different types of offenders" (Nagin, Farrington, and Moffitt, 1995) was cited only seven times. Farrington's advancement is notable as he did not even appear in the table in 1986-90. Robert J. Sampson was ranked third and his most-cited work, *Crime in the Making* (Sampson and Laub, 1993), was cited 37 times. The fourth most-cited scholar was Travis Hirschi; his most-cited work was *A General Theory of Crime* (Gottfredson and Hirschi, 1990), which was cited 74 times. Sampson and Hirschi were specialized scholars, whereas Cullen and Farrington were versatile. Overall, the most-cited works in the three American criminal justice journals tended to be on criminal career research, criminological theories, and/or rehabilitation.

Table 5-8 also shows the comparable ranking of the most-cited scholars in the three earlier time periods. Of the 30 most-cited scholars in 2001-05, eighteen (60 percent) were in the top 30 in 1996-00, eleven (37 percent) were in the top 30 in 1991-95, and seven (23 percent) were in the top 30 in 1986-90. All except two of the top twelve scholars in 1996-00 (Delbert S. Elliott, ranked 6, and David Huizinga, ranked 10) appeared in the top 30 in 2001-05.

The highest new entrants in Table 5-8 in 2001-05 were Robert J. Bursik (7) and Harold G. Grasmick (8); in point of fact, none of the scholars ranked 7 through 12 had appeared previously in this table. Scholars who made notable advances between 1996-00 and 2001-05 included Raymond Paternoster (from 24.5 to 5) and Robert J. Sampson (from 12 to 3). Scholars who moved downwards from 1986-90 to 2001-05 included John L. Hagan (from 5 to 16) and Robert Agnew (from 7 to 28.5). There was clearly more variability across time periods than was seen in the criminology journals. None of the three most-cited scholars in the three criminal justice journals in 1986-90 (Eric D. Poole, Robert M. Regoli, and Marvin E. Wolfgang) appeared in the 2001-05 list of most-cited scholars. Wolfgang, in particular, declined from 3 in 1986-90 to 9 in 1991-95, 27 in 1996-00, and 75 in 2001-05.

INTERNATIONAL JOURNALS

The three international journals that were analyzed were *Australian and New Zealand Journal of Criminology* (ANZ), *British Journal of Criminology* (BJC), and *Canadian Journal of Criminology and Criminal Justice* (CJC).

Australian and New Zealand Journal of Criminology (ANZ)

Between 2001 and 2005, 108 articles were published in ANZ by 194 authors, 73 percent of whom (141) were located in Australia and 5 percent of whom (10) were located in New Zealand. The other authors were most commonly from the United States (15) or the United Kingdom (11). The number of articles in ANZ did not change significantly compared to the previous time period (101 articles published in ANZ in 1996-00); however, there was a clear increase in the number of authors of those articles (from 142 in 1996-00).

These articles included a total of 7,558 cited authors, of which 475 were self-citations and 217 were co-author citations, resulting in 7,083 eligible cited authors (an average of 66 cited authors per article). This may be compared with 4,592 cited authors in 1996-00 (45 per article), 3,833 in 1991-95 (39 per article) and 3,620 in 1986-90 (43 per article). Although the number of cited authors per article had been fairly stable, it increased noticeably during the 2001-05 time period.

Table 5-9 shows the most-cited scholars in ANZ in 2001-05. There are actually 59 names in this table, as there were 19 scholars with tied ranks of 50. David Brown and Patrick O'Malley, both of whom appear in this table, refer to scholars in Australia, as opposed to the British David Brown and the American Patrick M. O'Malley.

The most-cited scholar was Lawrence W. Sherman, who was cited 53 times. His most-cited work, *Preventing Crime* (Sherman et al., 1997) was cited only seven times. Sherman's high ranking was primarily a function of the large number of his different works that were cited; he was a very versatile author, with 29 different works cited in 25 different articles in ANZ.

Table 5-9 also shows the comparable rankings of these scholars in the three earlier time periods. In both 1996-00 and 1991-95, the most cited scholar was John Braithwaite. In both time periods, his most-cited work was *Crime, Shame and Reintegration* (Braithwaite, 1989). Richard G. Fox, a specialized author, was the most-cited scholar in 1986-90. His most-cited work then was *Sentencing* (Fox and Freiberg, 1985).

Thirteen of the most-cited scholars in ANZ were female, more than in any of the other eight journals analyzed in this chapter. The highest-ranked female scholars were Kathleen Daly (4) and Heather Strang (9). Both were new entrants, neither having been among the 50 most-cited scholars in any of the earlier time periods studied. Strang publishes frequently with Sherman, which may help to account for her high citation count in 2001-05.

Of the most-cited scholars in 2001-05, eighteen (31 percent) had been ranked in the top 50 in 1996-00, nineteen (32 percent) had been ranked in the top 50 in 1991-95, and fifteen (25 percent) had been ranked in the top 50 in 1986-90. A number of scholars showed distinct changes in rankings, both up and down. Lawrence W. Sherman, for example, did not appear in the 1986-90 most-cited scholars list, was ranked 17.5 in 1991-95, fell to 29.5 in 1996-00, and then advanced to first in 2001-05. Such fluctuations are more likely in ANZ, as it has relatively few citations compared with some of the other journals under study. John Braithwaite, on the other hand, showed clear evidence of stability, being among the three most-cited scholars in all four time periods.

Scholars who showed notable advancement between 1996-00 and 2001-05 included Jock Young (from 19.5 to 7), Ross J. Homel (from 35.5 to 10), and Rob White (from 29.5 to 14). Scholars who moved downwards in rank between 1986-90 and 2001-05 include Stanley Cohen (from 3.5 to 50) and David Brown (from 10.5 to 50). Of the top nine scholars in 1996-00, seven survived to be in the top 50 in 2001-05 (neither Ken Pease nor Andrew Ashworth appeared in Table 5-9).

Table 5-9. Most-Cited Scholars in Australian and New Zealand Journal of Criminology

Rank in 2001-05	Rank in 1996-00	Rank in 1991-95	Rank in 1986-90	Name	Number of cites
1	29.5	17.5	--	Lawrence W. Sherman	53
2	1	1	3.5	John Braithwaite	48
3	--	29.5	43	David P. Farrington	34
4	--	--	--	Kathleen Daly	32
5	--	--	--	Robert J. Sampson	30
6	2	12	--	David Garland	27

Rank in 2001-05	Rank in 1996-00	Rank in 1991-95	Rank in 1986-90	Name	Number of cites
7	19.5	6.5	32.5	Jock Young	26
8	7.5	35.5	--	John Pratt[3]	22
9	--	--	--	Heather Strang	21
10	35.5	--	--	Ross J. Homel[1]	20
11	--	17.5	--	Clifford D. Shearing	19
12	--	--	--	David H. Bayley	16
14	--	--	--	Toni Makkai	15
14	3	4	--	Patrick O'Malley *	15
14	29.5	--	--	Rob White	15
16.5	--	--	43	Travis Hirschi	14
16.5	--	--	--	Bronwyn Lind	14
20.5	7.5	13.5	--	Michel Foucault	13
20.5	35.5	15	6.5	Arie Freiberg	13
20.5	--	--	--	John H. Laub	13
20.5	--	--	--	Terrie E. Moffitt	13
20.5	22.5	--	21	Allison M. Morris	13
20.5	--	13.5	6.5	Kenneth Polk	13
26	--	--	32.5	Alfred Blumstein	12
26	--	--	--	Shawn D. Bushway	12
26	--	--	--	David Dixon[2]	12
26	--	--	--	David Indermauer	12
26	--	--	--	Nick Tilley	12
34.5	--	--	--	Albert Bandura	11
34.5	22.5	45.5	21	Janet B.L. Chan	11
34.5	--	--	--	Ronald V. Clarke	11
34.5	--	--	21	Jacqueline Cohen	11
34.5	--	--	--	Michael R. Gottfredson	11
34.5	--	--	--	Wayne Hall	11
34.5	--	--	--	Gordon Hughes	11
34.5	--	--	--	Alison Liebling	11
34.5	--	--	--	Tim Prenzler	11
34.5	11	--	--	Jonathan Simon	11
34.5	--	--	--	Don Weatherburn	11
34.5	--	--	43	James Q. Wilson	11
50	--	45.5	32.5	Anthony E. Bottoms	10
50	16	45.5	10.5	David Brown *	10
50	--	--	--	Pat Carlen	10
50	--	--	--	Richard F. Catalano	10
50	7.5	8	3.5	Stanley Cohen	10
50	--	--	--	Adam Crawford	10
50	4.5	9.5	--	Chris Cunneen	10
50	--	--	--	Marcus Felson	10
50	--	--	--	J. David Hawkins	10
50	45	45.5	--	Tony Jefferson	10
50	--	--	--	Trevor Jones	10
50	--	24	--	John Lea	10
50	26	--	--	Gabrielle Maxwell	10
50	--	--	--	Patricia M. Mayhew	10
50	--	--	--	Tim Newburn	10
50	--	--	--	Michael Oakshott	10
50	--	--	--	Peter Reuter	10
50	--	--	--	Tim Stockwell	10
50	--	29.5	12.5	Marvin E. Wolfgang	10

[1] Editor, 1993-94; [2] Editor, 1995-97; [3] Editor, 1998-2005; * from Australia.

British Journal of Criminology (BJC)

A total of 217 articles were published in BJC in 2001-05. These articles were written by 417 individual authors, 57 percent of whom (237) were from the United Kingdom. There were also a large number of authors from United States (53) as well as 39 from Australia and 30 from Canada. Both the number of articles and the number of authors increased considerably from 1996-00, when the journal published 170 articles by 279 individual authors. In 2001-05, the 217 articles contained a total of 16,408 cited authors, of which 1,082 were self-citations and 662 were co-author citations. When the resulting 15,326 eligible cited authors (an average of 71 cited authors per article) is compared with 10,023 in 1996-00 (59 per article), 6,771 in 1991-95 (47 per article), and 5,665 in 1986-90 (44 per article), it is clear that the number of cited authors per BJC article has increased by about 61 percent over this time period.

Table 5-10 presents the 51 most-cited scholars in BJC in 2001-05. John Braithwaite was the most-cited scholar in BJC. He was cited 74 times and was a very versatile author, with 31 different works cited in 31 different articles. His most cited work, which was cited 14 times, was *Crime, Shame and Reintegration* (Braithwaite, 1989). Braithwaite has advanced steadily in the rankings of most-cited scholars in BJC, moving from 19 in 1986-90 to 10 in 1991-95, 8 in 1996-00, and 1 in 2001-05.

In 1996-00, Ken Pease was the most-cited scholar in BJC. He too was mainly a versatile author as his most-cited work then, *The Kirkholt Burglary Prevention Project* (Forrester, Chatterton, and Pease, 1988), was cited only six times. The most-cited scholar in 1991-95 was Patricia M. Mayhew. Her most-cited works then were *The 1988 British Crime Survey* (Mayhew, Elliott, and Dowds, 1989) and *The British Crime Survey* (Hough and Mayhew, 1983), each of which was cited nine times. The second most-cited scholar in 1991-95, J. Michael Hough, was also best-known for his work on the British Crime Survey, and was a co-author of one of Mayhew's two most-cited works. The most-cited scholar in 1986-90 was Stanley Cohen, a specialized author whose most-cited work then was *Visions of Social Control* (Cohen, 1985).

Twenty-six of the scholars (51 percent) in Table 5-10 had been ranked in the top 50 in 1996-00, 20 (39 percent) had been ranked in the top 50 in 1991-95, and 15 (29 percent) had been ranked in the top 50 in 1986-90. The highest ranked female scholars in BJC in 2001-05 were Allison M. Morris (a new entrant in the table at rank 12.5) and Patricia M. Mayhew (15).

Both David P. Farrington and Ken Pease showed distinct stability over time as both were among the eight most-cited scholars in all four time periods. A number of scholars advanced noticeably in the rankings between 1996-00 and 2001-05, including Clifford D. Shearing (from 11 to 4) and Tim Newburn (from 48 to 12.5). Stanley Cohen also advanced significantly, but his rankings showed considerable fluctuation, falling from first in 1986-90 to 12 in 1991-95 and 28 in 1996-00, and then rising back up to 6 in 2001-05. Scholars who moved down in rank between 1986-90 and 2001-05 included Anthony E. Bottoms (from 6 to 23), Patricia M. Mayhew (from 5 to 15), and J. Michael Hough (from 3.5 to 17.5). The highest new entrants among the most-cited scholars in 2001-05 were Allison M. Morris (12.5), Richard T. Wright (15), and Scott H. Decker (17.5). The nine most-cited scholars in 1996-00 all survived to be in the top 50 (actually in the top 35) in 2001-05. The highest ranked scholar in 1996-00 who did not appear in the 2001-05 table was Geoffrey Pearson (ranked 11), who was editor of BJC from 1999 to 2005.

Table 5-10. Most-Cited Scholars in *British Journal of Criminology*

Rank in 2001-05	Rank in 1996-00	Rank in 1991-95	Rank in 1986-90	Name	Number of cites
1	8	10	19	John Braithwaite	74
2	6	5.5	3.5	David P. Farrington	60
3	9	26.5	14	David Garland	51
4	11	--	--	Clifford D. Shearing	50
5	--	44.5	--	Robert J. Sampson	45
6	28	12	1	Stanley Cohen	40
7	17	3.5	2	Jock Young	39
8	1	3.5	8	Ken Pease	37
10	2	5.5	9	Ronald V. Clarke	35
10	13.5	17	44.5	Tony Jefferson	35
10	3	26.5	38.5	Robert Reiner	35
12.5	--	--	--	Allison M. Morris	34
12.5	48	--	--	Tim Newburn	34
15	17	--	--	Marcus Felson	33
15	7	1	5	Patricia M. Mayhew	33
15	--	--	--	Richard T. Wright	33
17.5	--	--	--	Scott H. Decker	32
17.5	4	2	3.5	J. Michael Hough	32
19	36.5	--	--	Richard V. Ericson	31
20.5	--	--	--	Adam Crawford	30
20.5	--	--	--	Kathleen Daly	30
23	13.5	8	6	Anthony E. Bottoms	29
23	--	--	--	J. Richard Sparks	29
23	17	--	--	Elizabeth A. Stanko	29
26.5	--	--	--	Benjamin Bowling	28
26.5	11	17	24	Michel Foucault	28
26.5	--	--	--	Michael Levi	28
26.5	43.5	17	--	Mike Maguire	28
29.5	20	13.5	--	Michael R. Gottfredson	27
29.5	--	44.5	--	Rolf Loeber	27
31.5	--	--	--	Lawrence E. Cohen	26
31.5	--	29	--	Lawrence W. Sherman	26
34	5	--	--	Anthony Giddens	25
34	--	--	--	Terance D. Miethe	25
34	23	--	--	Patrick O'Malley*	25
36	48	--	--	David Matza	24
37.5	--	--	--	Jason Ditton	23
37.5	--	--	--	Loraine R. Gelsthorpe	23
40.5	--	--	--	Les Johnston	22
40.5	--	--	--	Gabrielle Maxwell	22
40.5	20	--	--	Jonathan Simon	22
40.5	24.5	17	--	Wesley G. Skogan	22
45.5	--	--	--	R. Emerson Dobash	21
45.5	--	--	--	Russell P. Dobash	21
45.5	--	--	30	Stuart Hall	21
45.5	15	8	16.5	Travis Hirschi	21
45.5	--	--	--	Steven F. Messner	21
45.5	--	--	--	Edwin H. Sutherland	21
50	--	--	--	James Dignan	20
50	--	--	--	Dick Hobbs	20
50	--	--	--	Robert E. Park	20

* From Australia.

Table 5-11. Most-Cited Scholars in Canadian Journal of Criminology and Criminal Justice

Rank in 2001-05	Rank in 1996-00	Rank in 1991-95	Rank in 1986-90	Name	Number of cites
1	1	23	16	Julian V. Roberts[1]	37
2	9.5	--	11	James L. Bonta	34
3	2	2.5	1	Anthony N. Doob	32
4	15	37.5	2	Paul Gendreau	28
5	--	8	--	Travis Hirschi	25
6	40.5	31	--	David P. Farrington	23
7	6	13	9	Don A. Andrews	21
8	--	44.5	--	Lawrence W. Sherman	20
9.5	--	23	36	Michael R. Gottfredson	19
9.5	--	--	--	Philip C. Stenning	19
12	7.5	--	4.5	Francis T. Cullen	17
12	4	44.5	--	Richard V. Ericson	17
12	12	--	--	Jane B. Sprott	17
14	--	--	--	Peter J. Carrington[2]	16
16.5	--	--	--	R. Karl Hanson	15
16.5	--	23	4.5	Marc LeBlanc	15
16.5	--	--	--	Kent Roach	15
16.5	20.5	--	--	Robert J. Sampson	15
20	--	--	--	William L. Marshall	13
20	24	--	29	Lawrence L. Motiuk	13
20	--	18.5	--	Sharon Moyer	13
23.5	--	--	--	Robert Agnew	12
23.5	--	--	7	Ronald V. Clarke	12
23.5	--	--	--	Terrie E. Moffitt	12
23.5	--	--	--	Ivan Zinger	12
27	--	--	--	Claire Goggin	11
27	--	--	--	Denise C. Gottfredson	11
27	--	--	--	Raymond A. Knight	11
34	--	--	--	Bruce J. Arneklev	10
34	--	--	--	Robert J. Bursik	10
34	--	--	--	Patricia Erickson	10
34	--	--	22	Thomas Gabor	10
34	--	--	--	Harold G. Grasmick	10
34	5	--	14	John L. Hagan	10
34	--	--	--	Kevin D. Haggerty	10
34	--	--	--	Doris L. MacKenzie	10
34	--	--	--	Marc Ouimet	10
34	--	--	--	Albert J. Reiss	10
34	--	--	47.5	Michael H. Tonry	10
46.5	24	7	47.5	Nicholas Bala	9
46.5	--	--	--	Howard E. Barbaree	9
46.5	--	--	9	Maurice Cusson	9
46.5	--	--	--	John Duncanson	9
46.5	--	--	--	John Eck	9
46.5	--	--	--	Tim Hope	9
46.5	29	18.5	--	Leslie W. Kennedy	9
46.5	--	--	29	Pierre Landreville	9
46.5	--	--	29	Patricia M. Mayhew	9
46.5	--	--	--	Robert A. Prentky	9
46.5	--	--	--	Jennifer Quinn	9
46.5	--	--	--	Peter Reuter	9
46.5	--	--	--	Michelle Shepard	9
46.5	--	--	--	Brandon C. Welsh	9

[1] Editor, 1993-04; [2] Editor, 2005-present.

Canadian Journal of Criminology and Criminal Justice (CJC)

In 2001-05, a total of 124 articles were published in CJC by 228 authors, 90 percent of whom (206) were Canadian. Both the number of articles published in CJC and the number of authors of those articles increased noticeably from 1996-00, when there were 104 articles and 181 authors. As CJC primarily publishes articles with a Canadian focus, the low percentage of non-Canadian authors is not really surprising. In 2001-05, the non-Canadian authors were most commonly American (8) or British (5).

These 124 articles contained a total of 6,143 cited authors, of which 455 were self-citations and 316 were co-author citations, producing a total of 5,688 eligible citations (an average of 46 cited authors per article). This may be compared with 4,469 in 1996-00 (43 cited authors per article), 4,184 in 1991-95 (34 per article) and 4,049 in 1986-90 (30 per article). Overall, the number of cited authors per article in CJC increased by 53 percent over this time period.

Table 5-11 shows the most-cited scholars in CJC in 2001-05, those ranked up to 50. The table includes 53 scholars because there were 14 scholars with tied ranks of 46.5. The most-cited scholar was Julian V. Roberts, who was cited a total of 37 times. Roberts, who served as the editor of CJC from 1993 to 2004, was a versatile author, with 34 different works cited in 19 different articles, and no single work cited more than two times. His three most-cited works were *The Use of Victim Impact Statements in Sentencing* (Roberts, 2002), "The incarceration of Aboriginal offenders" (Roberts and Melchers, 2003), and "Empty promises" (Stenning and Roberts, 2001), with two cites each.

The second most-cited scholar, James L. Bonta (34 cites), was more specialized, with 17 different works cited in 12 different articles. His most cited work was *The Psychology of Criminal Conduct* (Andrews and Bonta, 1994), with 9 cites, although multiple editions of this work were included in this count. The highest ranked female scholars in CJC in 2001-05 were Jane B. Sprott (12) and Sharon Moyer (20). Three authors in the table were journalists: John Duncanson, Jennifer Quinn, and Michelle Shepard. Each was cited in only three different articles. A number of the most-cited scholars in 2001-05, including James L. Bonta, Paul Gendreau, Don A. Andrews, Francis T. Cullen, and R. Karl Hanson, were associated with research on rehabilitation and meta-analysis.

Table 5-11 also shows the comparable rankings of these scholars in CJC in 1996-00, 1991-95, and 1986-00. Julian V. Roberts was also the most-cited scholar in 1996-00. His most-cited work then was "Public opinion, crime, and criminal justice" (Roberts, 1992), which was cited six times. The most-cited scholar in 1991-95 was Murray A. Straus, whose most-cited work was *Behind Closed Doors* (Straus, Gelles, and Steinmetz, 1980). However, more than half of Straus' citations in CJC during that time period appeared in one article (Lenton, 1995), so he had a low prevalence. Anthony N. Doob was the most-cited scholar in 1986-90, and his most-cited work during that time period was *Sentencing* (Doob and Roberts, 1983).

Of the scholars appearing in Table 5-11, only 14 (26 percent) had been ranked in the top 50 in 1996-00, 13 (25 percent) had been ranked in the top 50 in 1991-95, and 17 (32 percent) had been ranked in the top 50 in 1986-90. Like ANZ, CJC is a journal with fewer citations, which may result in considerable variation in the rankings between one time periods. Among those scholars who showed some consistency of rankings was Julian V. Roberts, who was ranked 16 in 1986-90, 23 in 1991-95, and first in both 1996-00 and 2001-05. In addition,

Anthony N. Doob was ranked in the top 3 in all four time periods and Don A. Andrews was ranked in the top 13 in all four time periods. Philip C. Stenning was a new entrant at 9.5 in 2001-05 as he had not appeared among the most-cited scholars in any of the prior time periods. David P. Farrington advanced from 40.5 in 1996-00 to 6 in 2001-05. Only four of the top ten scholars in 1996-00 survived to be in the top 50 in 2001-05.

Table 5-12. Most-Cited Scholars in Three International Journals

Rank	Rank in 1996-00	Rank in 1991-95	Rank in 1986-90	Name	ANZ	BJC	CJC	TOTAL
1	17	3	12	David P. Farrington	48	49	45	142
2	--	--	--	Robert J. Sampson	46	46	34.5	126.5
3	--	11	--	Lawrence W. Sherman	50	19.5	43	112.5
4	1	2	4	John Braithwaite	49	50	0	99
5	2	9	42.5	David Garland	45	48	0	93
6	13	1	7	Jock Young	44	44	0	88
7	7	--	--	Clifford D. Shearing	40	47	0	87
8	--	4	29	Travis Hirschi	34.5	5.5	46	86
9	20.5	27	3	Ronald V. Clarke	16.5	41	27.5	85
10	--	8	--	Michael R. Gottfredson	16.5	21.5	41.5	79.5
11	--	--	--	Kathleen Daly	47	30.5	0	77.5
12	3	--	--	Richard V. Ericson	0	32	39	71
13	--	--	--	Allison M. Morris	30.5	38.5	0	69
14	--	--	--	Terrie E. Moffitt	30.5	0	27.5	58
15	6	7	--	Michel Foucault	30.5	24.5	0	55
16	5	22.5	--	Patrick O'Malley	37	17	0	54
17	16	--	--	Julian V. Roberts	0	0	50	50
18	10	--	--	James L. Bonta	0	0	49	49
19	20.5	18	14.5	Anthony N. Doob	0	0	48	48
20	--	--	--	Paul Gendreau	0	0	47	47
21	12	5	1	Stanley Cohen	1	45	0	46
22	8	--	--	Don A. Andrews	0	0	44	44
23.5	27.5	--	--	John Pratt	43	0	0	43
23.5	4	21	28	Ken Pease	0	43	0	43
25.5	27.5	--	--	Tony Jefferson	1	41	0	42
25.5	--	--	--	Heather Strang	42	0	0	42
27.5	25	13.5	6	Patricia M. Mayhew	1	36	4.5	41.5
27.5	--	--	--	Philip C. Stenning	0	0	41.5	41.5
29.5	--	--	--	Ross J. Homel	41	0	0	41
29.5	14	--	--	Robert Reiner	0	41	0	41

* From Australia.

THREE INTERNATIONAL JOURNALS COMBINED

A combined measure of influence based on all three international journals was computed. The 30 most-cited scholars on this combined measure are shown in Table 5-12. The most-cited scholars were David P. Farrington, Robert J. Sampson, and Lawrence W. Sherman, and all three were all among the most-cited scholars in all three journals. In addition to them, four others, Travis Hirschi, Ronald V. Clarke, Michael R. Gottfredson, and Patricia M. Mayhew, were also among the most-cited in all three international journals. The international journals showed more agreement than the three criminal justice journals (only four scholars were among the most cited in all three criminal justice journals) but much less agreement than the three criminology journals (only three of the 30 most-cited scholars in the three criminology journals were *not* among the most-cited scholars in all three journals). All of the top 16 scholars in international journals in 2001-05 were highly cited in at least two of these journals.

The most-cited works of the most-cited scholars in these three journals were determined. David Farrington's two most-cited works were "Explaining and preventing crime: The globalization of knowledge" (Farrington, 2000) and "Age and crime" (Farrington, 1986). Each had only four cites; Farrington was an extremely versatile author with 81 different works cited. Robert J. Sampson's most cited work was, not surprisingly, *Crime in the Making* (Sampson and Laub, 1993), which was cited 12 times. Lawrence W. Sherman's most-cited work was "Preventing crime: What works, what doesn't, what's promising" (Sherman et al., 1998), which was cited 18 times. John Braithwaite's most-cited work was *Crime, Shame, and Reintegration* (Braithwaite, 1989), which was cited 23 times. Sampson had 51 different works cited, Sherman had 42 different works cited, and Braithwaite had 45 different works cited.

Table 5-12 also shows the comparable rankings of these scholars in 1996-00, 1991-95 and 1986-90. Nineteen of the most-cited scholars in 2001-05 (63 percent) were in the top 30 in 1996-00, 14 (47 percent) were in the top 30 in 1991-95 and 10 (33 percent) were in the top 30 in 1986-90. Nine of the top 10 scholars in 1996-00 survived to be in the top 30 in 2001-05; only Anthony Giddens did not appear. John Braithwaite was among the four most-cited scholars in all four time periods. The highest new entrants in 2001-05 were Robert J. Sampson (2), Kathleen Daly (11), Allison M. Morris (13), and Terrie E. Moffitt (14). Scholars who advanced noticeably between 1996-00 and 2001-05 include David Farrington (from 17 to first), Jock Young (from 13 to 6), and Ronald V. Clarke (from 20.5 to 9). Scholars who moved downwards in rank from 1986-90 to 2001-05 include Patricia M. Mayhew (from 6 to 26.5) and Stanley Cohen (from 1 to 21).

CONCLUSIONS

This research is based on citations in only a small number of mainstream CCJ journals in the English-speaking world. This is both a strength and a weakness. The selected journals are all prestigious CCJ journals, allowing a research focus on citations in these specific journals. If a more generic source of citation data, such as SSCI, had been used, citations from a wide variety of journals that are either less prestigious or have little or nothing to do with criminology would have been included. However, the present research is limited to journals that were being published in 1986, when this analysis of citations began, and thus it is not possible to include more recent journals. For example, if the research was beginning today, the *European Journal of Criminology* would most likely have been included.

This study of citation trends in nine major CCJ journals over 20 years shows how the influence of one generation of scholars was gradually being replaced by the influence of the next generation. Highly cited scholars of the 1980s, such as Alfred Blumstein and Jacqueline Cohen, were gradually being cited less. Deceased scholars such as Douglas A. Smith, Michael J. Hindelang, and Marvin E. Wolfgang were also being cited less.

Robert J. Sampson, who was once taught by Alfred Blumstein, was the most highly-cited scholar in three major American criminology journals in 2001-05. Two other scholars who were greatly influenced by Blumstein (Daniel S. Nagin and David P. Farrington) were also among the most highly-cited scholars in these journals. Thus, as Blumstein's own citations decreased, his influence lived on in the next generation of scholars. The most highly-cited scholars in these journals still tended to focus on longitudinal/criminal career research and/or criminological theories. There was generally good agreement among the three criminology journals on the most-cited scholars.

The most highly-cited scholars in two of the three American criminal justice journals (JQ and JCJ) overlapped with those in American criminology journals, with the addition of some scholars who specialized in criminal justice topics such as rehabilitation, sentencing, and law enforcement (e.g. Francis T. Cullen, Lawrence W. Sherman, Wesley G. Skogan, and James Q. Wilson). However, the most highly-cited scholars in CJB tended to be Canadian researchers who focused on the effectiveness of rehabilitative treatment, psychopathy, or risk assessment.

The most-cited works of the most-cited authors show that some scholars (e.g., Robert J. Sampson, Travis Hirschi) were specialized, because they had a large number of citations of one or two seminal works, usually books and often theoretical in nature. Other scholars (e.g., Francis T. Cullen, David P. Farrington) were versatile, because they had many different works cited a few times each. Hence, there are two different ways in which scholarly influence operates in CCJ.

This analysis of citations over 20 years shows the emerging influence of a new generation of younger scholars, notably Robert J. Sampson, Raymond Paternoster, Daniel S. Nagin, Terrie E. Moffitt, John H. Laub, and, most recently, Alex R. Piquero. If these analyses could be continued for many more years, the complete trajectories of criminological citation careers could be documented. These kinds of analyses would greatly advance knowledge about the waxing and waning of scholarly influence in criminology.

In the three international journals, the most-cited scholars were Lawrence W. Sherman in ANZ, Julian V. Roberts in CJC, and John Braithwaite in BJC. In all three journals combined, the most-cited scholars were David P. Farrington, Robert J. Sampson, Lawrence W. Sherman, and John Braithwaite. The most-cited works of the most-cited authors show that some scholars were specialized while others were more versatile.

To a considerable extent, all nine journals tended to be parochial, with the majority of published articles by scholars from their own countries. BJC was the most international and least parochial of the four, with 57 percent of published articles written by scholars from the United Kingdom, followed by CJB (69 percent American). JQ and JRCD were the most parochial, with 97 percent and 94 percent (respectively) of the published articles written by scholars from the USA. Thus, the field of criminology does not appear to truly reflect the increasing globalization of the world as a whole. Ideally, criminology should become more global, with increasing communication and collaboration among criminologists from different countries, and with a greater emphasis on cross-national collaborative studies designed to compare and contrast theories and findings in different countries. Perhaps, in selecting articles for publication, major criminological journals should place more emphasis on scholarly quality and less emphasis on the location of the authors.

Over time, the average number of cited authors per article has tended to increase. This may reflect either the increasing volume of criminological literature over time or the increasing ease of accessing it. Twenty years ago, it was much more difficult for scholars to obtain and read source works, as they had to obtain printed copies of journal articles from their university library, or request them through inter-library loan. Today, more and more journals are available online in a full-text format, and can be accessed anywhere, as long as a scholar has internet access. It might be expected that, in light of the increasing accessibility of journal articles, scholars will cite more articles than books in the future.

In the next chapter, we review the most-cited scholars in all nine journals combined, their most-cited works, and the waxing and waning of criminological careers.

Chapter 6

MOST-CITED SCHOLARS AND WORKS
IN NINE MAJOR JOURNALS

In addition to examining individual journals, we also combined the citation rankings in all nine of the American and international criminology and criminal justice (CCJ) journals, to establish the most-cited scholars in all nine journals combined. This was determined by adding together the scores of scholars in American criminology, American criminal justice, and international journals (from Chapter 5). Table 6-1 identifies the 51 most-cited authors in all nine journals.

The five most-cited scholars in all nine journals were David P. Farrington, Robert J. Sampson, Travis Hirschi, Michael R. Gottfredson, and Francis T. Cullen. All five were highly cited in all three categories of journals. While only Farrington was among the most-cited scholars in all nine journals, Sampson, Hirschi, and Gottfredson were all among the most-cited scholars in eight of the nine journals (all except CJB), and Cullen was among the most-cited scholars in seven (all except ANZ and BJC). In general, Farrington was most highly-cited in international journals, Cullen was most highly-cited in criminal justice journals, and the rest were most highly-cited in criminology journals.

Table 6-1 also shows the comparable rankings of these scholars in 1996-00, 1991-95 and 1986-90. Travis Hirschi was the most-cited scholar in 1996-00 and 1991-95. Marvin E. Wolfgang, who does not appear in Table 6-1, was the most-cited scholar in 1986-90. Thirty two of these scholars (63 percent) had been ranked in the top 50 in 1996-00, 21 (41%) had been ranked in the top 50 in 1991-95, and 12 (29%) had been ranked in the top 50 in 1986-90. Noteworthy advances between 1986-90 and 2001-05 were made by Raymond Paternoster (from 49 to 8) and Lawrence W. Sherman (from 36.5 to 10). Four scholars advanced from outside the top 50 in 1986-90 to the top 10 in 2001-05: Robert J. Sampson (2), Terrie E. Moffitt (6), John H. Laub (7), and Daniel S. Nagin (9).

Scholars who moved downwards in rank between 1986-90 and 2001-05 included Alfred Blumstein (from 3 to 15), John L. Hagan (from 5 to 19), and James Q. Wilson (from 6 to 38). All except one of the top 15 scholars in 1996-00 survived to be in the top 50 (actually in the top 24) in 2001-05. The highest ranked scholars in 1996-00 who did not survive to be in the top 50 in 2001-05 were Douglas A. Smith (10), Ronald L. Akers (16), and Christy A. Visher (17).

Table 6-1. Most-Cited Scholars in Nine Journals

Rank	Rank in 1996-00	Rank in 1991-95	Rank in 1986-90	Name	CRIM	CJ	INT	TOTAL
1	2	3	10	David P. Farrington	135	113	142	390
2	5	7	--	Robert J. Sampson	148.5	99	126.5	374
3	1	1	4	Travis Hirschi	142.5	95	86	323.5
4	3	2	7	Michael R. Gottfredson	134	87.5	79.5	301
5	8	16	11	Francis T. Cullen	98	135.5	39	272.5
6	28	--	--	Terrie E. Moffitt	137	76.5	58	271.5
7	15	--	--	John H. Laub	127.5	84	30.5	242
8	13	26	49	Raymond Paternoster	135	92	0	227
9	25	30	--	Daniel S. Nagin	139	81	0	220
10	14	8	36.5	Lawrence W. Sherman	40	62	112.5	214.5
11	34	27	--	Rolf Loeber	105.5	84	21.5	211
12	19.5	--	--	Robert J. Bursik	106	87	17	210
13	9	--	--	Robert Agnew	112	45	27.5	184.5
14	--	--	--	Alex R. Piquero	102.5	78	0	180.5
15	11	4	3	Alfred Blumstein	110.5	35.5	25	171
16	29.5	--	--	Harold G. Grasmick	66	85.5	17	168.5
17	--	--	--	Stephen W. Raudenbush	103.5	58	0	161.5
18	6	6	9	Delbert S. Elliott	111.5	28.5	0	140
19	4	12	5	John L. Hagan	58.5	60.5	17	136
20	12	15	31	Wesley G. Skogan	46	70	10.5	126.5
21	--	--	--	Darrell J. Steffensmeier	85.5	34	0	119.5
22	23	22	--	John Braithwaite	0	20	99	119
23	35.5	--	--	Kenneth C. Land	113	5	0	118
24	7	11	--	David Huizinga	81	36	0	117
25	--	--	--	Paul Mazerolle	70	41.5	0	111.5
26	--	--	--	Steven F. Messner	56.5	41	5.5	103
27	24	32	--	Terence P. Thornberry	62	37	0	99
28	18	29	--	Don A. Andrews	0	50	44	94
29	27	9	12	Lawrence E. Cohen	49.5	24.5	19.5	93.5
30	29.5	--	--	David Garland	0	0	93	93
31.5	--	--	--	Robert Brame	53.5	39	0	92.5
31.5	--	--	--	Avshalom Caspi	92.5	0	0	92.5
33	--	--	--	William J. Wilson	64	25.5	0	89.5
34	38.5	33	26	Paul Gendreau	0	42	47	89
35	--	--	--	Jock Young	0	0	88	88
36	47	--	--	Clifford D. Shearing	0	0	87	87
37	--	--	--	Ronald V. Clarke	0	0	85	85
38	42	14	6	James Q. Wilson	12	51.5	16.5	80
39	40.5	--	39	Charles R. Tittle	48	31.5	0	79.5
40	--	--	--	Kathleen Daly	0	0	77.5	77.5
41	35.5	--	--	Richard V. Ericson	0	0	71	71
42	--	--	--	Marvin D. Krohn	70.5	0	0	70
43	--	--	--	Allison M. Morris			69	69
44	21	31	40	Albert J. Reiss	14	36.5	17	67.5
45	--	--	--	Mark Warr	17	50	0	67
46	--	--	--	David H. Bayley	0	26.5	39	65.5
47	--	--	--	Scott H. Decker	10.5	19	32.5	62
48	--	--	--	Doris L. MacKenzie	0	44.5	17	61.5
49	--	--	--	Robert E. Worden	0	58	0	58
50.5	45	--	--	Michel Foucault	0	0	55	55
50.5	--	--	--	Janet L. Lauritsen	21	34	0	55

Notes: CRIM = Criminology journals; CJ = Criminal Justice journals; INT = International journals.

The greatest numbers of highly-cited female scholars were in ANZ (12), CJC (10), CRIM (7), and CJB (7). The fewest were in JQ (3) and JRCD (4). The most highly-cited female scholar in all nine journals was Terrie E. Moffitt, who was ranked 6. Five female scholars appeared in this table of the most-cited scholars in nine journals in 2001-05, compared with four in 1996-00, six in 1991-95 and four in 1986-90.

PREVALENCE VERSUS FREQUENCY

As discussed in Chapter 4, the criminal career concepts of prevalence and frequency may be applied to citation analysis. Scholars with a high prevalence are those who are cited in many different articles. This could indicate either versatility (many different works by the scholar are being cited) or specialization (one or a small number of works by the scholar are repeatedly cited). Scholars with a high frequency are cited many times in only a few articles. High frequency must be associated with versatility, because each individual work cited will appear only once in the reference list of each article in which the scholar is being cited.

The numbers of different articles in which each of the ten most-cited scholars were cited in each journal and in all nine journals combined are shown in Table 6-2. Robert J. Sampson had the highest prevalence. He was cited in 332 different articles, or in 24.6% of the 1,347 articles that were published in the nine journals during the period 2001-05. A total of 74 different articles by Sampson were cited, suggesting that his high prevalence might be mainly due to his versatility (but see the discussion of the most-cited works below). Daniel S. Nagin had the lowest prevalence. He was cited in 163 different articles, or in 12.1% of the total number of published articles in the nine journals. Terrie E. Moffitt also had a relatively low prevalence, being cited in 167 different articles, or in 12.4% of the total number of published articles.

Travis Hirschi (41) and Michael R. Gottfredson (39) had the lowest number of different works cited, suggesting that their high prevalence might be attributable to their specialization. David P. Farrington (161) and Francis T. Cullen (111) had the highest number of different works cited, suggesting that their high prevalence was attributable to their versatility.

Table 6-2 also shows that Robert J. Sampson, Terrie E. Moffitt, John H. Laub, and Raymond Paternoster were most likely to be cited in CRIM articles. David P. Farrington, Travis Hirschi, and Michael R, Gottfredson were most likely to be cited in JRCD articles Francis T. Cullen was most likely to be cited in JCJ, Daniel S. Nagin was most likely to be cited in JQC, and Lawrence W. Sherman was most likely to be cited in ANZ.

MOST-CITED WORKS OF THE MOST-CITED SCHOLARS

In addition to determining the most-cited scholars in the nine journals, we also identified the most-cited works of the top ten scholars. These are shown in Table 6-.3. David P. Farrington's most cited work was "Life course trajectories of different types of offenders" (Nagin, Farrington, and Moffitt, 1995), which was cited 24 times, although "Age and crime" (Farrington, 1986) was almost as highly cited, with 23 cites. As mentioned, Farrington was an extremely versatile author, with a total of 161 different works cited. Of these, 73% were cited three times or less each and only 19% were cited five times or more.

Table 6-2. Number of Different Articles in Which Scholars are Cited (Prevalence Measure)

Journal	Farrington (161)	Sampson (74)	Hirschi (41)	Gottfredson (39)	Cullen (111)	Moffitt (75)	Laub (47)	Paternoster (56)	Nagin (57)	Sherman (65)	Total articles
ANZ	16 14.8%	11 10.2%	10 9.3%	8 7.4%	6 5.6%	7 6.5%	9 8.3%	2 1.9%	4 3.7%	25 23.1%	108 8.0%
BJC	21 9.7%	23 10.6%	17 7.8%	19 8.8%	11 5.1%	7 3.2%	8 3.7%	8 3.7%	8 3.7%	17 7.8%	217 16.1%
CJB	22 14.2%	7 4.5%	14 9.0%	14 9.0%	33 21.3%	15 9.7%	4 2.6%	7 4.5%	2 1.3%	8 5.2%	155 11.5%
CJC	13 10.4%	8 6.4%	12 9.7%	11 8.9%	13 10.4%	6 4.8%	6 4.8%	6 4.8%	3 2.4%	14 11.3%	124 9.2%
CRIM	49 26.6%	101 54.9%	63 34.2%	63 34.2%	30 16.3%	50 27.2%	63 34.2%	58 31.5%	50 27.2%	27 14.7%	184 13.7%
JCJ	28 11.6%	53 21.9%	45 18.6%	42 17.4%	63 26.0%	24 9.9%	32 13.2%	37 15.3%	27 11.2%	28 11.6%	242 18.0
JQ	27 18.8%	63 43.8%	39 27.1%	41 28.5%	36 25.0%	19 13.2%	38 26.4%	38 26.4%	22 15.3%	30 20.8%	144 10.7%
JQC	19 21.1%	24 26.7%	32 35.6%	27 30.0%	10 11.1%	19 21.1%	19 21.1%	22 24.4%	31 34.4%	10 11.1%	90 6.7%
JRCD	24 28.9%	42 50.6%	35 42.2%	34 41.0%	18 21.7%	20 24.1%	28 33.7%	25 30.1%	16 19.3%	15 18.1%	83 6.2%
TOTAL	219 16.3%	332 24.6%	267 19.8%	259 19.2%	220 16.3%	167 12.4%	207 15.4%	203 15.1%	163 12.1%	174 12.9%	1347 100%

Note: Numbers in parentheses show the total numbers of published works cited.

Table 6-3. Most-Cited Works of the Most-Cited Scholars

Rank	Author/Work	Citations of Work
1	**David P. Farrington (161 different works cited)**	
	"Life-course trajectories of different types of offenders" (Nagin et al., 1995)	24
	"Age and crime" (Farrington, 1986)	23
2	**Robert J. Sampson (74 different works cited)**	
	Crime in the Making (Sampson & Laub, 1993)	93
	"Neighborhoods and violent crime" (Sampson et al., 1997)	69
3	**Travis Hirschi (41 different works cited)**	
	A General Theory of Crime (Gottfredson & Hirschi, 1990)	184
	Causes of Delinquency (Hirschi, 1969)	114
4	**Michael R. Gottfredson (39 different works cited)**	
	A General Theory of Crime (Gottfredson & Hirschi, 1990)	184
	Victims of Personal Crime (Hindelang et al, 1978)	37
5	**Francis T. Cullen (111 different works cited)**	
	"The empirical status of Gottfredson and Hirschi's general theory of crime: A meta-analysis" (Pratt & Cullen, 2000)	33
	"Does correctional treatment work? (Andrews et al., 1990)	29
6	**Terrie E. Moffitt (75 different works cited)**	
	"Adolescence-limited and life-course-persistent antisocial behavior" (Moffitt, 1993)	87
	"Low self-control, social bonds, and crime" (Wright et al., 1999)	24
7	**John Laub (47 different works cited)**	
	Crime in the Making (Sampson & Laub, 1993)	108
	"Trajectories of change in criminal offending" (Laub et al., 1998)	27
8	**Raymond Paternoster (56 different works cited)**	
	"Using the correct statistical test for the equality of regression coefficients" (Paternoster et al., 1998)	41
	"Enduring individual differences and rational choice theories of crime" (Nagin & Paternoster, 1993)	39
9	**Daniel S. Nagin (57 different works cited)**	
	"Enduring individual differences and rational choice theories of crime" (Nagin & Paternoster, 1993)	40
	"Trajectories of change in criminal offending" (Laub et al., 1998)	28
10	**Lawrence W. Sherman (65 different works cited)**	
	Preventing Crime (Sherman et al., 1997)	31
	"Defiance, deterrence, and irrelevance" (Sherman, 1993)	23

Robert J. Sampson's most cited work was *Crime in the Making* (Sampson and Laub, 1993) which was cited 93 times. As noted in Table 6-2, Sampson had the highest prevalence of any of the most-cited scholars. This appears to be due to his versatility, as he had 74 different works cited. However, his citation pattern also demonstrates considerable specialization, as two of his works had a very large number of citations. Overall, 47% of his works were cited at least five times and 15% were cited at least 20 times.

With 184 citations, *A General Theory of Crime* (Gottfredson and Hirschi, 1990) was the most cited work of both Travis Hirschi and Michael R. Gottfredson. Both Hirschi and Gottfredson are more specialized authors. Hirschi had 41 different works cited, of which 66% received less than 4 cites and 44% were cited only once each. Only 34% of Hirschi's cited works had five or more citations. Hirschi had only one other work that received more than 36 citations; *Causes of Delinquency* (Hirschi, 1969) was cited 114 times. Gottfredson had 39 different works cited, of which 64% were cited no more than 4 times and 44% were cited only once each. Only 36% of Gottfredson's cited works received five or more citations and no other work by Gottfredson received more than 37 citations. For both authors, their high ranking was mainly attributable to the influence of their most-cited works.

Francis T. Cullen's most-cited work was "The empirical status of Gottfredson and Hirschi's general theory of crime: A meta analysis" (Pratt and Cullen, 2000), which was cited 33 times. As mentioned, Cullen was an extremely versatile author, with 111 different works cited. Of these 75% were cited four times or less and only 25% had five or more cites.

Terrie E. Moffitt's most-cited work was her seminal article on adolescence-limited and life-course-persistent offenders (Moffitt, 1993), which was cited 87 times. Moffitt was a versatile author, with 75 different works cited. Of these, only 10% were cited five or more times while 68% were cited four times or less and 32% were cited only once each. As with Hirschi and Gottfredson, Moffitt's influence is due primarily to her one seminal article; no other work by her received more than 24 citations.

John H. Laub's most-cited work was also *Crime in the Making* (Sampson and Laub, 1993) which was cited 108 times. Laub was a more specialized author, with only 47 different works cited, over half of which (53%) were cited five or more times. About 30% of his cited works received only one citation each while 40% were cited no more than three times. No other work by Laub received more than 27 cites, suggesting that his scholarly influence is to a considerable extent attributable to *Crime in the Making*.

Raymond Paternoster's most-cited work was "Using the correct statistical test for the equality of regression coefficients" (Paternoster, Brame, Mazerolle, and Piquero, 1998), which was cited 41 times. Like Laub, Paternoster was a more specialized author, with 56 different works cited, over half of which (52%) were cited at least five times. 43% of his works were cited no more than three times and only 18% received one citation each.

Daniel S. Nagin's most-cited work was "Enduring individual differences and rational choice theories of crime" (Nagin and Paternoster, 1993) with 40 citations. Nagin had 57 different works cited, 47% of which were cited at least five times. Over half of his works (53%) had four citations or less and 32% were cited only once.

Lawrence W. Sherman's most cited work was *Preventing Crime* (Sherman et al., 1997) which was cited 31 times. Sherman was a more versatile author, with 65 different works cited. Of these, 71% were cited four times or less and 42% received only one citation. Only 29% of his works were cited five or more times.

Overall, Farrington and Cullen were highly-cited primarily because of their versatility. They each had a large number of different works cited, but no single work was particularly highly cited. Similarly, Sherman is clearly a more versatile scholar, with no single work standing out as being highly cited.

On the other hand, Hirschi and Gottfredson were more specialized scholars. Each had a smaller number of different works cited, with one work (or in Hirschi's case, two works) being particularly highly cited. Moffitt was also a specialized scholar, with one seminal article accounting for a high percentage of her citations. Paternoster and Laub also appeared to be more specialized authors.

Sampson showed evidence of both versatility and specialization. He had considerably more different works cited than either Hirschi or Gottfredson, but many fewer than Farrington. However, like Hirschi, he also had two works that were particularly highly-cited.

TRAJECTORIES

The longitudinal nature of this study allows for an examination of how the citation patterns of scholars change over time. Figure 6-1 shows those scholars whose citation trajectories have generally shown a steady increase between 1986 and 2005. Francis T. Cullen, David P. Farrington, and Travis Hirschi all show clear indications of increasing citation trajectories. As shown in Figure 6-2, Terrie E. Moffitt, Daniel S. Nagin, and Alex R. Piquero also show rising numbers of citations, but their increases began much more recently, in the mid-1990s.

CONCLUSIONS

The primary limitation of this research is that it is based on citations in only a small number of central criminology and criminal justice journals. Therefore, it probably underestimates the influence of scholars who publish mainly in other journals. We have reported the total number of citations to better allow us to compare these results with those of our earlier research. However, it may be that the prevalence of citations, or the number of different articles in which a scholar is cited, may be a better measure of scholarly influence than is the total number of citations.

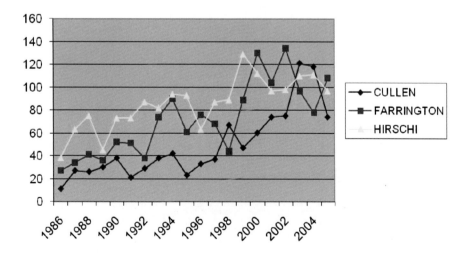

Figure 6-1. Increasing Trajectories.

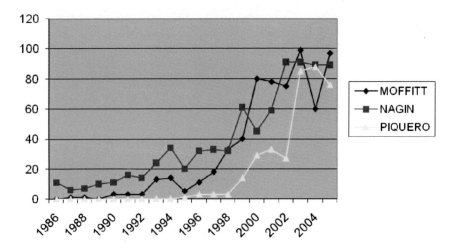

Figure 6-2. Recently Increasing Trajectories.

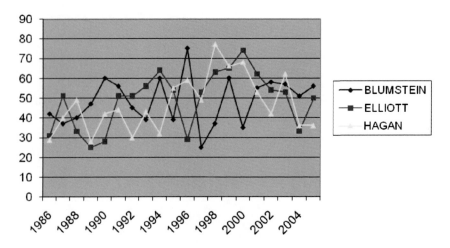

Figure 6.3. Constant Trajectories.

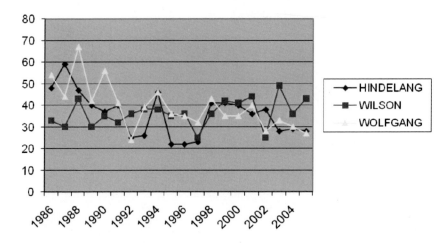

Figure 6-4. Decreasing Trajectories.

Other scholars have been more consistently cited over time. Figure 6-3 shows the trajectories of Alfred Blumstein, Delbert S. Elliott, and John L. Hagan. While their citations show considerable variation by year, overall they remain fairly stable. Finally, Figure 6-4 shows the citation trajectories of Michael J. Hindelang, James Q. Wilson, and Marvin E. Wolfgang. The citations of all three scholars have tended to decrease over time.

This examination of citation trends in nine major criminology and criminal justice journals over a period of 20 years clearly illustrates how the influence of an older generation of scholars has gradually been replaced by a younger generation. The "Kings" of the 1980s, such as Alfred Blumstein, Marvin E. Wolfgang, and Michael J. Hindelang in the United States, and Stanley Cohen and Jock Young in the United Kingdom, were gradually being cited less. Scholars who have died are clearly being cited less; Douglas A. Smith is a recent example of this. However, with the exception of Robert J. Sampson, John H. Laub, and Terrie E. Moffitt, the ten most-cited scholars in the nine journals are all older academics with long records of research and publications. Travis Hirschi, the third most-cited scholar, was Sampson's dissertation advisor.

The most-cited works of the most-cited authors show that some authors were specialized, with one or two seminal works (frequently books) receiving a large number of citations. However, other scholars were more versatile, because they had many different works that were each cited only a few times. Thus, it appears that there are two different ways in which scholarly influence operates in criminology and criminal justice.

The citation trajectories show that some scholars were increasingly being cited, while others were cited at a tolerably constant rate, and still others were being decreasingly cited. The citations of some scholars (e.g. Terrie E. Moffitt, Daniel S. Nagin, and Alex R. Piquero) seemed to accelerate in the mid to late 1990s. More citation trajectories of scholars and works should be calculated to document changes in scholarly influence. These would require comparable longitudinal citation data over time, such as we have assembled.

Chapter 7

CITATIONS IN TWENTY MAJOR CRIMINOLOGY AND CRIMINAL JUSTICE JOURNALS

As discussed in Chapter 4, one concern that has been raised regarding our analyses of citations in nine prestigious criminology and criminal justice (CCJ) journals is that only a small number of mainstream journals are covered. It could be argued that this may create a bias against scholars who are working in more specialized areas that are less well-represented in mainstream journals. There are at least 326 journals that focus at least in part on CCJ, many of which are very specialized (Vaughn, del Carmen, Perfecto, and Charand, 2004). In addition, it may be that the most-cited scholars are, at least to some extent, specific to particular journals, and that the results of any citation research would differ if other journals were included in the analysis.

One method of investigating these concerns is to study the most-cited scholars in specific sub-areas of CCJ, such as critical criminology (Wright and Friedrichs, 1998), law enforcement (Wright and Miller, 1998), or women and crime (Wright and Sheridan, 1997). This approach provides a considerable amount of information on which scholars and works are most influential and prestigious in a specific area of specialization.

Another alternative is to expand the number of CCJ journals being analyzed. One way to achieve this is to use the Web of Science databases, which includes the Social Sciences Citation Index (SSCI), or other electronic sources of citation data such as Scopus and Google Scholar. SSCI was used previously to identify the most-cited CCJ works (Cohn and Farrington, 1996). However, the disadvantages of electronic citation data sources have been discussed extensively in Chapter 1 and it is clear that no existing electronic source of citation data could provide reliable information about citation trends in CCJ over a long time period.

A third option, and the one employed here, is to expand the number of CCJ journals to include some that are slightly less mainstream. As described in Chapter 4, we increased the number of CCJ journals studied from the original nine up to twenty. The analysis of these twenty journals, first carried out in 1990 (Cohn et al., 1998), largely confirmed and amplified the parallel analyses of citations in the nine major journals in 1986-1990. Marvin E. Wolfgang, Alfred Blumstein, and James Q. Wilson were still among the most-cited authors. Generally, the most-cited works of the most-cited authors (e.g. Blumstein, Cohen, Roth, and Visher, 1986; Wolfgang, Figlio, and Sellin, 1972) were concerned with criminal career research. However, expanding the number of journals did reveal a number of other scholars and issues that were also influential. In particular, Francis T. Cullen's work on rehabilitation (Cullen and Gilbert, 1982) and Ronald V. Clarke's work on rational choice theory and situational crime prevention (Cornish and Clarke, 1986) were relatively more cited in the twenty-journal analysis.

This analysis was repeated for the year 1995 (Cohn and Farrington, 1999), using the same twenty journals. The most-cited scholars in 1995 were Lawrence W. Sherman, Travis Hirschi, Michael R. Gottfredson, David P. Farrington, and Robert J. Sampson. Both Sherman and Sampson became increasingly highly cited between 1990 and 1995. The most-cited works of the most-cited authors were *Policing Domestic Violence* (Sherman, 1992), *A General Theory of Crime* (Gottfredson and Hirschi, 1990), *Understanding and Controlling Crime* (Farrington, Ohlin, and Wilson, 1986), and *Crime in the Making* (Sampson and Laub, 1993). Again, the results show considerable overlap with the most-cited scholars in the nine journals during the five-year period from 1991-1995. Eight of the ten most-cited scholars in the twenty journals in 1995 were among the twenty most-cited scholars in the nine journals in 1991-1995.

Cohn and Farrington (2008) repeated the analysis again for the year 2000. The most-cited scholars in 2000 were Robert J. Sampson, David P. Farrington, Francis T. Cullen, Travis Hirschi, and Terrie E. Moffitt. The most-cited works of the most-cited authors were *Crime in the Making* (Sampson and Laub, 1993), "The development of offending and antisocial behavior from childhood" (Farrington, 1995), "Does correctional treatment work?" (Andrews et al., 1990), *A General Theory of Crime* (Gottfredson and Hirschi, 1990), and "Adolescence-limited and life-course-persistent antisocial behavior" (Moffitt, 1993). In contrast to previous years, these most-cited works included a number of articles as well as books. Again, there was considerable overlap with the most-cited scholars in the nine journals during the period 1996-2000, with eight of the twenty most-cited scholars in the twenty journals in 2000 also being among the twenty most-cited scholars in the nine journals in 1996-2000.

One interesting feature that was revealed by these comparisons is the relative importance of international scholars. International scholars are much more likely to be found on the most-cited scholar lists when examining twenty journals over one year than when looking at a smaller number of journals. For example, six of the most-cited international scholars on the twenty-journal list for 2000 (John Braithwaite, Michel Foucault, David Garland, Richard V. Ericson, Clifford D. Shearing, and Jock Young) were not among the twenty most-cited scholars in the nine journals.

This research has now been extended to examine the most-cited scholars in the same twenty journals in 2005. These have been compared not only with the most-cited scholars in twenty journals in 1990, 1995, and 2000, but also with the most-cited scholars in nine journals in 2001-2005 (see Cohn & Farrington, 2012).

CITATIONS IN TWENTY JOURNALS

Table 7-1 summarizes key statistics for the twenty journals, including the number of articles published in 2005, the number of authors of these articles, the percentage of these authors who were located in the United States, and the total number of eligible cited scholars (not including self-citations and institutional authors) in the journal. In the five American criminology journals, there were a total of 235 articles, with 620 authors (86 percent of whom were American) and a total of 21,105 cited scholars (an average of 90 per article). The five American criminal justice journals contained a total of 123 articles written by 275 authors (98 percent of whom were American) and a total of 10,448 cited scholars (an average of 85 per article). In the five international criminology journals, there were 153 articles, with 255 authors (11 percent American) and a total of 11,129 cited authors (an average of 73 per article). Finally, in the five international criminal justice journals, there were 133 articles written by 291 authors (62 percent American) and a total of 10,581 cited scholars (an average of 80 per article). Overall, this research examined 644 articles in these twenty journals in 2005 (an average of 32 articles per journal), with 1,441 authors (64 percent American) and 53,263 citations (an average of 2,663 cited scholars per journal, or 83 per article).

Table 7-1. Articles, Authors, and Cited Scholars

Title	Articles	Authors	%US	Cited scholars
American criminology journals				
Criminology (CRIM)	37	92	88.0	4,474
Journal of Quantitative Criminology (JQC)	19	53	88.7	1,531
Journal of Research in Crime and Delinquency (JRCD)	16	40	92.5	1,706
Journal of Interpersonal Violence (JIV)	120	301	71.4	8,830
Violence and Victims (VAV)	43	134	90.3	4,564
Total	235	620	86.2	21,105
American criminal justice journals				
Justice Quarterly (JQ)	20	42	100	2,221
Journal of Criminal Justice (JCJ)	53	120	90.8	4,441
Crime and Delinquency (CD)	24	63	100	2,421
Criminal Justice Review (CJR)	11	27	100	975
Federal Probation (FP)	15	23	100	390
Total	123	275	98.2	10,448
International criminology journals				
Australian and New Zealand Journal of Criminology (ANZ)	24	37	8.1	1,564
British Journal of Criminology (BJC)	47	82	9.8	3,695
Canadian Journal of Criminology and Criminal Justice (CJC)	29	49	4.1	1,376
Crime, Law, and Social Change (CLSC)	37	49	18.4	2,745
Criminologie (CRGE)	16	38	13.2	1,749
Total	153	255	10.7	11,129
International criminal justice journals				
Crime and Justice (CAJ)	6	9	66.7	1,617
Criminal Justice and Behavior (CJB)	31	88	65.9	2,992
International Journal of Comparative and Applied Criminal Justice (IJCA)	11	20	75.0	764
International Journal of Offender Therapy and Comparative Criminology (IJOT)	45	113	50.4	3,368
Social Justice (SJ)	40	61	52.5	1,840
Total	133	291	62.1	10,581
Total American journals	358	895	92.2	31,553
Total international journals	286	546	36.4	21,710
Total criminology journals	388	875	48.5	32,234
Total criminal justice journals	256	566	80.2	21,029
Total for all journals	644	1,441	64.3	53,263

Note: % US shows the percent of scholars located in the United States.

Table 7-2. Five Most-Cited Scholars in Each Journal

American criminology journals:	
CRIM:	R.J. Sampson (66); T.E. Moffitt (51); J.H. Laub (42); R. Paternoster (33); A. R. Piquero (33)
JQC:	D.S. Nagin (30); R.J. Sampson (21); J.H. Laub (17); D.S. Elliott (15); T. Hirschi (15)
JRCD:	R.J. Sampson (16); T. Hirschi (15); M.R. Gottfredson (14); J.H. Laub (13); T.E. Moffitt (13)
JIV:	M.A. Straus (74); M.P. Koss (50); D. Finkelhor (37); D.V. Cicchetti (31); J.C. Campbell (27); R.J. Gelles (27)
VAV:	M.A. Straus (84); K.D. O'Leary (33); J.C. Campbell (32); R.J. Gelles (30); L.K. Hamberger (30)
American criminal justice journals:	
JQ:	R.J. Sampson (28); H.G. Grasmick (19); R.J. Bursik (14); J. H. Laub (14); D. S. Nagin (14); D. J. Steffensmeier (14)
JCJ:	R.J. Sampson (32); R. Paternoster (26); R.J. Bursik (21); H.G. Grasmick (20); W.G. Skogan (20)
CD:	R.J. Sampson (12): M.D. Anglin (11); J. Petersilia (10); D.M. Bishop (9); J. A. Fagan (9); C.E. Frazier (9)
CJR:	S.D. Mastrofski (7); R.E. Worden (7); F.T. Cullen (5); J. Miller (5); D.H. Bayley (4); C.S. Koper (4); A.J. Reiss (4); F.E. Zimring (4)
FP:	P. Gendreau (13); F.T. Cullen (10); D.A. Andrews (8): J. L. Bonta (8); M.S. Umbreit (6)
International criminology journals:	
ANZ:	L.W. Sherman (19); D. H. Bayley (13); C. D. Shearing (12); K. Daly (11); T. Newburn (9); H. Strang (9)
BJC:	J. Braithwaite (21); R. T. Wright (19); S. Cohen (17); D. Garland (13); M. Levi (13); D. Matza (13); J. Young (13)
CJC:	L.W. Sherman (13); P.C. Stenning (11); D. L. MacKenzie (9); B. C. Welsh (9); D. P. Farrington (8); D.C. Gottfredson (8); T. J. Hope (8)
CLSC:	M. Levi (21): N. Passos (11); P. Reuter (9); R.H. Tillman (9); K. Calavita (8)
CRGE:	M. LeBlanc (16); T.E. Moffitt (16); A. Caspi (15); C.S. Widom (15); D.P. Farrington (14)
International criminal justice journals:	
CAJ:	R.J. Sampson (13): J. Braithwaite (11); M. H. Tonry (9); M.E.P. Seligman (8); M.B. Chamlin (7); C. DeFiebre (7); S.F. Messner (7)
CJB:	R.D. Hare (37); D.A. Andrews (33); J. L. Bonta (29): S.D. Hart (28); V. L. Quinsey (27); M. E. Rice (27)
IJCA:	M. Felson (15); J. Petersilia (15); P.J. Brantingham (10); P.L. Brantingham (10); R.V. Clarke (9); R.J. Sampson (9)
IJOT:	W. L. Marshall (23); J. L. Bonta (18); F.T. Cullen (16); D.A. Andrews (15); J. V. Becker (15)
SJ:	J. Young (14); D. Garland (10); F. Engels (8); K. Marx (8); Z. Bauman (7); E. Said (7)

Note: For abbreviations of journals, see Table 7-1. The most-cited five scholars are shown in general, but there can be more than five in cases of ties.

Table 7-2 shows the five most-cited scholars in each of the twenty journals in 2005. In *Criminology*, for example, the most-cited scholar was Robert J. Sampson, with 66 citations, followed by Terrie E. Moffitt (51), John H. Laub (42), Raymond Paternoster (33), and Alex R. Piquero (33). Robert J. Sampson was the most-cited scholar in six of the twenty journals, while Murray A. Straus and Lawrence W. Sherman were each most-cited in two journals. Robert J. Sampson was among the five most-cited scholars in eight of these journals, while Don A. Andrews, Francis T. Cullen, James L. Bonta, John H. Laub, and Terrie E. Moffitt each appeared three times in Table 7-2. The most-cited scholars in each journal reflect the different interests of the authors of each journal; for example the most-cited scholars in SJ were rarely cited in CRIM, and vice versa.

It is clear from Table 7-2 that even the most-cited scholars in a journal or group of journals account for a fairly small fraction of the total number of citations within that journal or group of journals. For example, Robert J. Sampson, the most highly cited scholar in CRIM, was cited 66 times, accounting for approximately 1.5 percent of all citations in CRIM that year. However, it is important to realize that the distribution of citations is highly skewed; researchers have found that most scholarly articles are never cited, or are cited only once or twice (Hamilton, 1990; 1991; Laband and Piette, 1994), while only a very small number are highly cited. Given that, there is a clear difference between being cited once and being cited 66 times, as Sampson was in CRIM. Impressively, Sampson was cited in 56 percent of all the articles in CRIM in 2005 (20 out of 36 articles; he was a co-author of one other article and his self-citations in that were not counted). Therefore, while the most-cited scholar in a journal may account for a relatively small fraction of citations overall, a large number of citations is nevertheless an objective indicator of influence.

MOST-CITED SCHOLARS

In order to compare the citations of scholars in each of the twenty journals, the most-cited scholars in each journal were ranked and given a score of 26 minus their ranking. Generally, this meant that those scholars who were ranked from 1 to 25 in each journal (according to their citations) received scores ranging from 25 to 1 (respectively). However, more than twenty-five scholars could score in a given journal if there were ties. For example, in CJC, Lawrence W. Sherman, the most cited scholar, was given a score of 25 and the next-most cited scholar, Philip C. Stenning, was given a score of 24. The next two scholars, Doris L. MacKenzie and Brandon C. Welsh, who were each ranked 3.5 because they were tied, were each given a score of 22.5. The ranking continued up to the nine scholars with six citations, who were each ranked 20. A total of 24 scholars were given a score in CJC; all other scholars cited in this journal were scored 0.

Table 7-3 shows the ten most-cited scholars in each group of five journals in 2005, and their comparative rankings in 2000, 1995, and 1990. The total score in 2005 is shown in the right-hand column. Robert J. Sampson was the most-cited scholar in American criminology journals in 2005 and 2000, compared with Travis Hirschi in 1995, and Marvin E. Wolfgang in 1990. Sampson was also the most-cited in American criminal justice journals in 2005, compared with Francis T. Cullen in 2000, Lawrence W. Sherman in 1995, and Joan Petersilia in 1990. David P. Farrington was the most cited in international criminology journals in 2005, compared with John Braithwaite in 2000, 1995, and 1990. Robert J. Sampson was the most-cited scholar in international criminal justice journals in 2005, compared with Robert D. Hare in 2000, Steven F. Messner in 1995, and Travis Hirschi in 1990.

There was very little overlap between the top ten scholars in one group of journals and the top ten scholars in another. Robert J. Sampson and John H. Laub were exceptions, coming in the top ten in three groups of journals (all except international criminology journals). James L. Bonta, David P. Farrington, and Terrie E. Moffitt came in the top ten in two groups of journals.

In American criminology journals, six of the top eleven scholars were highly-cited (among the top twenty-five) in CRIM, JQC, and JRCD; a seventh (Daniel S. Nagin) was highly cited in CRIM and JQC but not in JRCD. The other four (Murray A. Straus, Jacqueline C. Campbell, Kent D. O'Leary, and Richard J. Gelles) were highly-cited in JIV and VAV. This shows the effect of including these two somewhat more specialized journals. In American criminal justice journals, four of the ten most-cited scholars were highly cited in three of the five journals. In international criminal justice journals, the top four scholars were highly cited in three of the five journals and the other six were highly-cited in only two journals. The international criminology journals showed the least agreement; David P. Farrington was highly-cited in four journals, Clifford D. Shearing was highly-cited in three journals, five other scholars were highly-cited in two journals, and three (Philip C. Stenning, Terrie E. Moffitt, and Marc LeBlanc) were highly-cited in only one journal.

In American criminology journals, ten of the top eleven scholars in 2005 had also been in the top fourteen in 2000, six had been in the top fifteen in 1995, and six had been in the top eleven in 1990. All of the top six scholars in 2000 and four of the top five scholars in 1995 were still in the top ten in 2005. Five scholars were among the top eleven in all four years. However, two of the top five scholars in 1990 (Marvin E. Wolfgang and Jacqueline Cohen) were not among the thirty most-cited scholars in 2005. In American criminal justice journals, only two of the top ten scholars in 2005 had been in the top thirty in 2000, two had been in the top thirty in 1995, and only one had been in the top thirty in 1990. Francis T. Cullen was among the top fourteen scholars in all four years. The highest-ranked scholars in 2000 who were not in the top thirty in 2005 were Lawrence W. Sherman (3), Robert Agnew (5), and Travis Hirschi (6).

In international criminology journals, four of the top ten scholars in 2005 had been in the top thirty in 2000 (three in the top ten), three had been in the top thirty in 1995, and only two had been in the top thirty in 1990. John Braithwaite was among the top five scholars in all four years. The highest-ranked scholars in 2000 who were not in the top thirty in 2005 were Michel Foucault (2) and Richard V. Ericson (3). In international criminal justice journals, four of the top ten scholars in 2005 had been in the top thirty in 2000, two had been in the top thirty in 1995, and two had been in the top thirty in 1990. Robert D. Hare was among the top nineteen scholars in all four years.

Table 7-4 shows the ten most-cited scholars in each group of ten journals in 2005, and their comparative rankings (up to 30) in 2000, 1995, and 1990. The total score in 2005 is shown in the right-hand column. Robert J. Sampson was most-cited in American journals, as he was in 2000, compared with Travis Hirschi in 1995, and Marvin E. Wolfgang in 1990. Sampson was also most-cited in criminal justice journals in 2005, compared with Francis T. Cullen in 2000, Lawrence W. Sherman in 1995, and Travis Hirschi in 1990. David P. Farrington was most-cited in international journals in 2005, compared with John Braithwaite in 2000, Lawrence W. Sherman in 1995, and Francis T. Cullen in 1990. Farrington was also most-cited in criminology journals in 2005, compared with Robert J. Sampson in 2000, Travis Hirschi in 1995, and Marvin E. Wolfgang in 1990.

In American journals, nine of the top ten scholars in 2005 had been in the top thirty in 2000, six were in the top thirty in 1995, and five were in the top thirty in 1990. The highest ranked scholars in 2000 who were not in the top 30 in 2005 were Lawrence W. Sherman (5) and Robert Agnew (7). In international journals, eight of the top ten scholars in 2005 had been in the top thirty in 2000, compared with three in 1995 and three in 1990. The highest-ranked scholars in 2000 who were not in the top thirty in 2005 were Michel Foucault (2) and Richard V. Ericson (4).

Table 7-3. Most-Cited Scholars in Groups of Five Journals

	Rank in				Scholar	Score in
	2005	2000	1995	1990		2005
Five American criminology journals	1	1	5	10.5	Robert J. Sampson	74
	2	5	21	--	John H. Laub	67.5
	3	3	1	4	Travis Hirschi	66.5
	4	4	--	--	Terrie E. Moffitt	63.5
	5	2	4	6.5	David P. Farrington	55.5
	6	6	2	6.5	Murray A. Straus	50
	7	10	9	2	Michael R. Gottfredson	49
	8	--	--	--	Jacqueline C. Campbell	43.5
	10	14	15	8	Richard J. Gelles	42
	10	11.5	--	--	Daniel S. Nagin	42
	10	8	24.5	--	Kent D. O'Leary	42
Five American criminal justice journals	1	4	--	--	Robert J. Sampson	75
	2	1	12.5	14	Francis T. Cullen	66
	3	--	--	--	John H. Laub	47.5
	4	--	--	--	Harold G. Grasmick	45.5
	5	--	--	--	Robert J. Bursik	44.5
	6	--	--	--	Alex R. Piquero	35
	7.5	--	--	--	Cassia Spohn	32.5
	7.5	--	--	--	Jeffrey T. Ulmer	32.5
	9	--	24.5	--	Robert E. Worden	31
	10	--	--	--	Stephen D. Mastrofski	30.5
Five international criminology journals	1	--	15	20.5	David P. Farrington	76.5
	2	10	--	--	Clifford D. Shearing	52.5
	3	--	5.5	--	Lawrence W. Sherman	50
	4	--	--	--	Michael Levi	45.5
	5	1	1	1	John Braithwaite	44
	6	6	--	--	David Garland	38
	7	--	--	--	Philip C. Stenning	25
	9	23.5	--	--	James L. Bonta	24.5
	9	--	--	--	Marc LeBlanc	24.5
	9	--	--	--	Terrie E. Moffitt	24.5
Five international criminal justice journals	1	--	5	--	Robert J. Sampson	64.5
	2	--	--	--	James L. Bonta	54
	3	12	--	--	Don A. Andrews	52.5
	4	--	--	--	John H. Laub	38.5
	5	18.5	--	--	Marnie E. Rice	37.5
	6	1	18.5	6	Robert D. Hare	36
	7	--	--	--	Lawrence E. Cohen	33.5
	8	--	--	5	Paul Gendreau	33
	9.5	--	--	--	Marcus Felson	31.5
	9.5	24	--	--	Vernon L. Quinsey	31.5

Note: More than ten scholars are shown where there are ties. Ranks up to 30 in prior years are shown.

Table 7-4. Ten Most-Cited Scholars in Groups of Ten Journals

	Rank in				Scholar	Score in
	2005	2000	1995	1990		2005
Ten American Journals	1	1	6	18	Robert J. Sampson	149
	2	8.5	30	--	John H. Laub	115
	3	2	1	3	Travis Hirschi	89.5
	4	3	8	5	David P. Farrington	85
	5	8.5	29	26.5	Francis T. Cullen	79
	6	4	--	--	Terrie E. Moffitt	69.5
	7	13.5	4	4	Michael R. Gottfredson	68.5
	8	22	--	--	Raymond Paternoster	64.5
	9	18.5	--	--	Daniel S. Nagin	63.5
	10	--	--	--	Alex R. Piquero	56.5
Ten international journals	1	19	6	6.5	David P. Farrington	82
	2	15	--	--	Robert J. Sampson	80.5
	3	13	--	--	James L. Bonta	78.5
	4	1	4	2	John Braithwaite	68
	5	3	--	--	David Garland	62
	6	23	1	--	Lawrence W. Sherman	58.5
	7	7	--	21	Robert D. Hare	56
	8	--	--	--	John H. Laub	54.5
	9.5	--	--	--	Don A. Andrews	52.5
	9.5	5.5	--	--	Clifford D. Shearing	52.5
Ten criminology journals	1	2	3	3	David P. Farrington	132
	2	1	8.5	24.5	Robert J. Sampson	90
	3	7	--	--	Terrie E. Moffitt	88
	4	8	28	--	John H. Laub	83.5
	5	4	1	5	Travis Hirschi	66.5
	6	20.5	--	--	Daniel S. Nagin	55
	7	30	--	--	Clifford D. Shearing	52.5
	8.5	--	5	--	Lawrence W. Sherman	50
	8.5	9	2	10	Murray A. Straus	50
	10	17.5	4	2	Michael R. Gottfredson	49
Ten criminal justice journals	1	4	10	--	Robert J. Sampson	139.5
	2	1	4	11	Francis T. Cullen	89
	3	--	--	--	John H. Laub	86
	4	--	--	--	James L. Bonta	76.5
	5	15	12	--	Don A. Andrews	75
	6	9	20	19	Paul Gendreau	58
	7	3	--	5	Joan Petersilia	47.5
	8	--	--	--	Harold G. Grasmick	45.5
	9	--	--	--	Robert J. Bursik	44.5
	10	--	--	--	Mitchell B. Chamlin	38

Note: Ranks up to 30 in prior years are shown.

In criminology journals, nine of the top eleven scholars in 2005 had been in the top thirty in 2000, compared with seven in 1995 and five in 1990. The highest-ranked scholars in 2000 who were not in the top thirty in 2005 were Michel Foucault (5) and Richard V. Ericson (6). In criminal justice journals, five of the top ten scholars in 2005 had been in the top thirty in 2000, compared with four in 1995 and three in 1990. The highest-ranked scholars in 2000 who were not in the top thirty in 2005 were Lawrence W. Sherman (2) and Terrie E. Moffitt (6.5).

Table 7-5. Forty Most-Cited Scholars in All Twenty Journals

Rank in					2005		
2005	2000	1995	1990	Name	Crim score	CJ score	Total
1	1	5	38	Robert J. Sampson	90	139.5	229.5
2	13.5	--	--	John H. Laub	83.5	86	169.5
3	2	4	3	David P. Farrington	132	35	167
4	3	18	7	Francis T. Cullen	13	89	102
5	31	--	--	James L. Bonta	24.5	76.5	101
6	4	2	2	Travis Hirschi	66.5	30	96.5
7	5	--	--	Terrie E. Moffitt	88	6	94
8	--	--	--	Daniel S. Nagin	55	21.5	76.5
9	35.5	20	--	Don A. Andrews	0	75	75
10	6	1	29.5	Lawrence W. Sherman	50	23	73
11	27.5	3	5	Michael R. Gottfredson	49	19.5	68.5
12	7	9	10.5	John Braithwaite	44	24	68
13	23.5	--	--	Raymond Paternoster	40.5	24	64.5
14	9	--	--	David Garland	38	24	62
15	21	--	21.5	Paul Gendreau	0	58	58
16	--	--	--	Alex R. Piquero	21.5	35	56.5
17	20	--	--	Robert D. Hare	20	36	56
18	--	30	17	David Finkelhor	40.5	14	54.5
19	18.5	--	--	Clifford D. Shearing	52.5	0	52.5
20	--	31	--	Harold G. Grasmick	6.5	45.5	52
21	15	6	10.5	Murray A. Straus	50	0	50
22	--	--	--	David H. Bayley	24	25.5	49.5
23	13.5	--	18	Joan Petersilia	0	47.5	47.5
25.5	--	--	24	Lawrence E. Cohen	45.5	0	45.5
25.5	--	--	--	Michael Levi	32.5	13	45.5
25.5	--	--	--	Doris L. MacKenzie	20.5	25	45.5
25.5	18.5	26	--	Jock Young	12	33.5	45.5
28	--	33	--	Robert J. Bursik	0	44.5	44.5
29.5	17	--	35	Rolf Loeber	44	0	44
29.5	--	--	--	William L. Marshall	19	25	44
31	--	--	--	Jacqueline C. Campbell	43.5	0	43.5
33	--	12	12	Richard J. Gelles	42	0	42
33	27.5	--	--	Kent D. O'Leary	42	0	42
33	--	--	--	Marnie E. Rice	4.5	37.5	42
35.5	--	10	--	Mary P. Koss	41.5	0	41.5
35.5	--	--	--	Vernon L. Quinsey	10	31.5	41.5
37	--	--	--	Stephen D. Mastrofski	8.5	30.5	39
38	--	--	--	Avshalom Caspi	38.5	0	38.5
39	--	--	--	Mitchell B. Chamlin	0	38	38
40	--	21	--	Marcus Felson	6	31.5	37.5

Note: Ranks up to 40 in prior years are shown. CRIM = ten criminology journals. CJ = ten criminal justice journals.

Table 7-5 shows the forty most-cited scholars in all twenty journals in 2005 and their comparative rankings (up to 40) in 2000, 1995, and 1990. The most-cited scholar in 2005, as in 2000, was Robert J. Sampson, compared with Lawrence W. Sherman in 1995 and Marvin E. Wolfgang in 1990. Sampson advanced from 38 in 1990 to 5 in 1995 and first in 2000. The comparison of citation rankings over the years shows the advance of a new generation of scholars such as Sampson and John H. Laub (and even younger scholars such as Alex R.

Piquero), and the corresponding decline of older (and deceased) scholars such as Wolfgang and Michael J. Hindelang. David P. Farrington was among the most-cited four scholars in all four years, and Travis Hirschi was among the most-cited six scholars in all four years.

Nine of the top ten scholars in 2005 had been in the top forty in 2000; the new entry was Daniel S. Nagin. Conversely, eight of the top ten scholars in 2000 were still in the top forty in 2005. The highest ranked scholars in 2000 who were not in the top forty in 2005 were Michel Foucault (8) and Delbert S. Elliott (10). The highest-ranked scholars in 1990 who were not in the top forty in 2005 were Marvin E. Wolfgang (1), Alfred Blumstein (4), and Jacqueline Cohen (6). Seven of the top ten scholars in 2005 were mainly cited in American journals, while three (James L. Bonta, Don A. Andrews, and Lawrence W. Sherman) were mainly cited in international journals.

Table 7-6. Comparison of Twenty Journals in 2005 and Nine Journals in 2001-05

Twenty journals in 2005		Nine journals in 2001-05	
Rank	**Scholar**	**Rank**	**Scholar**
1	Robert J. Sampson	1	David P. Farrington
2	John H. Laub	2	Robert J. Sampson
3	David P. Farrington	3	Travis Hirschi
4	Francis T. Cullen	4	Michael R. Gottfredson
5	James L. Bonta	5	Francis T. Cullen
6	Travis Hirschi	6	Terrie E. Moffitt
7	Terrie E. Moffitt	7	John H. Laub
8	Daniel S. Nagin	8	Raymond Paternoster
9	Don A. Andrews	9	Daniel S. Nagin
10	Lawrence W. Sherman	10	Lawrence W. Sherman
11	Michael R. Gottfredson	11	Rolf Loeber
12	John Braithwaite	12	Robert J. Bursik
13	Raymond Paternoster	13	Robert Agnew
14	David Garland	14	Alex R. Piquero
15	Paul Gendreau	15	Alfred Blumstein
16	Alex R. Piquero	16	Harold G. Grasmick
17	Robert D. Hare	17	Stephen W. Raudenbush
18	David Finkelhor	18	Delbert S. Elliott
19	Clifford D. Shearing	19	John L. Hagan
20	Harold G. Grasmick	20	Darrell J. Steffensmeier

Note: The nine journals were: CRIM, JQC, JRCD, JQ, JCJ, CJB, BJC, CJC, and ANZ.

As already indicated, citation counts are correlated with other indicators of scholarly prestige. For example, many of the scholars listed in Table 5 have been honored by the American Society of Criminology. Robert J. Bursik, Francis T. Cullen, David P. Farrington, Travis Hirschi, John H. Laub, Joan Petersilia, and Lawrence W. Sherman are past Presidents of the Society, and Robert J. Sampson is the current President, through 2013. Nineteen of the most-cited scholars are Fellows of the ASC and fifteen have received awards from the Society. John Braithwaite, David P. Farrington, David Garland, and Jock Young have all received the Sellin-Glueck Award for international contributions to criminology. Robert J.

Sampson, John H. Laub, Terrie E. Moffitt, and John Braithwaite have all received the Stockholm Prize in Criminology.

Table 7-6 compares results obtained with twenty journals in one year and with nine journals in five years, showing that there was a considerable overlap of the most-cited scholars. Twelve of the twenty most-cited scholars in twenty journals in 2005 were among the twenty most-cited scholars in nine journals in 2001-05. However, it was noticeable that six international scholars on the twenty-journal list (Don A. Andrews, James L. Bonta, John Braithwaite, Paul Gendreau, Robert D. Hare, and Clifford D. Shearing) were missing from the top twenty on the nine-journal list, most likely because the nine-journal list gave less weight to international journals. Sixteen of the top twenty scholars on the twenty-journal list (all except David Garland, Paul Gendreau, David Finkelhor, and Clifford D. Shearing) were in the top fifty on the nine-journal list, an impressive level of agreement. Nevertheless, it is clear that international scholars such as John Braithwaite, and scholars in less mainstream areas such as David Finkelhor, tend to be given higher rankings in the twenty-journal analysis than in the nine-journal analysis.

FURTHER ANALYSES

Table 7-7 shows the top two most-cited works of the ten most-cited scholars in all twenty journals in 2005. The most-cited work of the most-cited scholar, Robert J. Sampson, was *Crime in the Making* (Sampson and Laub, 1993) with thirty citations. The number of citations of this work differed from those of John H. Laub because of the exclusion of self-citations. As in prior years, the majority of the most-cited works of the ten most-cited scholars in 2005 were books rather than journal articles. Five works from the 2000 table of the most-cited works of the most-cited scholars appear in the 2005 table: the most-cited works of Sampson, Laub, Cullen, Hirschi, and Moffitt.

Table 7-8 shows the total number of citations of the ten most-cited scholars in 2005, together with the number of different articles in which they were cited (prevalence), and the average number of citations per article (frequency). Because of the scoring system which gave equal weight to each journal, some authors with high scores (e.g. James L. Bonta and Don A. Andrews) had fewer citations than others; they were highly-cited in journals that contained relatively few citations.

As an example, John H. Laub had 147 total citations and was cited in 67 different articles. His average number of citations per article was therefore 2.2. As mentioned above, a high frequency of citations per article, or being cited many times in a few articles, may be a poorer measure of influence on a large number of other scholars than a high prevalence of citations. James L. Bonta and Don A. Andrews had a relatively high frequency of citations combined with a relatively low prevalence. Counting the total number of citations may overestimate the influence of these scholars and underestimate the influence of scholars with a high prevalence and a low frequency, such as Francis T. Cullen and Travis Hirschi. The total number of citations, however, is the most widely used measure. Robert J. Sampson had both a high prevalence and a high frequency.

Table 7-7. Most-Cited Works of the Most-Cited Scholars

Rank	Author/Work	Number of Citations
1	Robert J. Sampson	
	Crime in the Making (Sampson & Laub, 1993)	30
	"Neighborhoods and violent crime" (Sampson et al., 1997)	20
2	John H. Laub	
	Crime in the Making (Sampson & Laub, 1993)	32
	Shared Beginnings, Divergent Lives (Laub & Sampson, 2003)	13
3	David P. Farrington	
	"The criminal career paradigm" (Piquero et al., 2003)	9
	"Age and crime" (Farrington, 1986)	7
4	Francis T. Cullen	
	"Does correctional treatment work?" (Andrews et al., 1990)	16
	"The empirical status of Gottfredson and Hirschi's general theory of crime" (Pratt & Cullen, 2000)	9
5	James L. Bonta	
	The Psychology of Criminal Conduct* (Andrews & Bonta, 2003)	24
	"Does correctional treatment work?" (Andrews et al., 1990)	18
6	Travis Hirschi	
	A General Theory of Crime (Gottfredson & Hirschi, 1990)	41
	Causes of Delinquency (Hirschi, 1969)	27
7	Terrie E. Moffitt	
	"Adolescence-limited and life-course-persistent antisocial behavior" (Moffitt, 1993)	25
	"Sex differences in antisocial behavior" (Moffitt et al., 2001)	11
8	Daniel S. Nagin	
	"Enduring individual differences and rational choice theories of crime" (Nagin & Paternoster, 1993)	9
	"Personal capital and social control" (Nagin & Paternoster, 1994)	8
9	Don A. Andrews	
	The Psychology of Criminal Conduct* (Andrews & Bonta, 2003)	24
	"Does correctional treatment work?" (Andrews et al., 1990)	18
10	Lawrence W. Sherman	
	Preventing Crime (Sherman et al., 1998)	12
	"The specific deterrent effects of arrest for domestic assault" (Sherman & Berk, 1984)	8

* including earlier editions.

The total number of citations can also be disaggregated into the number of different works cited and the average number of citations per work. Some scholars (defined above as versatile) may be highly cited primarily because they have a large number of different works cited, while others (defined above as specialized) may be highly cited because a small number of works are each cited many times. Table 7-9 shows three measures of specialization or versatility: the number of different works cited, the average number of citations per work, and the percentage of total citations accounted for by the two most-cited works. For example, Robert J. Sampson had a total of 239 citations of 58 different works, with an average of 4.1 citations per work. His most-cited work, *Crime in the Making* (Sampson and Laub, 1993) was cited thirty times and therefore accounted for 13 percent of his citations. His next most-cited work was "Neighborhoods and violent crime" (Sampson, Raudenbush, and Earls, 1997), with twenty citations. His two most-cited works therefore accounted for 21 percent of all his citations (50 out of 239).

Table 7-8. Prevalence and Frequency

Rank	Author	Total citations	No. of different articles	Citations/ Article
1	Robert J. Sampson	239	81	3.0
2	John H. Laub	147	67	2.2
3	David P. Farrington	157	71	2.2
4	Francis T. Cullen	124	74	1.7
5	James L. Bonta	93	39	2.4
6	Travis Hirschi	125	69	1.8
7	Terrie E. Moffitt	148	71	2.1
8	Daniel S. Nagin	110	52	2.1
9	Don A. Andrews	98	38	2.6
10	Lawrence W. Sherman	103	59	1.7

Note: This shows the number of different articles in the twenty journals (out of a total of 644) in which the author was cited.

Table 7-9. Specialization and Versatility

Rank	Author	No. of different works	Citations/Work	% accounted for by top two works
1	Robert J. Sampson	58	4.1	21
2	John H. Laub	36	4.1	31
3	David P. Farrington	86	1.8	10
4	Francis T. Cullen	60	2.1	20
5	James L. Bonta	26	3.6	45
6	Travis Hirschi	21	6.0	54
7	Terrie E. Moffitt	61	2.4	24
8	Daniel S. Nagin	41	2.7	15
9	Don A. Andrews	35	2.8	42
10	Lawrence W. Sherman	45	2.3	19

Note: This shows the number of different works by an author that were cited in the twenty journals, plus the percentage of total cites that were accounted for by the two most-cited works of that author.

On the criterion of the largest number of different works cited, David P. Farrington (86), Terrie E. Moffitt (61), Francis T. Cullen (60), and Robert J. Sampson (58) were the most versatile, whereas Travis Hirschi (21), James L. Bonta (26), Don A. Andrews (35), and John H. Laub (36) were the most specialized. On the criterion of the average number of citations per work, Travis Hirschi (6.0), Robert J. Sampson (4.1), and John H. Laub (4.1) were the most specialized. Those with few citations per work were not necessarily versatile, because versatility depends also on the number of different works cited. Scholars with a low frequency of citation per work and a large number of different works cited (e.g., David P. Farrington, Francis T. Cullen, Terrie E. Moffitt) were the most versatile.

Travis Hirschi was the most specialized in that two of his works accounted for a large fraction of all his citations. His two most-cited works, *A General Theory of Crime* (Gottfredson and Hirschi, 1990) and *Causes of Delinquency* (Hirschi, 1969), accounted for 54 percent of all his citations. On this criterion, James L. Bonta (45 percent), and Don A. Andrews (42 percent) were also specialized, whereas David P. Farrington (10 percent), Daniel S. Nagin (15 percent) and Lawrence W. Sherman (19 percent) were the most versatile.

CONCLUSIONS

Expanding the number of CCJ journals from nine to twenty identified many of the same most-cited scholars found in other research that involved fewer journals. However, the rankings of some international scholars and some scholars working in less mainstream CCJ areas were improved when the number of journals was increased. The use of additional journals has both advantages and disadvantages. The obvious advantages of increased coverage were to some extent counteracted by the disadvantages of including progressively less mainstream CCJ journals. Continuing to expand the analysis to even more journals would require the inclusion of more peripheral or specialized journals, thus further diluting the importance of mainstream CCJ topics. It would, however, increase the visibility of scholars who publish in more specialized fields. The present results depend to a considerable extent on the choice of journals to be analyzed.

The use of only one year of citations in each journal inevitably caused more variability in the results over time than would occur in analyses based on five years. However, while the most-cited scholar in one journal could possibly be affected by one article that extensively cited a single author, the focus here is on identifying the most-cited scholars in groups of five, ten, or twenty journals. Studying groups of journals, which are less vulnerable to such distortion, reduces the variability of the results and increases both the validity and reliability of the findings. Against the variability argument, there was considerable agreement between the results of this research and results obtained in earlier studies using the same set of journals, as well as results obtained using more years of data from smaller numbers of journals.

Chapter 8

PUBLICATION PRODUCTIVITY IN CRIMINOLOGY AND CRIMINAL JUSTICE

Studies of publication productivity are based on the assumption that scholars who publish more works have more influence and prestige on their field of study than those who publish fewer works. The publication productivity of faculty has been mainly used to evaluate the prestige of criminology and criminal justice (CCJ) programs, rather than as a way of determining the prestige of individual faculty members. The main objection to this method is that publication productivity might be a measure of quantity rather than quality. However, measures of publication productivity are highly correlated with citation counts (Gordon and Vicari, 1992), suggesting that the most productive scholars are indeed also the most influential. Steiner and Schwartz (2007) pointed out that the analysis of publications avoids the time lag problem inherent in citation analysis: the need to allow time for a particular scholar or publication to have an influence on the field.

An important methodological issue is how to deal with multiple-authored works. As Tewksbury and Mustaine (2011) demonstrated, both the number of multiple-authored works and the average number of authors per work have increased greatly over time in CCJ, while the percentage of solo-authored articles has declined significantly. Kleck and Barnes (2011) employed a weighting system to deal with this problem, weighting articles both by the number of authors of the article and by each scholar's place in the order of authors. In addition, researchers have often taken account of the prestige of the journals in their analyses (e.g., Sorensen, Patterson, and Widmayer, 1992).

PUBLICATION PRODUCTIVITY OF DEPARTMENTS

Table 8-1 summarizes studies of publication productivity of departments, in chronological order. One of the first studies to use publication productivity in evaluating university-level CCJ departments was conducted by Parker and Goldfeder (1979). They identified a total of 52 institutions offering graduate degrees in the field of criminal justice (although not all programs were actually called "criminal justice" or "criminology").

Table 8-1. Publication Productivity of Departments

Study	Unusual features	Data sources	Time period	Results – top 5 most productive departments
Parker and Goldfeder (1979)	Included graduate CJ degree programs that did not grant PhDs	British J of Criminology Crime and Delinquency Federal Probation J of Criminal Justice J of Criminal Law and Criminology Criminology J of Police Science and Administration J of Research on Crime and Delinquency Police Chief Social Problems	June 1972-July 1977	U of Albany U of New Haven Rutgers U Indiana State U American U (average number of publications per faculty member)
DeZee (1980)	Included graduate programs in CCJ and sociology depts. providing degrees in criminology	23 journals	1970-1978	U of Albany East Texas State U Pennsylvania State U U of Pennsylvania Portland State U (faculty productivity adjusted by number of faculty)
Fabianic (1981)		Crime and Delinquency Criminology J of Criminal Justice J of Criminal Law and Criminology J of Police Science and Administration J of Research in Crime and Delinquency	1974-1988	U of Albany Pennsylvania State U U of Southern California John Jay College Ohio State U (number of credited articles)
Taggart and Holmes (1991)	Only examined first authors	Criminology J of Criminal Justice Justice Quarterly	1976-1988 (Crim/JCJ) 1984-1988 (JQ)	Pennsylvania State U U of Albany Michigan State U U of Alabama-Birmingham (4 universities tied for 5th place) (total number of first authorships)

Study	Unusual features	Data sources	Time period	Top 5 most productive departments
Sorensen, Patterson, and Widmayer (1992)		Many journals (based on CJPI, CJA, SSCI, Index to Legal Periodicals)	1986-1991	Rutgers U U. of California-Berkeley U of Maryland U of Albany Washington State U (average number of articles per fac. member)
Sorensen (1994)		British J of Criminology Crime and Delinquency Criminal Justice and Behavior Criminology J of Criminal Justice J of Criminal Law and Criminology J of Quantitative Criminology J of Research in Crime and Delinquency Justice Quarterly Law and Society Review	1983-1992	U of Maryland U of Albany Rutgers U U of Florida Indiana U (weighted number of publications)
Cohn and Farrington (1998c)	Only studied US CCJ programs registered with AADPCJC	Criminal Justice and Behavior Criminology J of Criminal Justice J of Quantitative Criminology J of Research in Crime and Delinquency Justice Quarterly	1991-1995	U of Maryland U of Cincinnati U of Missouri-St. Louis Washington State U Penn. State U (journal pub. per fac. member)
Cohn, Farrington, and Sorensen (2000)	Studied publications of PhD graduates in 12 US CCJ programs	CJPI Criminology	1985-1996	U of Maryland Michigan State U U of California-Irvine Florida State U Sam Houston St. U (acad. pub. per scholar)
Fabianic (2001)	Studied publications of PhD graduates	Crime and Delinquency Criminal Justice and Behavior Criminology J of Criminal Justice J of Quantitative Criminology J of Research in Crime and Delinquency Justice Quarterly Law and Society	1991-1995	U of Albany Florida State U U of Wisconsin U of North Carolina U of Illinois (weighted publications)

Table 8-1. (Continued)

Study	Unusual features	Data sources	Time period	Top 5 most productive departments
Fabianic (2002)	PhD and masters level CCJ programs examined	Crime and Delinquency Criminal Justice and Behavior Criminology J of Criminal Justice J of Quantitative Criminology J of Research in Crime and Delinquency Justice Quarterly Law and Society	1995-1999	U of Cincinnati Michigan State U U of Missouri-St. Louis U of Central Florida U of Maryland (weighted number of publications per faculty member – doctoral and masters programs combined) U of Cincinnati U of Missouri-St. Louis U of Maryland Pennsylvania State U Temple U (weighted number of publications per faculty member – PhD programs only)
Sorensen and Pilgrim (2002)		Crime and Delinquency Criminal Justice and Behavior Criminology J of Criminal Justice J of Criminal Law and Criminology J of Quantitative Criminology J of Research in Crime and Delinquency Justice Quarterly	1995-1999	U of Cincinnati U of Maryland Temple U U of Albany Sam Houston State U (weighted number of articles by faculty affiliation)
Steiner and Schwartz (2006)		Crime and Delinquency Criminal Justice and Behavior Criminology J of Criminal Justice J of Criminal Law and Criminology J of Quantitative Criminology J of Research in Crime and Delinquency Justice Quarterly	2000-2004	U of Maryland U of Cincinnati Pennsylvania State U U of Florida (3 universities tied for 5th place) (weighted publications)

Study	Unusual features	Data sources	Time period	Top 5 most productive departments
Steiner and Schwartz (2007)	Publication productivity of PhD program graduates	Crime and Delinquency Criminal Justice and Behavior Criminology J of Criminal Justice J of Criminal Law and Criminology J of Quantitative Criminology J of Research in Crime and Delinquency Justice Quarterly Law and Society Review	2000-2004	U of Maryland U of Albany Florida State U U of Cincinnati Rutgers U (weighted publications)
Kleck, Wang, and Tark (2007)	Publication productivity at all but 1 of the CCJ PhD granting universities in US and Canada	ISI Web of Science Proquest CJPI	2000-2005	U of Cincinnati U of Florida U of Maryland John Jay College Pennsylvania State U (total weighted counts of articles published in refereed journals)
Kleck and Barnes (2011)	Only CCJ doctoral programs examined	ISI Web of Science Proquest CJPI	2005-2009	Florida State U U of Cincinnati Arizona State U Sam Houston State U Michigan State U (weighted publications)
Oliver et al. (2009)	Textbooks studied	586 criminal justice textbooks	Available in 2006	U of Massachusetts-Boston California State U – San Bernardino Normandale Community College Boise State U Texas A & M U
Davis & Sorensen (2010)	Meta-analysis	Journals, textbooks, peer assessments	1979-2007	U of Cincinnati U of Albany U of Maryland U of Florida

Note: CJ = Criminal Justice; CCJ = Criminology and Criminal Justice; U = University;

CJPI = Criminal Justice Periodical Index; CJA = Criminal Justice Abstracts,

SSCI = Social Science Citation Index;

AADPCJC = American Association of Doctoral Programs in Criminology and Criminal Justice.

They examined ten criminal justice journals over the five year period, June 1972 to July 1977, to identify articles authored or coauthored by faculty who were affiliated with these institutions at the time of publication, and ranked the departments based on the number of substantive articles written by faculty, for a measure of overall productivity. Parker and Goldfeder found that only three departments published more than 20 articles, and only nine departments published 10 or more. At eight of the 52 institutions, only one faculty member had authored a published article during the five-year period, and 18 of the institutions had no articles contributed by faculty to any of the ten journals examined. Parker and Goldfeder also adjusted for faculty size, ranking departments by the average number of publications per faculty member. The University at Albany (formerly SUNY-Albany) was the most prolific department on both total publications and publications per faculty member, with an average of two publications per faculty member over the five year time period.

Some of the departments that were highly ranked on total productivity dropped considerably in the rankings after controlling for faculty size. For example, John Jay College of Criminal Justice, which was ranked second in total productivity, fell to rank 19 after controlling for faculty size, and the University of Southern California, which was ranked fourth in total productivity, fell to rank 25 when faculty size was controlled for. On the other hand, Rutgers University and Indiana State University were both ranked 13 in total productivity but rose to rank 3 and 4 respectively when the number of publications per faculty member was examined.

As Oliver, Swindel, Marks, and Balusek (2009: 61) pointed out, one of the main results of Parker and Goldfeder's (1979) research was to "inspire a long line of research examining different journals, different time frames, and different subsets of criminal justice academia." DeZee (1980) identified 71 schools that offered graduate degrees in criminology or criminal justice, or that had outstanding sociology departments providing degrees in criminology. He selected 23 prestigious journals based on rankings given by a random sample of members of the American Society of Criminology (ASC) and the Academy of Criminal Justice Sciences (ACJS) and examined all issues of these journals during the years 1970 to 1978 for articles and research notes authored by faculty from the selected departments. These counts were weighted on the basis of a peer ranking of journal prestige and by the number of faculty in each department. Like Parker and Goldfeder (1979), DeZee (1980) also found that the University at Albany accounted for the largest number of articles and the highest faculty productivity adjusted for the number of faculty.

Fabianic (1981) studied the institutional affiliations of authors in six criminal justice journals in 1974-88 and found that academic institutions offering nationally recognized doctoral programs in criminal justice usually had faculty publications in these journals, although many published authors were affiliated with departments that did not offer the Ph.D. degree. Again, the University at Albany was the most productive. He also found that slightly over 25 percent of all articles in the six journals were authored by individuals who were not affiliated with any academic institution but were probably practitioners employed in the criminal justice system.

Taggart and Holmes (1991) examined the institutional affiliation of primary (first) authors of articles published in *Criminology* and the *Journal of Criminal Justice* between 1976 and 1988, and in *Justice Quarterly* between 1984 and 1988 (the first five years of its publication). A total of 850 articles were published during this period that were first-authored by academics. A total of 54 universities had at least four or more first authorships in

Criminology or *Journal of Criminal Justice* or at least two or more in *Justice Quarterly*. Twenty programs had first authors in at least two of the journals but only five had first authors in all three. The programs with the most first-authorships in these three journals were Pennsylvania State University, the University at Albany, Michigan State University, and the University of Alabama-Birmingham.

Sorensen, Patterson, & Windmayer (1992) looked at the publication productivity of faculty at 23 universities offering doctoral degrees in CCJ or closely related disciplines. They obtained publication information from 1986-1990 for faculty who were at these doctoral institutions during the 1991-1992 academic year, from the *Criminal Justice Periodical Index* (CJPI), *Criminal Justice Abstracts* (CJA), the *Social Science Citation Index* (SSCI), and the *Index to Legal Periodicals*. After ranking the departments based on the average number of articles per faculty member, Sorensen et al. (1992) found that Rutgers University was the most productive department, followed by the University of California-Berkeley, the University of Maryland, the University at Albany, and Washington State University.

Sorensen (1994) examined the scholarly productivity of academic institutions during the 10-year period 1983 to 1992, focusing on peer-reviewed publications in 10 high-ranked CCJ journals, all except one of which (*British Journal of Criminology*) were American journals. Unlike earlier studies that only examined the first author of an article (e.g., Taggart and Holmes, 1991) or distributed credit among multiple institutions in cases of coauthored works (e.g., Fabianic, 1981), Sorensen included the affiliations of all authors. He found that 14 institutions, many of which offered doctoral degrees in CCJ, had at least 20 articles published in these 10 journals during the time period under study. Sorensen also inversely weighted the data by the number of coauthors of each article but found that in most cases this weighting did not greatly influence the rankings. Using the weighted rankings, the top five programs were the University of Maryland, the University at Albany, Rutgers University, the University of Florida, and Indiana University.

Cohn and Farrington (1998c) measured program quality by counting the number of publications of faculty members in six major American CCJ journals during the 1991 to 1995 time period. They calculated the publication rate per faculty member and found that the University of Maryland was the most productive department, followed by the University of Cincinnati and the University of Missouri-St. Louis.

Cohn, Farrington, and Sorensen (2000) evaluated the quality of 12 American doctoral programs in CCJ by counting the number of publications of their Ph.D. graduates in the almost 150 criminology and criminal justice journals indexed in CJPI as well as in *Criminology*, which at that time was not indexed in CJPI. Publications were examined in the three years prior to each scholar's graduation, the year of graduation, and all years following graduation, through 1996. Because CJPI includes a very large number of journals, many of which are law-related (e.g., *American University Law Review*) or practitioner-oriented (e.g., *The Police Chief*), a subset of 20 more scholarly or "academic" mainstream CCJ journals were identified; publication rates in all journals and in the subset of academic journals were determined.

In addition to investigating publication patterns during the early part of scholarly careers, Cohn et al. (2000) also ranked doctoral programs based on the productivity of their Ph.D. graduates. They found that Michigan State University, the University of California-Irvine, and Sam Houston State University had the highest rate of journal publications by Ph.D. graduates. When only academic publications were considered, graduates from the University of Maryland, Michigan State University, the University of California-Irvine, and Florida State University had the highest rate of publications by Ph.D. graduates. They then compared these rankings with those obtained by Cohn and Farrington (1998c) using faculty publications and found that faculty publications were much more highly correlated with the academic publication rate of the Ph.D. graduates than with their total publication rate in all journals. They also found that about half of all Ph.D. graduates had no publications at all in these journals.

Fabianic (2001) looked at the institutional backgrounds of those scholars who made the most frequent contributions to criminal justice journals from 1991-1995. He examined eight top criminology and criminal justice journals, weighting publications by the number of authors, and found that scholars with doctorates from the University at Albany were the most productive, followed by Florida State University, the University of North Carolina, and the University of Illinois. Overall, he found that 30 institutions, making up 21 percent of the total number of doctorate-granting programs, produced scholars who authored about two-thirds of all published material.

Fabianic (2002) then used the publication productivity of faculty in eight top CCJ journals in 1995-99 to examine 18 doctoral programs and 17 masters-level programs in criminal justice. Unweighted publication counts were examined, as well as weighted counts, based on the number of authors of an article. Not surprisingly, publication rates were higher for doctoral programs than for masters-level programs. When doctoral and masters-level programs were examined together, Fabianic (2002) found that five schools were consistently ranked very high: the University of Cincinnati, Michigan State University, the University of Maryland, the University of Missouri-St. Louis, and the University of Central Florida (which at that time did not offer a Ph.D.).

Fabianic (2002) also compared his results with those obtained by Cohn and Farrington (1998c), although this required him to drop some programs from each study and to only examine doctoral programs, omitting departments that only offered masters-level programs. Overall, he found a very high Spearman rank correlation of 0.79 between the publication rankings of the two studies for 16 criminal justice doctoral programs. Although the order was different, the top four programs (the University of Cincinnati, the University of Missouri-St. Louis, the University of Maryland, and Pennsylvania State University) appeared in both lists, and seven out of the next eight top-ranked programs were common to both studies.

Sorensen and Pilgrim (2002) built on the work of Fabianic (1981) and Sorensen (1994), examining the institutional affiliations of authors in eight top CCJ journals between 1995 and 1999. Twenty-four CCJ departments with at least seven articles published in these journals were identified; these institutions accounted for about one-third of the total published articles and authorships in these journals during the time period of the study. The top five institutions were the University of Cincinnati, the University of Maryland, Temple University, the University at Albany, and Sam Houston State University. Sorensen and Pilgrim (2002) also found that programs offering doctoral degrees in CCJ tended to dominate the rankings. Only one of the top 13 institutions did not offer a Ph.D. in CCJ, while conversely, only one of the remaining 12 programs did have a doctoral program.

Steiner and Schwartz (2006) replicated and extended Sorensen and Pilgrim's (2002) study, using data from the subsequent five years (2000 to 2004), and replicated Fabianic's (2002) research by calculating the average number of publications of faculty at the most productive graduate programs in criminal justice. They used the same eight journals studied by Sorensen and Pilgrim (2002) but were unable to compare their results with those of Cohn and Farrington (1998c) because different journals were analyzed in the earlier study. They found that the University of Cincinnati had the most publications between 2000 and 2004, followed by the University of Maryland, the University at Albany, the University of Florida, and Pennsylvania State University.

However, when publications were weighted by the number of authors, the order changed slightly, with the University of Maryland being the most productive program, followed by the University of Cincinnati. In addition, the University at Albany fell out of the top five and was replaced by Northeastern University. When the average number of publications of faculty in the top graduate programs were examined, the University of Maryland had the most publications per faculty member, followed by the University of Cincinnati, the University at Albany, the University of Florida, and the University of South Carolina. As in the earlier research, it was clear that institutions with doctoral programs had the highest publication productivity.

Steiner and Schwartz (2007) assessed the quality of 24 CCJ doctoral programs based on the publication records of Ph.D. graduates through 2004. Rather than using CJPI, as did Cohn et al. (2000), they examined publications in nine top journals in CCJ. They found that graduates from the University of Maryland produced the most weighted publications, followed by the University at Albany and Florida State University. The University of Cincinnati had the highest proportion of graduates who published and the highest proportion of graduates who published a first-authored article.

Kleck, Wang, and Tark (2007) studied the productivity of faculty in 33 CCJ Ph.D. granting programs in the U.S. and Canada between 2000 and 2005, using both the Web of Science database and CJPI. They found that faculty in these programs focused their research on criminology-related topics but published primarily outside the mainstream CCJ journals that had been analyzed in earlier research. The most productive faculties were those at the University of Cincinnati and the University of Florida. However, they also found that the University of Florida fell to sixth when Alex R. Piquero, who produced a disproportionately large amount of the university's article publications, was removed from the analysis. Kleck and Barnes (2011) recently updated this research, analyzing the publication productivity of CCJ faculty in 34 doctoral programs between 2005 and 2009; there is a four month overlap between the two studies. They identified the most productive faculties as Florida State University and the University of Cincinnati.

The findings of Kleck et al. (2007) were significantly different from those of many earlier faculty productivity studies, probably because of the wider array of publication outlets considered. For example, based on published articles weighted by journal quality, Kleck and Barnes (2011) found that the University of Cincinnati and the University of Florida were the two most productive doctoral faculties. Research by Sorensen and Pilgrim (2002) had ranked the University of Florida sixteenth. Part of this difference may be due to the inclusion of Alex R. Piquero as a member of the Florida faculty; he was not a member of this faculty when Sorensen and Pilgrim conducted their research. However, Kleck and Barnes found that, even if Piquero had been excluded from the analysis, the University of Florida ranked much higher than in the earlier study. They suggest that this is at least partly due to the small number of journals upon which Sorensen and Pilgrim based their publication counts.

Oliver, Swindel, Marks, and Balusek (2009) evaluated criminal justice programs by looking at the institutional affiliation of authors of criminal justice textbooks (rather than citations in textbooks). As well as examining unweighted data, Oliver et al. (2009) also used three different weighting techniques. They first weighted the data based on the number of co-authors of a textbook; the first author received a half-credit weight and the remainder was divided equally among the rest of the authors. The second weighted books based on edition, giving a weighting of one credit to books in their first edition and a weighting of two to textbooks in the second or later edition. Finally, a weighted score based on the prestige of the book (with original research being most prestigious and workbooks being least prestigious) combined with the numbered edition of the book was determined.

A total of 586 books that were available at the 2006 annual meeting of the Academy of Criminal Justice Sciences, written by 627 different authors from 305 institutions, were analyzed and reported in various ways. When publications were divided by the number of faculty members, the top five institutions were University of Massachusetts-Boston, California State University-San Bernardino, Normandale Community College, Boise State University, and Texas A & M University. When the results were compared with those of Sorensen and Pilgrim (2002) and Steiner and Schwartz (2006), which examined institutional affiliations in leading journals, the results were not at all similar, suggesting that most institutions were ranked high in publishing either journal articles or books, but not in both.

Overall, we have reviewed 15 studies of publication productivity of departments. About half of the studies were restricted to departments with Ph.D. programs. In the eight oldest studies, the University at Albany was rated in the top five departments six times, Pennsylvania State University and the University of Maryland four times, and Rutgers University three times. In the seven later studies, the University of Cincinnati was rated in the top five departments five times, the University of Maryland four times, and the University at Albany and Florida State University three times each.

In all fifteen studies, the University at Albany was rated in the top five departments nine times, the University of Maryland eight times, the University of Cincinnati and Pennsylvania State University six times each, and Rutgers University five times. Interestingly, Cohn and Farrington (1998c) in their citation analysis concluded that the top four programs were the University of Maryland, the University of Cincinnati, Rutgers University, and the University at Albany (see Chapter 3). Davis and Sorensen (2010) carried out a meta-analysis of studies of departments, based on both citations and publications, and concluded that the University of Cincinnati, the University at Albany, the University of Maryland, and the University of Florida had the highest prestige. All these analyses are reasonably concordant.

We conclude that the existing research on publication productivity indicates that the most productive departments are the University of Cincinnati, the University at Albany, and the University of Maryland. The University at Albany was identified in the six oldest studies; the University of Maryland was not identified in the four oldest studies but was identified in eight of the next nine; and the University of Cincinnati was identified in five of the six most recent studies. It is possible that these results reflect changes in the publication productivity of departments over time.

Table 8-2. Publication Productivity of Scholars

Study	Unusual features	Data sources	Time period	Most productive scholars
Cohn, Farrington, and Sorensen (2000)	Studied publications of PhD graduates in 12 US CCJ programs	CJPI Criminology	1988-1996	Most productive scholars not listed in rank order
Rice, Cohn, and Farrington (2005)	Studied 22 most productive scholars identified by Cohn et al (2000)	20 academic CCJ journals	N/A	Alex R. Piquero Michael S. Vaughn Joan Petersilia Robert Brame Jon R. Sorensen (based on weighted publications)
Shutt and Barnes (2008)	Examined CCJ and sociology PhD graduates	70 CCJ journals	1988-2008	Alex R. Piquero Richard Tewksbury Michael S. Vaughn Robert Brame James Frank (based on weighted publication counts)
Long, Boggess, and Jennings (2011)	Looked at top 10 "stars" identified by Shutt and Barnes (2008)	Harzing Publish or Perish software	N/A	Alex R. Piquero Joan Petersilia Robert Brame Richard Tewksbury Pamela Wilcox (ranks for total # citations and total # citations/year)
Rice, Terry, Miller, and Ackerman (2007)	Only examined female scholars	22 academic CCJ journals: 20 journals of Rice et al. (2005) plus Australian and New Zealand Journal of Criminology and Law and Society Review	N/A	Leah E. Daigle Jean M. McGloin Nicole L. Piquero Elaine E. Doherty Beth M. Huebner (based on publications standardized by years in discipline)
Khey et al. (2011)	Only looked at female scholars	Harzing Publish or Perish software	N/A	Robin S. Engel Angela R. Gover Nicole L. Piquero Jean M. McGloin Laura J. Hickman

Table 8-2. (Continued)

Study	Unusual features	Data sources	Time period	Most productive scholars
Frost et al (2007)	Publications of ASC and ACJS members	CVs	2001 and earlier	Most productive scholars not listed
Jennings et al (2008a)	Publications of faculty in CCJ doctoral programs	CVs	2000 and earlier	Most productive scholars not listed
Stack (2001)	Publications of faculty in CCJ master's-level programs	SSCI	1988-2000	Most productive scholars not listed
Steiner and Schwartz (2006)	Publications of faculty members	Crime and Delinquency Criminal Justice and Behavior Criminology J of Criminal Justice J of Criminal Law and Criminology J of Quantitative Criminology J of Research in Crime and Delinquency Justice Quarterly	2000-2004	Alex R. Piquero Francis T. Cullen Robin S. Engel Greg Pogarsky
Steiner and Schwartz (2007)	Examined graduates of 24 CCJ doctoral programs	Crime and Delinquency Criminal Justice and Behavior Criminology J of Criminal Justice J of Criminal Law and Criminology J of Quantitative Criminology J of Research in Crime and Delinquency Justice Quarterly Law and Society Review	2000-2004	Most productive scholars not listed
Orrick and Weir (2011)	Only examined first or solo authors	Crime and Delinquency Criminal Justice and Behavior Criminology J of Criminal Justice J of Criminal Law and Criminology J of Quantitative Criminology J of Research in Crime and Delinquency Justice Quarterly	2000-2009	Alex R. Piquero Daniel P. Mears Robin S. Engel* Glenn D. Walters* John L. Worrall* *tied for rank 3rd

Study	Unusual features	Data sources	Time period	Most productive scholars
Jennings et al (2008b)	Executive board members of ASC, ACJS, and ACJS regional affiliates	CVs of board members	N/A	Brandon Applegate Steven Messner J. Mitchell Miller Justin Patchin Gary LaFree
Oliver et al. (2009)	Textbooks studied	586 criminal justice textbooks	Available in 2006	Cliff Roberson Frank Schmalleger Victor E. Kappeler Larry J. Siegel Joycelyn M. Pollock (weighted by coauthors)
Fabianic (2012)	Publications of faculty members	Faculty CVs	N/A	Most productive scholars not listed

Notes: CCJ = Criminology and Criminal Justice; CJPI = Criminal Justice Periodical Index; N/A = studies without clearly defined time periods

PUBLICATION PRODUCTIVITY OF SCHOLARS

Table 8-2 summarizes studies of the publication productivity of scholars. In addition to using publications to rank academic departments, Cohn et al. (2000) also identified 22 Ph.D. graduates with the highest publication rates in academic journals. These scholars, whom they referred to as publication "stars," accounted for 39 percent of all publications by these graduates in academic journals. In a follow-up to this study, Rice, Cohn, and Farrington (2005) examined the research trajectories of 20 of these stars in the 20 academic journals identified by Cohn et al. (2000), and in a subset of seven "elite" journals. (Of the 22 Ph.D. graduates that they originally identified, one had since died and a second was semi-retired and raising meat goats in the Catskill Mountains of New York.) Rice et al. (2005) took account of a variety of measures of publication, both unweighted and weighted, and standardized these based on the number of years since graduation.

The relative ranking of the "stars", and of the Ph.D. granting institutions, was found to be greatly affected by the measures that were used. For example, the low rate of multiple authorship of Joan Petersilia and Katheryn K. Russell-Brown in both academic and elite journals affected their placement when their publications were weighted by the number of co-authors. Russell-Brown was ranked 11 in elite unweighted publications but, when her publications were weighted, she moved up to sixth. In general, Rice et al. (2005) found that those scholars employed at Carnegie Research I institutions (Robert Brame, Stephen G. Brandl, James Frank, Joan Petersilia, Alex R. Piquero, Katheryn K. Russell-Brown, Claire C. Souryal-Shriver, Ruth Triplett, and Michael S. Vaughn) tended to have the highest publication frequencies, regardless of the criterion examined.

Shutt and Barnes (2008) responded to Rice et al. (2005), replicating some elements of the original research. They retained the original cohort of 22 criminal justice "stars" and added an additional 20 scholars who had graduated from sociology doctoral programs during the same time period (1988-1997). After removing a number of "stars" from the study because they declined to participate or did not meet certain qualifications for inclusion, the final cohort included 32 scholars, 16 CCJ and 16 sociology Ph.D. graduates. Shutt and Barnes also expanded the scope of the study to include 70 CCJ journals (instead of the 20 examined by Rice et al.), based on information from the curriculum vitae of the scholars, and weighted journals based on the average peer ranking reported by Sorensen, Snell, and Rodriguez (2006).

Based on publication counts from the 70 CCJ journals, five of the top ten scholars had a Ph.D. in CCJ while the other five held sociology doctorates. When weighted publication counts were used, the top ten still included five CCJ and five sociology degree-holders. Shutt and Barnes (2008: 218) argued that "sociological criminologists continue to realize and exert tremendous influence throughout the discipline [of criminology and criminal justice]." They found that many of the sociology "stars" worked in CCJ departments, held editorships of CCJ journals, and held offices in CCJ associations.

Long, Boggess, and Jennings (2011) used "Harzing Publish or Perish" software to examine the weighted publication counts of the ten "stars" identified by Shutt and Barnes (2008). Harzing Publish or Perish is a software program that analyzes academic citations obtained from Google Scholar and provides a variety of statistics, including total and average citations and publications as well as ten different indices such as the g-index, and a number of variations on the Hirsch *h*-index (see Chapter 1). It can also consider issues such as solo versus multiple authorship and age-weighting. Long et al. (2011) compared the *h*-index ranking system with the conclusions of Rice et al. (2005) and Shutt and Barnes (2008) and found that their results were extremely similar to those obtained in the earlier research. For example, in all studies, Alex R. Piquero was ranked first and Richard Tewksbury was either in the second or third position in the rankings. Robert Brame was ranked fourth by both Long et al. (2011) and Shutt and Barnes (2008); in Rice et al. (2005) he was ranked either second or third, depending on whether information was weighted to take account of multiple authors.

Rice et al. (2007) examined the productivity of female scholars in CCJ, looking at 88 female scholars who graduated from doctoral programs in CCJ between 1996 and 2006. They looked at publications in 22 academic journals and identified 20 "academic stars" with the greatest number of published and in-press articles, finding that 70 percent were employed at research universities and 50 percent were employed at institutions with the highest Carnegie research classification. They also examined publications of these academic stars in nine "elite" journals (the eight journals used by Rice et al. (2005), with the addition of the *Australian and New Zealand Journal of Criminology*). Publication rankings were affected by both journal category (academic vs. elite) and by standardizing publication frequencies according to the number of years each scholar had been out of graduate school. Rice et al. (2007) also found that these academic stars were much more likely to collaborate with others than to produce solo-authored papers; seven produced no solo-authored works in the 22 academic journals.

Khey et al. (2011) used Harzing Publish or Perish software to re-rank 19 of the 29 top female academic stars identified by Rice et al (2007); one scholar was not able to be re-ranked due to software limitations and because she had a very "common" name. This process allowed them to examine not only articles published in the 22 academic and 9 elite journals used by Rice et al. (2007) but also articles published in other journals, books, book chapters, monographs, and other works. Overall, their rankings were comparable to those of Rice et al. There were several noticeable exceptions, such as Nicole L. Piquero, whose ranking was higher and more stable, and Angela R. Gover and Lois Presser, who were ranked much higher by Khey et al. (2011) than by Rice et al. (2007). Khey et al. attributed these differences to the restricted list of journal outlets used in the earlier research and to the fact that Harzing Publish or Perish allows for both citation as well as publication analysis of an author's publications.

Frost, Phillips, and Clear (2007) looked at the publication productivity of criminology and criminal justice scholars in five-year periods, specifically examining productivity before and after tenure. They conducted a phone survey of a random sample of 211 members of ASC and ACJS taken from the 1997-1998 membership guides. In 2001-2002, they obtained current CVs from 131 of the members of this sample, making it possible to examine publishing trajectories over time. Overall, Frost et al. (2007) found that average publication productivity tended to increase following the receipt of tenure, and then stabilized. Additionally, scholars affiliated with research-oriented universities (those identified by the Carnegie Foundation's Classification of Institutions of Higher Education as Research I or II or Doctoral I or II) were more productive in terms of publications. Frost et al. also examined "highly productive scholars," defined as those for whom less than one year passed between published journal articles over the course of their careers.

Building on the work of Cohn et al. (2000), Rice et al. (2005), Rice et al. (2007), and Frost et al. (2007), Jennings, Gibson, Ward, and Beaver (2008a) studied the scholarly productivity of 204 criminology and criminal justice faculty members in doctoral programs to examine publication trajectories and careers. CVs were used to obtain year-by-year counts of peer-reviewed publications and publications in the eight elite journals studied by Sorensen and Pilgrim (2002) and Steiner and Schwartz (2007) for scholars during the first six years after the completion of their Ph.D. degree (which necessarily limited the study to scholars receiving their Ph.D. no later than 2000).

Jennings et al. (2008a) found three distinct publishing trajectories. First, there was a high productivity trajectory, in which a small group of scholars show high publication productivity, especially in elite journals. Second, there was a low productivity trajectory, in which members publish few or no articles at all during the first six years after receiving their Ph.D. When elite journal publications were considered, over 50 percent of the sample had published virtually no articles in elite journals. Finally, there was a third trajectory of scholars with a publishing rate that fell between the high and low productivity groups. Consistent with Frost et al.'s (2007) finding that scholars tend to become more productive over time and do not slow down, Jennings et al. (2008a) discovered an acceleration effect for all three groups, so that on average, each group appeared to become more productive, although at different rates.

Stack (2001) examined the impact of the field in which a scholar's terminal degree is earned upon scholarly productivity among faculty members in criminal justice departments. As discussed in Chapter 3, only master's level departments located in universities that offer doctoral degrees in other disciplines, but not in criminal justice, were included in the study. Publications data were obtained from the SSCI from 1988 through 2000. Overall, the study found that faculty members with Ph.D. degrees in criminal justice tended to be more productive than those with terminal degrees in law and less productive than those with Ph.D. degrees in sociology. There was no difference in productivity between faculty members with criminal justice degrees and those with other non-criminal justice terminal degrees.

As discussed above, Steiner and Schwartz (2006) looked at publications of faculty members in CCJ graduate programs. In addition to identifying the most productive departments, they also identified those scholars within the departments who were the most productive. After weighting articles by number of co-authors, only ten scholars were found to have published in the leading criminology and criminal justice journals more than four times. The most highly-published scholar was Alex R. Piquero, followed by Francis T. Cullen, Robin S. Engel, and Greg Pogarsky. Steiner and Schwartz (2006) pointed out, however, that while certain departments had publication stars, most of the faculty in the top-ranked departments published in these journals.

Steiner and Schwartz (2007) looked at the publication records of Ph.D. graduates of 24 CCJ doctoral programs and identified a group of 61 "stars" (5 percent of the total number of graduates) that included all scholars who had published at least three times between 2000 and 2004 in the target journals. The University of Maryland produced the largest number of these "stars" (as was also found by Cohn et al., 2000), followed by the University at Albany and the University of Cincinnati. Cohn et al.'s finding that a program's total publications were greatly affected by these stars was also supported.

Orrick and Weir (2011) built upon the work of Sorensen and Pilgrim (2002) and Steiner and Schwartz (2007) by examining the publication productivity of faculty in 34 American and Canadian doctoral programs, using the same eight CCJ journals. As was found in much of the earlier research in this area, a small number of scholars accounted for a disproportionate amount of the research published in these top journals. The most prolific sole and lead authors were Alex R. Piquero and Daniel P. Mears.

Jennings, Schreck, Sturtz, and Mahoney (2008b) examined publication productivity in seven elite journals of the elected executive board members of ASC and ACJS, as well as members of the boards of five regional affiliates of ACJS. CVs were obtained for 17 of the 26 board members identified by the researchers. While publishing in the elite journals is rare, Jennings et al. found that the executive board members of ASC had nearly three times the elite publication productivity compared with ACJS executive board members across comparable positions. Among the regional affiliates, the Southern Criminal Justice Association (SCJA) had the highest publication productivity. Specifically, the board members with the highest elite publication productivity were Brandon K. Applegate (former president of SCJA), Steven F. Messner (first vice president of ASC), and J. Mitchell Miller (first vice president of SCJA). All of the recent executive board members of ASC ranked in the top ten, with two in the top five.

Oliver, Swindel, Marks, and Balusek (2009) investigated the authors of 586 criminal justice textbooks that were available at the 2006 annual meeting of the Academy of Criminal Justice Sciences, written by 627 different authors from 305 institutions. In terms of publication productivity, the top five authors were Cliff Roberson, Frank Schmalleger, Victor E. Kappeler, Larry J. Siegel, and Joycelyn M. Pollock.

Fabianic (2012) looked at publication productivity of scholars at various stages in their careers, specifically focusing on 151 faculty members attached to 22 departments offering doctoral programs in criminology or criminal justice. Only faculty members who had achieved the rank of associate professor or professor by 1990 or later were included in the study. Programs were grouped into two tiers based on the program rankings provided by *U.S. News and World Report* (2009). Fabianic (2012) found that faculty publication rates overall did not vary by program group. However, when publications in a group of eight highly ranked "core" journals (the same journals used by Sorensen and Pilgrim, 2002), were examined, Fabianic found that faculty members in the higher tier published in the core journals at a significantly higher rate than those in the lower tier, both in the period preceding their promotion to associate professor and also as an associate professor. Conversely, faculty members in the lower-ranked programs published books more frequently than those faculty members in the more highly-ranked departments.

CONCLUSIONS

A number of studies of scholarly influence have been based on analyses of numbers of publications. Some of these have focused on publications by departments, while others have focused on publications by individuals. Most of the studies of individual scholars have focused on Ph.D. graduates or female scholars rather than all faculty members. In the next chapter, we investigate the publication productivity of all criminologists.

In general, the older analyses were carried out manually and were based on a small number of journals, while the later analyses used more modern electronic and internet-based methods. We believe that the older studies, although more limited, are likely to contain fewer errors.

Chapter 9

PUBLICATIONS OF MEMBERS
OF THE AMERICAN SOCIETY OF CRIMINOLOGY

In Chapter 8, we reviewed previous studies of publication productivity as a measure of scholarly influence. We noted that most studies of publication productivity were designed to evaluate the prestige and influence of criminology and criminal justice (CCJ) programs rather than individual faculty members. In this chapter, we study the publication productivity of individuals.

In an attempt to cover as large a number of criminologists as possible, we assessed the publication productivity of all individuals who were members of the American Society of Criminology (ASC) in 2000 and in 2005 and who were members of a university or college faculty or employed in research institutes. The goal was to analyze those ASC members who were "at risk" of publishing, to establish how many actually published in CCJ journals and to identify the most prolific publishers.

We obtained ASC membership lists in January 2000 and November 2005. As the focus was on members who were "at risk" of publishing, we deleted all students, all members who did not have a university or research institute affiliation, anyone who did have such an affiliation but who was not in a CCJ or closely-related department, and anyone whose position in CCJ could not be verified. We also deleted any duplicate listings. For 2000, this was relatively easy, as the data included each member's titles and affiliations. However, as the 2005 data only included contact information for members, every member had to be checked individually, to determine if he or she met the criteria for inclusion. In many cases, the contact information was a university or agency address; in those situations, the university website was checked to determine if the individual was a faculty member or a student. In other cases, however, the contact information was a home address, and an internet search had to be conducted to identify the individual's affiliation.

Once we had removed all names from the membership lists that did not meet our criteria for inclusion, a spreadsheet was created that included the name, position/title, affiliation, and country of each ASC member. All scholars were looked up in the online version of the Criminal Justice Periodical Index (CJPI) to obtain information on their publications during a two year period including the membership year: 1999-00 and 2004-05. All articles were included, with the exception of book reviews, obituaries, introductions, and editorials. For each publication, we recorded the year of publication, the journal in which the article was published, and the number of co-authors (if any). In addition, as CJPI classified journals as "scholarly" and "technical", we noted into which of these categories each publication fell. Of the 309 journals included in CJPI in 2005, 180 were labeled as scholarly, or peer reviewed; those classified as "technical" were primarily trade publications and magazines. We also counted how many of the publications were in journals that we had classified as "academic" in prior articles (Cohn et al., 2000; Rice et al., 2005). Table 9-1 shows the 20 CCJ journals that were classified as "academic".

Table 9-1. Twenty "Academic" Journals

Journal Title	Abbreviation
British Journal of Criminology	BJC
Canadian Journal of Criminology and Criminal Justice	CJC
Crime and Delinquency	CD
Criminal Justice and Behavior	CJB
Criminal Justice Review	CJR
Criminology	CRIM
Howard Journal of Criminal Justice	HJCJ
International Journal of Comparative and Applied Criminal Justice	IJCA
International Journal of Offender Therapy and Comparative Criminology	IJOT
Journal of Contemporary Criminal Justice	JCCJ
Journal of Crime and Justice	JoCJ
Journal of Criminal Justice	JCJ
Journal of Criminal Justice Education	JCJE
Journal of Criminal Law and Criminology	JCLC
Journal of Interpersonal Violence	JIV
Journal of Quantitative Criminology	JQC
Journal of Research in Crime and Delinquency	JRCD
Justice Quarterly	JQ
Social Justice	SJ
Women and Criminal Justice	WCJ

We were very surprised to find that the number of eligible ASC members on January 14, 2000 (1,764) was much less than the comparable number on November 22, 2005 (2,955). We asked the ASC Executive Director Chris Eskridge about this and he informed us that members who had not paid by January 1, 2000, were not included in the ASC membership list for 2000. They were only included when they did pay, and some did not pay until later in the year. Therefore, our membership list retrieved on January 14, 2000 included those who had paid on time (including those who had joined at the 1999 ASC meeting and those who paid for three years at a time) but it excluded the late payers. In contrast, our membership list for 2005 was obtained on November 22, after the ASC meeting, and it would have included all ASC members in 2005. All those who were intending to join would have joined by November, and the list would have included a considerable number who joined at the 2005 ASC meeting. Therefore, the 2005 list is a more complete list of ASC members than the 2000 list.

RESULTS

In 2000, as mentioned, 1,764 ASC members were "at risk" of publishing. Of these, only 589 (33.4%) actually published at least one article in a CCJ journal in either 1999 or 2000. A total of 1,163 articles were published by these members, or an average of 1.97 publications per scholar. There were 996 scholarly publications (86% of all publications), of which 647 (65%) were publications in the 20 academic journals.

Table 9-2. Total Publications

1999-00			2004-05		
Name	Total	% Scholarly	Name	Total	% Scholarly
Craig T. Hemmens	21	48	Alex. R. Piquero	23	100
Alex R. Piquero	15	87	Brian Payne	15	100
Edward W. Gondolf	14	100	Francis T. Cullen	14	100
Francis T. Cullen	13	100	David W. Webb	14	7
David P. Farrington	13	100	Daniel J. Mabrey	10	0
Doris L. MacKenzie	13	85	Julian V. Roberts	10	100
James W. Marquart	11	73	Eric G. Lambert	9	100
Todd R. Clear	10	20	Edward J. Latessa	9	33
Steven F. Messner	10	100	Randy R. Gainey	8	100
Brian Payne	10	100	Terrie E. Moffitt	8	100
Martin Killias	9	78	William A. Pridemore	8	100
Randy R. Gainey	8	100	Rick K. Ruddell	8	50
John K. Cochran	7	100	Jacqueline C. Campbell	7	100
Sheila R. Maxwell	7	86	Alvin Cohn	7	86
Matthew B. Robinson	7	100	Richard Dembo	7	86
Dennis J. Stevens	7	29	David P. Farrington	7	100
Stephen G. Tibbetts	7	86	Michael L. Prendergast	7	100
Mary A. Farkas	6	100	Arnie M. Schuck	7	0
Edward J. Latessa	6	50	Faye S. Taxman	7	57
Raymond Paternoster	6	100	Richard Davis	6	0
Michael S. Vaughn	6	83	James A. Inciardi	6	100
Lening Zhang	6	100	Shane D. Johnson	6	100
Marcelo F. Aebi	5	80	Carl Leukefeld	6	100
Leanne F. Alarid	5	80	Jianhong Liu	6	83
Jeffrey A. Fagan	5	100	Arthur J. Lurigio	6	83
Jack R. Greene	5	80	Donald R. Lynam	6	100
Valerie Hans	5	80	J. Mitchell Miller	6	100
Michael J. Lynch	5	100	Byongook Moon	6	100
Michael D. Reisig	5	100	Daniel S. Nagin	6	100
Robert T. Sigler	5	100	Eugene A. Paoline	6	100
Eric Silver	5	100	Raymond Paternoster	6	100
Howard N. Snyder	5	60	Joseph A. Schafer	6	100
Michael H. Tonry	5	80	Hung-en Sung	6	100
Christopher J. Uggen	5	80	William C. Terrill	6	100
Michael Welch	5	100	Ronald Weitzer	6	83

In 2005, as mentioned, 2,955 ASC members were "at risk" of publishing, and only 891 of them (30.2%) actually published at least one article in a CCJ journal in either 2004 or 2005. The total number of publications by these members was 1,734, or an average of 1.95 publications per scholar. There were 1,505 scholarly publications (87% of all publications), of which 899 (60%) were publications in the 20 academic journals. Since the percentages and means for 2005 were similar to those for 2000, we conclude that, at least in regard to their publications, the missing ASC members in 2000 were a random sample of all ASC members.

Table 9-2 shows the scholars with the most publications in CCJ journals in 1999-00 and 2004-05. In 1999-00, Craig T. Hemmens published 21 articles in CCJ journals, but only 10 of these (48%) were in scholarly journals. The next most productive scholar, Alex R. Piquero, published 15 articles, 13 of which (87%) were in scholarly journals. Only 10 scholars published 10 or more articles, and only 35 scholars published 5 or more articles. The top 10 scholars (0.6% of all scholars) published 130 articles (11.2% of all articles). The top 35 scholars (2.0% of all scholars) published 277 articles (23.8% of all articles). Of these, only three were not affiliated with institutions in the United States: David P. Farrington was at Cambridge University in England and both Martin Killias and Marcelo F. Aebi were at the University of Lausanne in Switzerland.

In 2004-05, Alex R. Piquero published 23 articles in CCJ journals, all of which were in scholarly journals. The next most productive scholar, Brian Payne, published 15 articles, all of which were in scholarly journals. Only six scholars published 10 or more articles, and only 35 scholars published 6 or more articles. The top six scholars (0.2% of all scholars) published 86 articles (5.0% of all articles). The top 35 scholars (1.2% of all scholars) published 281 articles (16.2% of all articles). Of these, only two were not affiliated with institutions in the United States: Julian V. Roberts was at Oxford University (but only from 2004; before that he was at Ottawa University) and David P. Farrington was at Cambridge University, both in England.

Of the 35 most productive scholars in 1999-00, only seven survived to be among the most productive scholars five years later, in 2004-05: Alex R. Piquero, Francis T. Cullen, David P. Farrington, Brian Payne, Randy R. Gainey, Edward J. Latessa, and Raymond Paternoster. All except Latessa mainly or exclusively published articles in scholarly journals. Remarkably, Alex R. Piquero and Francis T. Cullen were among the six most prolific scholars in both time periods.

Table 9-3 shows the persons with the most scholarly publications in 1999-00 and 2004-05. In 1999-00, Edward W. Gondolf published 14 articles in scholarly journals, and Francis T. Cullen, David P. Farrington, and Alex R. Piquero each published 13. The percentages of these articles that were published in the 20 academic CCJ journals varied from 50% for Gondolf to 92% for Piquero. In 2004-05, Alex R. Piquero published 23 articles in scholarly journals, while Brian Payne published 15, and Francis T. Cullen published 14. Most of these articles were in the 20 academic journals. Francis T. Cullen, David P. Farrington, Alex R. Piquero, Brian Payne, and Randy R. Gainey were among the ten most prolific scholars in both time periods.

Of the 47 ASC members who had the most scholarly publications in 2004-05, 17 were not on the ASC membership list in 2000. We wondered if some of these might have been excluded because they paid late. Of the 17, five only obtained their Ph.D. in 1999-2002, and so would have been excluded as student members. Two were probably not members because they were in disparate fields (one in nursing and one in political science). We contacted five of the others and four said that they would not have been ASC members at that time. Of the other six, four had four or more publications in scholarly journals in 1999-2000: John L. Worrall (7), Robert Brame (6), Julian V. Roberts (5), and George S. Yacoubian (5).

Table 9-4 shows the scholars with the most publications in the 20 academic CCJ journals in 1999-00, and the journals in which they published. Alex R. Piquero and Francis T. Cullen were the most prolific scholars. Similarly, Table 9-5 shows the scholars with the most publications in the 20 academic CCJ journals in 2004-05. Piquero and Cullen were again at the top, along with Brian Payne.

Table 9-3. Scholarly Publications

1999-00	Total	% Academic	2004-05	Total	% Academic
Edward W. Gondolf	14	50	Alex R. Piquero	23	87
Francis T. Cullen	13	85	Brian Payne	15	73
David P. Farrington	13	54	Francis T. Cullen	14	71
Alex R. Piquero	13	92	Julian V. Roberts	10	50
Doris L.MacKenzie	11	72	Eric G. Lambert	9	56
Craig T. Hemmens	10	70	Randy R. Gainey	8	75
Steven F. Messner	10	90	Terrie E. Moffitt	8	38
Brian Payne	10	70	William A. Pridemore	8	50
Randy R. Gainey	8	75	Jacqueline C. Campbell	7	29
James W. Marquart	8	100	David P. Farrington	7	71
John K. Cochran	7	43	Michael L. Prendergast	7	14
Martin Killias	7	29	Alvin Cohn	6	0
Matthew B. Robinson	7	43	Richard Dembo	6	0
Mary A. Farkas	6	100	James A. Inciardi	6	33
Sheila R. Maxwell	6	83	Shane D. Johnson	6	50
Raymond Paternoster	6	100	Carl Leukefeld	6	83
Stephen G. Tibbetts	6	67	Donald R. Lynam	6	50
Lening Zhang	6	83	J. Mitchell Miller	6	83
Jeffrey A. Fagan	5	60	Byongook Moon	6	83
Michael J. Lynch	5	40	Daniel S. Nagin	6	83
Michael D. Reisig	5	80	Eugene A. Paoline	6	83
Robert T. Sigler	5	20	Raymond Paternoster	6	100
Eric Silver	5	40	Joseph A. Schafer	6	83
Michael S. Vaughn	5	60	Hung-en Sung	6	17
Michael Welch	5	40	William C. Terrill	6	67
Marcelo F. Aebi	4	50	Kate Bowers	5	60
Leanne F. Alarid	4	25	Robert Brame	5	10
Velmer S. Burton	4	100	Scott D. Camp	5	60
Mitchell B. Chamlin	4	75	Liqun Cao	5	80
Scott H. Decker	4	100	James Frank	5	40
Edna Erez	4	75	Edward W. Gondolf	5	60
Finn-Age Esbensen	4	75	Sergio Herzog	5	60
T. David Evans	4	100	Jodi Lane	5	100
Bonnie Fisher	4	25	Jianhong Liu	5	80
Jack R. Greene	4	75	Arthur J. Lurigio	5	40
Valerie Hans	4	0	John D. McCluskey	5	60
Matthew L. Hiller	4	0	Edward P.Mulvey	5	80
John P. Hoffmann	4	75	Greg Pogarsky	5	100
Paul J. Mazerolle	4	100	Jean J. P. Proulx	5	80
Terrie E. Moffitt	4	75	Michael D. Reisig	5	80
Martin D. Schwartz	4	100	Terrance J. Taylor	5	40
Michael H. Tonry	4	50	Richard E. Tremblay	5	80
Christopher J. Uggen	4	75	James D. Unnever	5	60
N. Prabha Unnithan	4	50	Ronald Weitzer	5	40
Ronald Weitzer	4	75	John L. Worrall	5	80
Wayne N. Welsh	4	100	George S. Yacoubian	5	0
John T. Whitehead	4	75	Jihong S. Zhao	5	100
L. Thomas Winfree	4	50			
Richard A. Wright	4	75			

Table 9-4. Academic Publications in 1999-00

Name	Total	Journals
Alex R. Piquero	12	2000: CRIM(2), JRCD, JQ, JCJ; 1999: JQ(2), CRIM(3), JCJE, JRCD
Francis T. Cullen	11	2000: JQ, CRIM(4), JRCD, JCJ, CD; 1999: CD(2), JCJ
Steven F. Messner	9	2000: IJOT, JRCD(2), JQ; 1999: JQC, CRIM, IJOT, BJC, JRCD
Doris L. MacKenzie	8	2000: JRCD, CD, IJOT, JQ, JCJ; 1999: JRCD, JCJE, IJOT
David P. Farrington	7	2000: CD, JCJE, CJB, CRIM; 1999: JCJ, BJC, IJOT
Edward W. Gondolf	7	2000: WCJ, JRCD, JIV(2), IJOT, WCJ; 1999: JIV
Craig T. Hemmens	7	2000: CD, JCJ(2), IJOT; 1999: IJOT, IJCA, CD
James W. Marquart	7	2000: JCJ(2); 1999: JCJ(2), CD(2), IJOT
Mary A. Farkas	6	2000: IJOT(2), JoCJ; 1999: JCJ, WCJ(2)
Randy R. Gainey	6	2000: JQ, CRIM(2), JCJ, JCJE, IJOT
Raymond Paternoster	6	2000: CRIM(2), JQC; 1999: CRIM, JRCD, JQC
Sheila R. Maxwell	5	2000: CD, CRIM, IJOT; 1999: IJCA, JCJ
Brian Payne	5	2000: JQ, JCJ, JCJE, IJOT; 1999: JCJ
Lening Zhang	5	2000: IJOT, JRCD; 1999: IJOT, BJC, JCJ
Velmer S. Burton	4	2000: CRIM, JRCD, JCJ; 1999: JCJ
Scott H. Decker	4	2000: JCJ(20, JQ; 1999: JQ
T. David Evans	4	2000: CRIM, JCJ; 1999: JCJ(2)
Paul J. Mazerolle	4	2000: JQ, CRIM, JCJ; 1999: JRCD
Michael D. Reisig	4	2000: JQ, JCJ; 1999: CRIM, IJCA
Stephen G. Tibbetts	4	2000: JQ, JoCJ; 1999: JQ, CRIM
Wayne N. Welsh	4	2000: CRIM, JRCD; 1999: CRIM, JRCD

Note: for abbreviations see Table 9-1.

Table 9-5. Academic Publications in 2004-05

Name	Total	Journals
Alex R. Piquero	20	2005: CRIM(2), JCJ(4), JIV, JCLC, JQC(2), JRCD; 2004: JQC(2), JCJ(2), CRIM, JRCD, CD, JCCJ, IJOT
Brian Payne	11	2005: JCJE(2), JCJ(2), WCJ; 2004: JCJ(4), CD, WCJ
Francis T. Cullen	10	2005: JQ, JIV, JQC, CRIM, JRCD, JCJ; 2004: JRCD, CD, JQ, WCJ
Randy R. Gainey	6	2005: JQ, CRIM; 2004: JCJ(4)
Raymond Paternoster	6	2005: JQC, JQ; 2004: JOC, JCCJ(2), JRCD
Arnie M. Schuck	6	2005: JQC, CJC, JCJ, WCJ; 2004: JQ, JCJ
Robert Brame	5	2005: JQ, JQC; 2004: JCCJ(2), CD
David P. Farrington	5	2005: JCJE, JQC, CJC; 2004: BJC(2)
Eric G. Lambert	5	2005: JCJ(2); 2004: CJR, JoCJ, WCJ
Jodi Lane	5	2005: JCJ, CD, JoCJ; 2004: CJR, JCJ
Carl Leukefeld	5	2005: IJOT(3); 2004: IJOT(2)
J. Mitchell Miller	5	2005: JCJE, JCJ; 2004: JCJ(2), JQ
Byongook Moon	5	2005: JCJ; 2004: IJOT, IJCA, JCJ(2)
Daniel S. Nagin	5	2005: CRIM(3); 2004: JQC(2)
Eugene A. Paoline	5	2005: IJOT, JCJ, JoCJ; 2004: JoCJ, WCJ
Greg Pogarsky	5	2005: JQ; 2004: JQC(2), JCJ, CRIM
Joseph A. Schafer	5	2005: JCJE(2), JCJ; 2004: JCJ(2)
Jihong S. Zhao	5	2005: JCJ(3), CD; 2004: JCJ

Note: for abbreviations see Table 9-1.

One issue that may be raised when examining publication productivity is that of the number of co-authors of a given work. Scholars who work regularly with a large number of co-authors may be more prolific simply because of the increased productivity often afforded by collaboration. To address this, we weighted all publications inversely by the total number of authors. A single-authored paper was counted as 1.0, while a paper with two authors was counted as 0.5 for each author, a paper with three authors counted as 0.33 for each author, and so on. In this way, scholars received more credit for solo authored publications than for articles that involved one or more co-authors. Table 9-6 shows the weighted scores for academic publications. Of the 1,764 scholars examined in 1999-00, only 21 achieved weighted scores of greater than 2.0 in academic journals. Similarly, only 19 scholars out of 2,955 in 2004-05, achieved weighted scores greater than 2.0 in academic journals. The most prolific author in both time periods was Alex R. Piquero, with 6.40 weighted publications in 1999-00 and 6.72 in 2004-05. The other scholars who appear in both time periods are Francis T. Cullen, David P. Farrington, Randy R. Gainey and Brian Payne.

Table 9-6. Weighted Academic Publications

1999-00		Weighted Publications	2004-05		Weighted Publications
Rank	Name		Rank	Name	
1	Alex R. Piquero	6.40	1	Alex R. Piquero	6.72
2	Edward W. Gondolf	4.67	2	Brian Payne	5.25
3	Mary A. Farkas	4.50	3	Francis T. Cullen	4.07
4	Sheila R. Maxwell	3.83	4	Arnie M. Schuck	3.67
5	Craig T. Hemmens	3.75	5.5	Jianhong Liu	3.50
6.5	David P. Farrington	3.67	5.5	Julian V. Roberts	3.50
6.5	Doris L. MacKenzie	3.67	7.5	Sergio Herzog	3.00
8	Francis T. Cullen	3.37	7.5	Judith Rumgay	3.00
9	Brian Payne	3.33	9	Daniel S. Nagin	2.83
10	Steven F. Messner	3.14	10	Greg Pogarsky	2.67
11	Matthew B. Robinson	3.00	11	John L. Worrall	2.58
12	James W. Marquart	2.92	12	Lorine A. Hughes	2.50
13	Randy R. Gainey	2.83	13	Byongook Moon	2.33
15.5	Jay S. Albanese	2.50	14.5	Randy R. Gainey	2.25
15.5	Meda Chesney-Lind	2.50	14.5	William C. Terrill	2.25
15.5	Scott H. Decker	2.50	16.5	John H. Laub	2.17
15.5	Ronald Weitzer	2.50	16.5	Joseph A. Schafer	2.17
18.5	Martin D. Schwartz	2.33	18.5	Liqun Cao	2.08
18.5	Christopher J. Uggen	2.33	18.5	David P. Farrington	2.08
20	Sun Joon Jang	2.25			
21	Raymond Paternoster	2.07			

CONCLUSIONS

Our research shows that only about one-third of ASC members who are "at risk" of publishing actually publish any articles in CCJ journals during a two-year time period. We investigated which publications were in scholarly or academic journals. Alex R. Piquero and Francis T. Cullen were among the three most prolific publishers in academic journals during both time periods.

Chapter 10

CONCLUSION

We have now come to the end of our journey. We have studied scholarly influence in criminology and criminal justice (CCJ) using mainly citation analysis but also employing publication productivity. Citation analysis is a valid measure of scholarly influence because it is highly correlated with other measures such as peer rankings, the receipt of academic prizes, and election to prestigious posts in scholarly societies. Publication productivity is not as valid a measure of scholarly influence as citations, because there is no guarantee that a publication will influence, or even be read by, other scholars. However, publication counts are highly correlated with citation counts.

CITATION ANALYSIS

Since we began our research in 1988, the use of citation analysis has increased enormously, largely because of the availability of internet sources such as the Web of Science, Google Scholar, and Scopus. The journal impact factor, based on citations of articles one to two years after publication, has become enormously important and seems to be widely accepted as the main measure of the prestige of scholarly journals. And yet, as we pointed out in Chapter 1, this one to two year time window is much too short to capture most of the citations of CCJ works. As we demonstrated, a highly-cited CCJ article, such as "Adolescence-limited and life-course-persistent antisocial behavior" (Moffitt, 1993), may not become highly-cited until at least 5-10 years after its publication.

Citation analyses based on internet sources and carried out mechanically are inevitably unsatisfactory and full of errors, as we discussed in Chapter 1. Among the main problems are the inclusion of self-citations, the failure to correct errors in the original lists of references, the incorrect amalgamation of different persons with the same name and initials, and changes in coverage over time. Other problems include the fact that Google Scholar sets no standards for inclusion of material (presumably including everything on the internet?) and provides no information about coverage.

The methods that we have used overcame these problems. First, we have expended huge amounts of time to correct mistakes in reference lists, to distinguish different people with the same name and initials, to amalgamate the same people with different names, and to discover the scholars hidden by "et al." in reference lists. We were only able to do this because we have analyzed a limited number of the most prestigious journals in criminology and criminal justice and because of our personal knowledge of many scholars. Second, we eliminated all self-citations. Third, we analyzed the same journals over time, using exactly the same scoring methods that give equal weight to each journal, so that we could carry out longitudinal analyses of changes in the most-cited scholars over a twenty-year time period. We believe that our citation analyses, although relatively limited in scope, produce more valid results than any citation analyses based on any internet source. And we believe that our citation analyses provide valid information about changes over time in scholarly influence in criminology and criminal justice.

MOST-CITED SCHOLARS IN NINE JOURNALS

One of the main contributions of this book lies in its detailed tables identifying the most-cited scholars, and in the information about trends over time. In addition, the most-cited works of the most-cited scholars are revealed. For example, the most-cited scholars in three major American criminology journals in 2001-05 were Robert J. Sampson, Travis Hirschi, Daniel S. Nagin, and Terrie E. Moffitt. Their most-cited works in these journals were *Crime in the Making* (Sampson and Laub, 1993*), A General Theory of Crime* (Hirschi and Gottfredson, 1990), "Enduring individual differences and rational choice theories of crime" (Nagin and Paternoster, 1993), and "Adolescence-limited and life-course persistent antisocial behavior" (Moffitt, 1993). All of these most-cited works were published a decade before their citations were measured (on average). Noteworthy advances in rankings over time were made by Robert J. Sampson, Terrie E. Moffitt, Stephen W. Raudenbush, Alex R. Piquero, and Francis T. Cullen, while John L. Hagan, Lawrence E. Cohen and Michael J. Hindelang declined. However, Hindelang was still ranked 41 in 2001-05 (out of thousands of cited scholars), two decades after he died in 1982.

The most-cited scholars in three major American criminal justice journals in 2001-05 were Francis T. Cullen, David P. Farrington, Robert J. Sampson, and Travis Hirschi. Their most-cited works in these journals were "Does correctional treatment work?" (Andrews et al., 1990), "Life-course trajectories of different types of offenders" (Nagin et al., 1995), *Crime in the Making* (Sampson and Laub, 1993), and *A General Theory of Crime* (Gottfredson and Hirschi, 1990). Noteworthy advances in rankings were made by Robert J. Sampson, Robert J. Bursik, Harold G. Grasmick, and Raymond Paternoster, while John L. Hagan, Robert Agnew, and Marvin E. Wolfgang (who died in 1998) decreased.

The most-cited scholars in three major international journals in 2001-05 were David P. Farrington, Robert J. Sampson, Lawrence W. Sherman, and John Braithwaite. Their most-cited works in these journals were "Explaining and preventing crime" (Farrington, 2000), "Age and crime" (Farrington, 1986), *Crime in the Making* (Sampson and Laub, 1993), *Preventing Crime* (Sherman et al., 1998), and *Crime, Shame, and Reintegration* (Braithwaite, 1989). Noteworthy advances in rankings over time were made by Robert J. Sampson, Kathleen Daly, Allison M. Morris and Terrie E. Moffitt, while Stanley Cohen and Patricia M. Mayhew decreased. ANZ and CJC contained the largest number of highly cited female scholars.

The most-cited scholars in all nine major journals in 2001-05 were David P. Farrington, Robert J. Sampson, Travis Hirschi, Michael R. Gottfredson, Francis T. Cullen, and Terrie E. Moffitt. Their most-cited works were "Life-course trajectories of different types of offenders" (Nagin et al., 1995), *Crime in the Making* (Sampson and Laub, 1993), *A General Theory of Crime* (Hirschi and Gottfredson, 1990), "The empirical status of Hirschi and Gottfredson's general theory of crime" (Pratt and Cullen, 2000), and "Adolescence-limited and life-course-persistent antisocial behavior" (Moffitt, 1993). The most-cited works of the most-cited scholars were mainly theoretical or concerned with developmental/life course, longitudinal, or criminal career research. It is not until we reach the tenth most-cited scholar, Lawrence W. Sherman, that the most-cited work is on a different topic: *Preventing Crime* (Sherman et al., 1997). Interestingly, one of the reasons why this work was highly cited is because it was one of the first criminological works that was freely available online during the early days of the internet.

Over time, younger scholars tended to advance while older scholars tended to decline in their citation rankings. Between 1986-90 and 2001-05, noteworthy advances in rankings were made by Robert J. Sampson, Terrie E. Moffitt, John H. Laub, Raymond Paternoster, Daniel S. Nagin, and Lawrence W. Sherman. Moving in the other direction were deceased scholars such as Marvin E. Wolfgang, Michael J. Hindelang, and Douglas A. Smith. David P. Farrington, Travis Hirschi, and Michael R. Gottfredson were among the top ten scholars in all four time periods.

Several different types of citation trajectories over the twenty-year period were identified: steadily increasing (Francis T. Cullen, David P. Farrington, Travis Hirschi) sharply increasing (Terrie E. Moffitt, Daniel S. Nagin, Alex R. Piquero), stable (Alfred Blumstein, Delbert S. Elliott, John L. Hagan), and decreasing (Michael J. Hindelang, James Q. Wilson, Marvin E. Wolfgang). Although the numbers of citations of Blumstein, Elliott, and Hagan were relatively stable over time, their rankings tended to decline because the numbers of citations of all scholars in general tended to increase over time.

Some scholars (especially David P. Farrington and Francis T. Cullen) were versatile, since they were highly cited primarily because they had many different works cited, with no particular work receiving a large number of citations. Other scholars (especially Travis Hirschi, Michael R. Gottfredson, and John H. Laub) were more specialized, since their large number of citations was driven to a considerable extent by one or two highly-cited works. Still other scholars (e.g. Robert J. Sampson, Terrie E. Moffitt) were both versatile and specialized, since they had many different works cited and also one or two highly-cited seminal works.

MOST-CITED SCHOLARS IN TWENTY JOURNALS

When our citation analysis was extended to twenty major journals in 2005, we found that Robert J. Sampson was among the five most-cited scholars in eight of the twenty journals, while Don A. Andrews, Francis T. Cullen, James L. Bonta, John H. Laub, and Terrie E. Moffitt were each among the five most-cited scholars in three journals. The most-cited scholars in five American criminology journals were Robert J. Sampson, John H. Laub, Travis Hirschi, Terrie E. Moffitt, and David P. Farrington; in five American criminal justice journals they were Robert J. Sampson, Francis T. Cullen, John H. Laub, Harold G. Grasmick, and Robert J. Bursik; in five international criminology journals they were David P. Farrington, Clifford D. Shearing, Lawrence W. Sherman, Michael Levi, and John Braithwaite; and in five international criminal justice journals they were Robert J. Sampson, James L. Bonta, Don A. Andrews, John H. Laub, and Marnie E. Rice.

There was very little overlap between the top ten scholars in one group of journals and the top ten scholars in another. Robert J. Sampson and John H. Laub were exceptions, coming in the top ten in three groups of journals (all except international criminology journals). James L. Bonta, David P. Farrington, and Terrie E. Moffitt came in the top ten in two groups of journals.

In all twenty journals in 2005, the most-cited scholars were Robert J. Sampson, John H. Laub, David P. Farrington, Francis T. Cullen, and James L. Bonta. Noteworthy advances over the years were made by Robert J. Sampson, John H. Laub, James L. Bonta, Terrie E. Moffitt, and Daniel S. Nagin. David P. Farrington was in the top four in all four years, while Travis Hirschi was in the top six in all four years. Moving downwards were Marvin E. Wolfgang, Alfred Blumstein, and Jacqueline Cohen.

There was considerable agreement on the most-cited scholars between the twenty-journal analysis and the nine-journal analysis. Twelve of the twenty most-cited scholars in twenty journals in 2005 were among the twenty most-cited scholars in nine journals in 2001-05. However, it was noticeable that six international scholars on the twenty-journal list (Don A. Andrews, James L. Bonta, John Braithwaite, Paul Gendreau, Robert D. Hare, and Clifford D. Shearing) were missing from the top twenty on the nine-journal list, most likely because the twenty-journal list gave more weight to international journals (ten out of twenty, compared with three out of nine).

POLICY IMPLICATIONS

The results of our research may have important public policy implications. An examination of the most-cited scholars and works indicates those topics that criminological researchers consider to be of most importance in different time periods. The most-cited works may also reflect current policy concerns, and an awareness of the topics that criminologists consider to be important and influential should guide policy makers and legislators in the development of new public policies. We will illustrate this by discussing the results reported in our analysis of twenty major journals.

The most-cited works of five of the six most-cited scholars in 1990 (Cohn et al., 1998) focused on criminal career research. This research should inform criminal justice decision making because it can provide useful information about the likely future course of criminal careers. The other most-cited scholar was Travis Hirschi, and his most-cited work was the theoretical book *Causes of Delinquency* (Hirschi, 1969). According to Laub (2004, p.18), "successful theories... provide influential guides to public policy". The main policy implication of this theory is that efforts should be made to increase individuals' bonding to society. The seventh most-cited scholar was Francis T. Cullen, and his most-cited work was *Reaffirming Rehabilitation* (Cullen and Gilbert, 1982), which has clear implications for effective correctional treatment. The eighth most-cited scholar was Ronald V. Clarke, and his most-cited work was *The Reasoning Criminal* (Cornish and Clarke, 1986). This book propounded a rational choice theory of offending that has important implications for situational crime prevention.

The most-cited works of the most-cited scholars in 1995 (Cohn and Farrington, 1999) also have clear policy implications. *Policing Domestic Violence* (Sherman, 1992) was the most-cited work of the most-cited scholar, and this book reported research that encouraged police to arrest male domestic violence offenders. The most-cited work of the next two scholars was *A General Theory of Crime* (Gottfredson and Hirschi, 1990), which proposed that offending depended on self-control. A clear implication of this theory is that policy makers should develop early intervention programs to improve juveniles' self control at a young age, perhaps focusing on parent training (Piquero, Jennings, and Farrington, 2010). The next most-cited work, *Understanding and Controlling Crime* (Farrington, Ohlin, and Wilson, 1986) set out methods of advancing knowledge about the development of criminal careers and how this knowledge might be used to reduce offending.

Similar policy implications can be drawn from the most-cited works of the most-cited scholars in 2000 (Cohn and Farrington, 2008). The most-cited work of the most-cited scholar was *Crime in the Making* (Sampson and Laub, 1993), which reported on the development of offending and proposed that the most important theoretical construct was informal social control. The main implication of this theory is that bonding to the family, the school and the community should be increased, through programs such as those providing job training and structured routine activities in adulthood. Another implication is that desistance can be encouraged by fostering bonding to adult institutions such as employment and marriage. Other proposals are that informal social control in communities could be improved by increasing community cohesiveness or "collective efficacy" (Sampson, Raudenbush, and Earls, 1997), and that it is important to minimize labelling or stigmatization of offenders by reducing the use of incarceration.

Some of the other most-cited scholars in 2000 were the same as in earlier years: David P. Farrington for the development of offending, Francis T. Cullen for the effectiveness of correctional treatment, Travis Hirschi for the general theory of crime, and Lawrence W. Sherman for policing domestic violence. However, a new entry was *Crime, Shame, and Reintegration* by John Braithwaite (1989), with a policy implication of restorative justice programs for offenders.

Another new entry in 2000 was Terrie E. Moffitt's (1993) theory, which implies that different types of programs are needed for adolescence-limited and life-course-persistent offenders. For adolescence-limited offenders, it is especially important to limit contact with delinquent peers. Research on co-offending (Reiss and Farrington, 1991) suggests that it is essential to identify and target "recruiters", offenders who repeatedly commit crimes with younger, less experienced offenders, and who seem to be dragging increasing numbers of young people into crime. Programs that put antisocial peers together may have harmful effects (Dishion, McCord, and Poulin, 1999). Moffitt also suggests that, in order to target the "maturity gap" of adolescence-limited offenders, it is important to provide opportunities for them to achieve status and material goods by legitimate means.

The most-cited works of the most-cited scholars in 2005 show both continuity and change in their theoretical concerns and policy implications. The most-cited work of the most-cited scholar was still *Crime in the Making* (Sampson and Laub, 1993). The criminal career paradigm and developmental research were still important, as was rational choice theory, the effectiveness of correctional treatment, and the theories of Moffitt (1993) and of Gottfredson and Hirschi (1990). A newly identified work with clear policy implications for reducing crime was *Preventing Crime* by Lawrence W. Sherman and his colleagues (1997). *The Psychology of Criminal Conduct,* by Don A. Andrews and James L. Bonta (2003), was also identified as important, possibly because of its emphasis on the policy issues of risk assessment and correctional effectiveness.

PUBLICATION PRODUCTIVITY

We also investigated scholarly influence by studying the number of publications of scholars. Publication counts have been used to identify the most productive departments. From our review, we concluded that these were SUNY-Albany, the University of Maryland, the University of Cincinnati, and Pennsylvania State University. SUNY-Albany was especially identified in older studies, while the University of Cincinnati was especially identified in more recent studies, possibly indicating changes in publication productivity over time.

We studied the publication productivity of members of the American Society of Criminology (excluding students) in 1999-2000 and 2004-05, in over 300 scholarly and technical journals listed in the *Criminal Justice Periodical Index.* Only about one-third of ASC members published any articles during these two-year time windows. Of those who did publish, the average number of published articles was only two per scholar in each two-year period, or one article per year. A small percentage of ASC members (1-2%) accounted for a relatively large percentage of articles published (16-24%). In future research, the Gini coefficient could be used to measure the degree of concentration of publication productivity.

The most prolific publishers (in the top ten) in scholarly journals in both time periods were Alex R. Piquero, Francis T. Cullen, David P. Farrington, Brian Payne, and Randy R. Gainey. After inversely weighting for the number of authors, Alex R. Piquero was the most prolific publisher in both time periods. He was also the most prolific publisher in the twenty most "academic" journals in both time periods. Francis T. Cullen was also among the top three publishers in "academic" journals in both time periods.

THE WAY FORWARD

We hope that this book has demonstrated how much information the analyses of citations and publications have yielded about a wide variety of topics. The most pressing need in the future is for funding to carry out citation and publication analyses of larger numbers of journals and books in criminology and criminal justice. With funding, it would be possible to expand these analyses to later periods of time, and to trace citation careers of scholars and works over long time periods. The aim should be to trace complete citation and publication trajectories of scholars, and citation trajectories of works, and to investigate to what extent the later trajectory can be predicted from the first few years. It is also important to investigate how long a scholar's influence persists after his or her death. We believe that it would be useful to apply criminal career concepts such as onset, duration, termination, frequency, versatility, specialization, and escalation to the study of citation and publication careers.

With funding, it would be possible to compare the results of citation and publication analyses with a variety of alternative methods of measuring prestige and influence, such as surveys of criminologists and criminal justice scholars, numbers of publications, and receipt of honors and major offices in scholarly societies. With funding, more extensive analyses of what topics are addressed by articles and books could be carried out, to identify and aim to predict changes in key topics over time. In particular, the influence of publication productivity on the number of citations should be studied.

It would be possible to carry our more extensive analyses of the most-cited works of the most-cited scholars, to document changes over time in the most influential scholars and works in more detail, and also to identify highly-cited works by less highly-cited scholars. Ideally, vitae of the most influential scholars should be collected, so that all their publications, and citations of all their works, could be studied. It would also be important to relate the changing influence of scholars and works to changes in theoretical, empirical, methodological, and political concerns, and to the changing priorities of funding agencies. A crucial question is why certain scholars and topics (rather than others) become pre-eminent in certain time periods.

Further advances in the methodology of citation analysis are needed. In particular, the prevalence of citations (the number of different articles or books in which a work is cited) seems a more valid measure of influence than the more usual measure of the number of citations. In the interests of comparability over time, we had to keep measuring the number of citations. It would be desirable to develop a classification system for types of citations: whether they are favorable or unfavorable, to what extent they are perfunctory, how central to the argument they are, and so on. Measures of the number of words devoted to discussing a work, or the number of pages on which a work is cited, would also be useful. In addition, the prestige of citing and cited journals could be taken into account in inclusion criteria for citation analysis and in weighting citations. Also, the number and ordering of authors should be considered in citation and publication analyses.

It is important to study the waxing and waning of scholarly influence over time. However, this requires using exactly the same methods and sources over time. This was a problem for us, as we could not include recently established influential journals such as *Criminology and Public Policy, Journal of Experimental Criminology,* or *European Journal of Criminology* in our citation analyses without reducing the comparability of our results over time.

In order to overcome problems of undesirable citation behavior (e.g. citing friends and departmental colleagues deliberately to boost their citations rather than because of their salience for the argument), research on citation behavior is needed. With funding, it would be possible to survey authors of books and journal articles to ask them why they cited certain scholars rather than others. It is important to investigate the extent to which authors obey the law of least effort and only read articles that are immediately available on the internet, as opposed to books that have to be purchased or obtained from libraries. It is known that sales of scholarly books (other than textbooks) have declined greatly as the use of the internet has increased (although this decline may be reversed as more e-books are published).

This survey could include questions designed to investigate to what extent citation behavior is designed to curry favor with journal editors, likely reviewers, key staff members of funding agencies, and other individuals with power (e.g. heads of departments and presidents of scholarly societies). The effects of the specific interests of journal editors on the topics of articles published should be investigated. Systematic studies of similarities and dissimilarities between journals in topics covered and citations should be carried out, together with an investigation of how these change when the editor changes. In addition to eliminating self-citations, coauthor citations could be excluded from analyses, and even citations of scholars in the same department or the same university.

Overall, we believe that citation analysis is a very useful method of investigating changes in scholarly influence over time. However, funding is needed to transform it from its Cinderella status to an accepted discipline, to overcome future threats to its validity, and to establish it as a valuable method of documenting changes in influential scholars and topics in criminology and criminal justice over time. Funding is also needed for more extensive analyses of publication productivity.

FINAL CONCLUSION

Over a twenty-year period from 1986-2005, the most influential topics in major criminological journals (based on the most-cited works of the most-cited scholars) were either concerned with developmental/life course or longitudinal/criminal career research, or with major theories by leading scholars such as Robert J. Sampson and John H. Laub, Michael R. Gottfredson and Travis Hirschi, Terrie E. Moffitt, Ronald V. Clarke, and John Braithwaite (or concerned with both topics in the cases of Sampson/Laub and Moffitt). Other influential topics were correctional effectiveness (especially the work of Francis T. Cullen, Don A. Andrews, and James L. Bonta) and policing and crime prevention topics covered by the work of Lawrence W. Sherman. All of these topics should be carefully considered by policy makers and practitioners.

Our study of changes in scholarly influence over time shows the declining influence of one generation of older and deceased scholars such as Marvin E. Wolfgang and Michael J. Hindelang, as they are replaced by the next influential generation of younger scholars such as Robert J. Sampson and Terrie E. Moffitt. And this process is continuing as even younger scholars such as Alex R. Piquero (the most prolific publisher in our analyses) become increasingly influential. These kinds of changes are only to be expected in general, but more research on scholarly influence is needed to explain, predict, and specify them in more detail, using unbiased, objective, transparent, and quantitative methods such as analyses of citations and publications.

REFERENCES

Adam, David. (2002). The counting house. *Nature, 415* (14 February), 726-729.

Allen, Harry E. (1983). Comment: A reaction to 'An analysis of citations in introductory criminology textbooks,' JCJ 10(3). *Journal of Criminal Justice, 11*, 177–178.

Andrews, Donald A., & Bonta, James L. (1994). *The psychology of criminal conduct.* (1st edition), Cincinnati, OH: Anderson.

Andrews, Donald A., & Bonta, James L. (1998). *The psychology of criminal conduct.* (2nd edition), Cincinnati, OH: Anderson.

Andrews, Donald A., & Bonta, James L. (2003). *The psychology of criminal conduct.* (3rd edition), Cincinnati, OH: Anderson.

Andrews, Donald A., Zinger, Ivan., Hoge, Robert D., Bonta, James, Gendreau, Paul, & Cullen, Francis T. (1990). Does correctional treatment work? A clinically relevant and psychologically informed meta-analysis. *Criminology, 28*, 369-404.

Bagby, R. Michael, Parker, James D.A., & Bury, Alison S. (1990). A comparative citation analysis of attribution theory and the theory of cognitive dissonance. *Personality and Social Psychology Bulletin, 16*, 274–283.

Bain, Read (1962). The most important sociologists? *American Sociological Review, 27*, 746–748.

Barbaree, Howard E., & Marshall, William L. (1989). Erectile responses among heterosexual child molesters, father-daughter incest offenders and matched nonoffenders: Five distinct age-preference profiles. *Canadian Journal of Behavioral Science, 21*, 70-82.

Barbui, Corrado, Cipriani, Andrea, Malvini, Lara, & Tansella, Michele (2006). Validity of the impact factor of journals as a measure of randomized controlled trial quality. *Journal of Clinical Psychiatry, 67*, 37-40.

Bauer, Kathleen & Bakkalbasi, Nisa (2005). An examination of citation counts in a new scholarly communication environment. *D-Lib Magazine* [On-line serial], 11(9). Available from: http://dlib.org/dlib/september05/bauer/09bauer.html

Blackburn, Richard S., and Mitchell, Michelle (1981). Citation analysis in the organizational sciences. *Journal of Applied Psychology, 66*, 337–342.

Blumstein, Alfred, Cohen, Jacqueline, Roth, Jeffrey A., & Visher, Christy A. (Eds.) (1986). *Criminal careers and "career criminals."* Washington, D.C.: National Academy Press.

Bornmann, Lutz & Daniel, Hans-Dieter (2007). Multiple publication on a single research study: Does it pay? The influence of number of research articles on total citation counts in biomedicine. *Journal of the American Society for Information Science and Technology, 58*, 1100-1107.

Bott, David M., & Hargens, Lowell L. (1991). Are sociologists' publications uncited? Citation rates of journal articles, chapters, and books. *American Sociologist, 22*, 147–158.

Braithwaite, John (1989). *Crime, shame and reintegration.* Cambridge: Cambridge University Press.

Brody, Tim, Harnad, Stevan, & Carr, Leslie (2006). Earlier Web usage statistics as predictors of later citation impact. *Journal of the American Association for Information Science and Technology, 57* (8), 1060-1072.

Buchanan, Robert A. (2006). Accuracy of cited references: The role of citation databases. *College and Research Libraries, 64* (4), 292-303.

Bugeja, Michael, Dimitrova, Daniela V., & Hong, Hyehyun (2008). Online citations in history journals: Current practice and views from journal editors. *American Journalism, 25*(4), 83-100.

Buss, Allan R. (1976). Evaluation of Canadian psychology departments based upon citation and publication counts. *Canadian Psychological Review, 17*, 143–150.

Callaham, Michael, Wears, Robert L., & Weber, Ellen (2002). Journal prestige, publication bias, and other characteristics associated with citation of published studies in peer-reviewed journals. *Journal of the American Medical Association, 287*, 2847-2850.

Cano, V., & Lind, N.C. (1991). Citation life cycles of ten citation classics. *Scientometrics, 22*, 297–312.

Chapman, Antony J. (1989). Assessing research: Citation-count shortcomings. *The Psychologist, 8*, 336–344.

Chew, Mabel, Villanueva, Elmer V., & Van Der Weyden, Martin B. (2007). Life and times of the impact factor: Retrospective analysis of trends for seven medical journals (1994-2005) and their Editor's views. *Journal of Research in Social Medicine, 100*, 142-150.

Chikate, R.V., & Patil, Suresh Krishna (2008). Citation analysis of theses in library and information science submitted to University of Pune: A pilot study. *Library Philosophy and Practice* [On-line serial].

Christenson, James A., & Sigelman, Lee (1985). Accrediting knowledge: Journal stature and citation impact in social science. *Social Science Quarterly, 66*, 964–975.

Cloward, Richard A., & Ohlin, Lloyd E. (1960). *Delinquency and opportunity: A theory of delinquent gangs.* New York: The Free Press.

Cohen, Albert K. (1955). *Delinquent boys: The culture of the gang.* New York: The Free Press.

Cohen, Stanley (1985). *Visions of social control: Crime, punishment and classification.* Cambridge, UK: Polity.

Cohn, Ellen G. (2011a). Changes in scholarly influence in major international criminology journals, 1986-2005. *Canadian Journal of Criminology and Criminal Justice, 53* (2), 157-188.

Cohn, Ellen G. (2011b). Changes in scholarly influence in major American criminology and criminal justice journals between 1986 and 2005. *Journal of Criminal Justice Education, 22* (4), 493-525.

Cohn, Ellen G. Farrington, David P., & Wright, Richard A. (1998). *Evaluating criminology and criminal justice.* CT: Greenwood Press.

Cohn, Ellen G., & Farrington, David P. (1990). Differences between British and American criminology: An analysis of citations. *British Journal of Criminology*, *30*, 467–482.

Cohn, Ellen G., & Farrington, David P. (1994a). Who are the most influential criminologists in the English-speaking world? *British Journal of Criminology*, *34*, 204–225.

Cohn, Ellen G., & Farrington, David P. (1994b). Who are the most-cited scholars in major American criminology and criminal justice journals? *Journal of Criminal Justice*, *22*, 517–534.

Cohn, Ellen G., & Farrington, David P. (1995). The validity of citations as a measure of influence in criminology. *British Journal of Criminology*, *35*, 143-145.

Cohn, Ellen G., & Farrington, David P. (1996). *Crime and justice* and the criminology and criminal justice literature. *Crime and justice: A review of research*, *20*, 265-300.

Cohn, Ellen G., & Farrington, David P. (1998a). Changes in the most-cited scholars in major international journals between 1986-90 and 1991-95. *British Journal of Criminology*, *38*, 156-170.

Cohn, Ellen G., & Farrington, David P. (1998b). Changes in the most-cited scholars in major American criminology and criminal justice journals between 1986-1990 and 1991-1995. *Journal of Criminal Justice*, *26*(2), 99-116.

Cohn, Ellen G., & Farrington, David P. (1998c). Assessing the quality of American doctoral program faculty in criminology and criminal justice, 1991-1995. *Journal of Criminal Justice Education, 9*(2), 187-210.

Cohn, Ellen G., & Farrington, David P. (1999). Changes in the most-cited scholars in twenty criminology and criminal justice journals between 1990 and 1995. *Journal of Criminal Justice*, *27*(4), 345-359.

Cohn, Ellen G., & Farrington, David P. (2007a). Changes in scholarly influence in major international criminology journals between 1986 and 2000. *Australian and New Zealand Journal of Criminology, 40* (3), 335-360.

Cohn, Ellen G., & Farrington, David P. (2007b). Changes in scholarly influence in major American criminology and criminal justice journals between 1986 and 2000. *Journal of Criminal Justice Education, 18* (1), 6-34.

Cohn, Ellen G., & Farrington, David P. (2008). Scholarly influence in criminology and criminal justice journals in 1990-2000. *Journal of Criminal Justice*, *36* (1), 11-21.

Cohn, Ellen G., & Farrington, David P. (2012). Scholarly influence in criminology and criminal justice journals in 1990-2005. *Criminal Justice Review*, forthcoming.

Cohn, Ellen G., Farrington, David P., & Sorensen, Jonathan R. (2000). Journal publications of Ph.D. graduates from American criminology and criminal justice programs, 1988-1997. *Journal of Criminal Justice Education, 11*(1), 35-49.

Cole, Jonathan & Cole, Stephen (1971). Measuring the quality of sociological research: Problems in the use of the Science Citation Index. *American Sociologist*, *6*, 23–29.

Cole, Jonathan R., & Cole, Stephen. (1972). The Ortega hypothesis. *Science*, *178* (27 Oct.), 368–375.

Cole, Stephen (1975). The growth of scientific knowledge: Theories of deviance as a case study. In L.A. Coser (Ed.), *The idea of social structure: Papers in honor of R.K. Merton* (pp. 175-200). New York: Harcourt Brace Jovanovich.

Cornish, Derek B. & Clarke, Ronald V. (Eds) (1986). *The reasoning criminal: Rational choice perspectives on offending*. New York: Springer-Verlag.

Courtney, John C., Kawchuk, Karman B., & Spafford, Duff (1987). Life in print: Citation of articles published in volumes 1–10 of the Canadian Journal of Political Science/Revue canadienne de science politique. *Canadian Journal of Political Science, 20*, 625–637.

Cronin, Blaise, Snyder, Herbert, & Atkins, Helen (1997). Comparative citation rankings of authors in monographic and journal literature: A study of sociology. *Journal of Documenation, 53*(3), 263-273.

CrossRef (2010). History/Mission. Retrieved January 31, 2012 from http://www.crossref.org/01company/02history.html

Cullen, Francis T., & Gilbert, Karen E. (1982). *Reaffirming rehabilitation.* Cincinnati, OH: Anderson.

Cullen, Francis T., Link, Bruce G., Wolfe, Nancy T., & Frank, James (1985). The social dimensions of correctional officer stress. *Justice Quarterly, 2*, 505-33.

Davis, Jaya & Sorensen, Jonathan R. (2010). Doctoral programs in criminal justice and criminology: A meta-analysis of program ranking. *Southwest Journal of Criminal Justice, 7* (1), 6-23.

De Lacey, Gerald, Record, Carol, & Wade, Jenny (1985). How accurate are quotations and references in medical journals? *British Medical Journal, 291* (Sept. 28), 884–886.

Dess, Howard M. (2006). Database reviews and reports: Scopus. *Issues in Science and Technology Librarianship*, Winter.

DeZee, Matthew R. (1980). *The productivity of criminology and criminal justice faculty.* Chicago, IL: Joint Commission on Criminology and Criminal Justice Education and Standards.

Diamond, Arthur M. (1986). What is a citation worth? *Journal of Human Resources, 21*, 200–215.

Dishion, Thomas J., McCord, Joan, and Poulin, François (1999). When interventions harm: Peer groups and problem behavior. *American Psychologist, 54,* 755-764.

Doerner, William G., DeZee, Matthew R., & Lab, Steven P. (1982). Responding to the 'call for papers.' *Criminology, 19*, 650–658.

Doob, Anthony N., & Roberts, Julian V. (1983). *Sentencing: An analysis of the public's view.* Ottawa: Department of Justice.

Douglas, Robert J. (1992). How to write a highly cited article without even trying. *Psychological Bulletin, 112*, 405–408.

Dumé, Belle (2006a). Hottest topic in physics revealed. *PhysicsWorld.Com.* Retrieved February 10, 2010 from http://physicsworld.com/cws/article/news/24845

Dumé, Belle (2006b). Revealed – the world's most creative physicist. *Physics World, 19* (9), 9.

Dunford, Franklyn W., Huizinga, David, & Elliott, Delbert S. (1990). The role of arrest in domestic assault: The Omaha Police experiment. *Criminology, 28,* 183-206.

Duy, Joanna & Vaughan, Liwen (2006). Can electronic journal usage data replace citation data as a measure of journal use? An empirical examination. *The Journal of Academic Librianship, 32* (5), 512-517.

Egghe, Leo (2006). Theory and practice of the g-index. *Scientometrics*, 69 (1), 131-152.

Endler, Norman S. (1977). Research productivity and scholarly impact of Canadian psychology departments. *Canadian Psychological Review*, 18 (2), 152-168.

Endler, Norman S., Rushton, J. Phillipe, and Roediger, Henry L. (1978). Productivity and scholarly impact (citations) of British, Canadian, and US departments of psychology (1975). *American Psychologist*, 33, 1064–1083.

Eysenbach, Gunther (2006). Citation advantage of open access articles. *PLoS Biology*, [Online serial], 4 (5).

Fabianic, David A (1981). Institutional affiliation of authors in selected criminal justice journals. *Journal of Criminal Justice*, 9(3), 247-252.

Fabianic, David A. (1979). Relative prestige of criminal justice doctoral programs. *Journal of Criminal Justice*, 7, 135–145.

Fabianic, David A. (1980). Perceived scholarship and readership of criminal justice journals. *Journal of Police Science and Administration*, 8, 15–20.

Fabianic, David A. (2001). Frequently published scholars and educational backgrounds. *Journal of Criminal Justice, 29*, 119-125.

Fabianic, David A. (2002). Publication productivity of criminal justice faculty in criminal justice journals. *Journal of Criminal Justice*, 30, 549-558.

Fabianic, David A. (2012). Publication profiles at point of promotion of criminal justice faculty. *Journal of Criminal Justice Education, 23* (1), 65-80.

Farrington, David P. (1986). Age and crime. In Michael Tonry & Norval Morris (Eds.), *Crime and justice*, Vol. 7 (pp.189-250). Chicago: University of Chicago Press.

Farrington, David P. (1995). The development of offending and antisocial behaviour from childhood: Key findings from the Cambridge study in delinquent development. *Journal of Child Psychology and Psychiatry, 36*, 929-964.

Farrington, David P. (2000). Explaining and preventing crime: The globalization of knowledge. *Criminology*, 38, 1-24.

Farrington, David P., Ohlin, Lloyd E., and Wilson, James Q. (1986). *Understanding and controlling crime: Toward a new research strategy*. New York: Springer-Verlag.

Ferber, Marianne A. (1986). Citations: Are they an objective measure of scholarly merit? *Signs: Journal of Women in Culture and Society* 11, 381–389.

Fingerman, Susan (2006). Web of Science and Scopus: Current features and capabilities. *Issues in Science and Technology Librarianship*, Fall.

Forrester, David H., Chatterton, Michael R., & Pease, Ken (1988). *The Kirkholt Burglary Prevention Project, Rochdale*. London: Home Office (Crime Prevention Paper No. 13).

Fox, Richard G., & Freiberg, Arie (1985). *Sentencing: State and Federal Law in Victoria*. Melbourne: Oxford University Press.

Frost, Natasha A., Phillips, Nickie D., and Clear, Todd R. (2007). Productivity of criminal justice scholars across the career. *Journal of Criminal Justice Education, 18* (3), 428-443.

Funkhouser, Edward T. (1996). The evaluative use of citation analysis for communications journals. *Human Communication Research*, 22(4), 563-574.

Gabbidon, Shaun L. & Greene, Helen T. (2001). The presence of African American scholarship in early American criminology texts (1918-1960). *Journal of Criminal Justice Education, 12* (2), 301-310.

Garfield, Eugene (1972). Citation analysis as a tool in journal evaluation. *Science, 178*, 471-479.

Garfield, Eugene (1977a). The 250 most-cited primary authors, 1961–1975. Part I. How the names were selected. *Current Contents, 77* (49), 5–15.

Garfield, Eugene (1977b). The 250 most-cited primary authors, 1961–1975. Part II. The correlation between citedness, Nobel prizes and academy memberships. *Current Contents, 77* (50), 5–15.

Garfield, Eugene (1977c). The 250 most-cited primary authors, 1961–1975. Part III. Each author's most-cited publication. *Current Contents, 77* (51), 5–20.

Garfield, Eugene (1977d). A list of 100 most cited (chemical) articles. *Current Contents, 10*, 5–12.

Garfield, Eugene (1979). Is citation analysis a legitimate evaluation tool? *Scientometrics, 1*, 359–375.

Garfield, Eugene (2003). The meaning of the impact factor. *International Journal of Clinical and Health Psychology*, 3 (2), 363-369.

Garfield, Eugene, & Welljams-Dorof, Alfred (1990). Language use in international research: A citation analysis. *Annals of the American Academy of Political and Social Science, 511*, 10–24.

Gastwirth, Joseph L. (1972). The estimation of the Lorenz curve and Gini index. *Review of Economics and Statistics, 54*(3), 306-316.

Geis, Gilbert & Meier, Robert F. (1978). Looking backward and forward: Criminologists on criminology as a career. *Criminology, 16*, 273–288.

Giblin, Matthew J., & Schafer, Joseph A. (2008). Comprehensive examination reading lists as indicators of scholar impact and significance. *Journal of Criminal Justice, 36*, 81-89.

Gilbert, G. Nigel (1977). Referencing as persuasion. *Social Studies of Science, 7*, 113–122.

Glänzel, Wolfgang & Garfield, Eugene (2004). The myth of delayed recognition. *The Scientist, 18* (11), 8.

Goodrich, June E., & Roland, Charles G. (1977). Accuracy of published medical reference citations. *Journal of Technical Writing and Communication, 7*, 15–19.

Google Scholar (2012). Google Scholar help. Retrieved January 31, 2012 from http://scholar.google.com/intl/en/scholar/help.html

Gordon, Randall A., & Vicari, Pamela J. (1992). Eminence in social psychology: A comparison of textbook citation, Social Sciences Citation Index, and research productivity rankings. *Personality and Social Psychology Bulletin. 18*, 26–38.

Gorenflo, David W., & McConnell, James V. (1991). The most frequently cited journal articles and authors in introductory psychology textbooks. *Teaching of Psychology, 18*, 8–12.

Gottfredson, Michael R., & Hirschi, Travis (1990). *A general theory of crime.* Stanford, CA: Stanford University Press.

Greene, Jack R., Bynum, Timothy S., & Webb, Vincent J. (1985). Paradigm development in crime-related education: The role of the significant others. *Criminal Justice Review, 10*, 7–17.

Grégoire, Denis A., Noël, Martin X., Déry, Richard, & Béchard, Jean-Pierre (2006). Is there conceptual convergence in entrepreneurship research? A co-citation analysis of *Frontiers of Entrepreneurship Research*, 1981-2004. *Entrepreneurship Theory and Practice, 30* (3), 333-373.

Haddow, Gaby (2008). Quality Australian journals in the humanities and social sciences. *Australian Academic and Research Libraries, 39* (2), 79-91.

Hagan, John L. (1974). Extra-legal attributes and criminal sentencing: An assessment of a sociological viewpoint. *Law and Society Review, 8*, 357-8.

Hamermesh, Daniel S., Johnson, George E., & Weisbrod, Burton A. (1982). Scholarship, citations and salaries: Economic reward in economics. *Southern Economic Journal, 49,* 472–481.

Hamilton, David P. (1990). Publishing by – and for? – the numbers. *Science, 250,* 1331-1332.

Hamilton, David P. (1991). Research papers: Who's uncited now? *Science, 251,* 25.

Hanson, David J. (1975). The dissemination of Ph.D. results: Further findings. *American Sociologist, 10* (4), 237-238.

Heinzkill, Richard (2007). References in scholarly English and American literary journals thirty years later: A citation study. *College and Research Libraries, 68* (2), 141-153.

Henneken, Edwin A., Kurtz, Michael J., Eichhorn, Guenther, Accomazzi, Alberto, Grant, Carolyn, Thompson, Donna, & Murray, Stephen S. (2006). Effect of e-printing on citation rates in astronomy and physics. *JEP: Journal of Electronic Publishing* [On-line serial], *9* (2).

Hindelang, Michael J., Gottfredson, Michael R., & Garofalo, James (1978). *Victims of personal crime: An empirical foundation for a theory of personal victimization.* Cambridge, MA: Ballinger.

Hindelang, Michael J., Hirschi, Travis, & Weis, Joseph G. (1981). *Measuring delinquency.* Beverly Hills, CA: Sage.

Hirsch, J.E. (2005). An index to quantify an individual's scientific research output. *PNAS, 102* (November 15), 16569-16572.

Hirschi, Travis (1969). *Causes of delinquency.* Berkeley, CA: University of California Press.

Hough, J. Michael, & Mayhew, Patricia M. (1983). *British Crime Survey: First report.* London: Her Majesty's Stationery Office.

Hutson, Scott R. (2002). Gendered citation practices in *American Antiquity* and other archaeology journals. *American Antiquity, 67* (2), 331-342.

Jascó, Peter (2008a). Savvy searching: Google Scholar revisited. *Online Information Review, 32* (1), 102-114.

Jascó, Peter (2008b). The pros and cons of computing the h-indeusing Google Scholar. *Online Information Review, 32* (3), 437-452.

Jascó, Peter (2009a). Google Scholar's ghost authors. *Library Journal, 134* (18), 26-27.

Jascó, Peter (2009b). A final joy write: Panorama of past pans. *Online: Exploring Technology and Resources for Information Professionals, 33* (6), 51-53.

Jascó, Peter (2009c). Peter's digital reference shelf: Scopus. Available online at http://www.gale.cengage.com/reference/peter/200906/scopus.html

Jennings, Wesley G., Gibson, Chris L., Ward, Jeffrey T., & Beaver, Kevin M. (2008a) "Which group are you in?": A preliminary investigation of group-based publication trajectories of criminology and criminal justice scholars. *Journal of Criminal Justice Education, 19,* (2), 227-250.

Jennings, Wesley G., Higgins, George E., & Khey, David N. (2009). Exploring the stability and variability of impact factors and associated rankings in criminology and criminal justice journals, 1998-2007. *Journal of Criminal Justice Education,* 20 (2), 157-172.

Jennings, Wesley G., Schreck, Christoper J., Sturtz, Michael, & Mahoney, Margaret (2008b) Exploring the scholarly output of academic organization leadership in criminology and criminal justice: A research note on publication productivity. *Journal of Criminal Justice Education, 19* (3), 404-416.

Jones, Alan Wayne (2005). Créme de la crème in forensic science and legal medicine: The most highly cited articles, authors, and journals 1981-2003. *International Journal of Legal Medicine, 119*, 59-65.

Khey, David N., Jennings, Wesley G., Higgins, George E., Schoepfer, Andrea, & Langton, Lynn (2011). Re-ranking the top female academic "stars" in criminology and criminal justice using an alternative method: A research note. *Journal of Criminal Justice Education, 22* (1), 118-129.

Kleck, Gary & Barnes, James C. (2011). Article productivity among the faculty of criminology and criminal justice doctoral programs, 2005-2009. *Journal of Criminal Justice Education, 22* (1), 43-66.

Kleck, Gary, Wang, Shun-Yung K., & Tark, Jongyeon (2007). Article productivity among the faculty of criminology and criminal justice doctoral programs, 2000-2005. *Journal of Criminal Justice Education, 18* (3), 385-405.

Laband, David N., & Piette, Michael J. (1994). A citation analysis of the impact of blinded peer review. *Journal of the American Medical Association, 272*, 147-149.

LaBonte, Kristen B. (2005). Citation analysis: A method for collection development for a rapidly developing field. *Issues in Science and Technology Librarianship*, [On-line serial], *43*.

Land, Kenneth C., McCall, Patricia L., & Nagin, Daniel S. (1996). A comparison of Poisson, negative binomial, and semiparametric mixed Poisson regression models with empirical applications to criminal careers research. *Sociological Methods and Research, 24*, 387–442.

Laub, John H. (2004). The life course of criminology in the United States: The American Society of Criminology 2003 Presidential address. *Criminology, 42* (1), 1-26.

Laub, John H., & Sampson, Robert J. (2003). *Shared beginnings, divergent lives: Delinquent boys to age 70*. Cambridge, MA: Harvard University Press.

Laub, John H., Nagin, Daniel S., & Sampson Robert J. (1998). Trajectories of change in criminal offending: Good marriages and the desistance process. *American Sociological Review, 63*, 225-238.

Lawrence, Steve (2001). Free online availability substantially increases a paper's impact. *Nature, 411*, 521. Available online at http://www.nature.com/nature/debates/e-access/Articles/lawrence.html

Lee, Kirby P., Schotland, Marieka, Bacchetti, Peter, & Bero, Lisa A. (2002). Association of journal quality indicators with methodological quality of clinical research articles. *Journal of the American Medical Association, 287*, 2805-2808.

Lenton, Rhonda L. (1995). Power versus feminist theories of wife abuse. *Canadian Journal of Criminology, 38*, 305-30.

Levi, Michael (1995). The use and misuse of citations as a measure of influence in criminology. *British Journal of Criminology, 35*, 138-142.

Lindsey, Duncan (1980). Production and citation measures in the sociology of science: The problem of multiple authorship. *Social Studies of Science, 10*, 145–162.

Logan, Elisabeth L., & Shaw, W. M. (1991). A bibliometric analysis of collaboration in a medical speciality. *Scientometrics, 20*, 417–426.

Lok, Candy K.W., Chan, Matthew T.V., & Martinson, Ida M. (2001) Risk factors for citation errors in peer-reviewed nursing journals. *Journal of Advanced Nursing, 34*, 223-229.

Lokker, Cynthia, McKibbon, K. Ann, McKinlay, R. James, Wilczynski, Nancy L., & Haynes, R. Brian (2008). Prediction of citation counts for clinical articles at two years using data available within three weeks of publication: Retrospective cohort study. *British Medical Journal, 336,* 665-667.

Long, Heather, Boggess, Lyndsay N., & Jennings, Wesley G. (2011). Re-assessing publication productivity among academic "stars" in criminology and criminal justice. *Journal of Criminal Justice Education, 22* (1), 102-117.

Long, J. Scott, McGinnis, Robert, & Allison, Paul D. (1980). The problem of junior-authored papers in constructing citation counts. *Social Studies of Science, 10,* 127–143.

Lotz, Roy, & Regoli, Robert M. (1977). Police cynicism and professionalism. *Human Relations, 30,* 175-86.

Marenin, Otwin (1993). Faculty productivity in criminal justice Ph.D. programs: Another view. *Journal of Criminal Justice Education, 4,* 189–192.

Marshall, William L., & Barbaree, Howard E. (1988). The long-term evaluation of a behavioral treatment program for child molesters. *Behavior Research and Therapy, 26,* 499-511.

Mayhew, Patricia M., Elliott, David, & Dowds, Lizanne (1989). *The 1988 British Crime Survey.* (Home Office Research Study no. 111.) London: Her Majesty's Stationery Office.

McElrath, Karen (1990). Standing in the shadows: Academic mentoring in criminology. *Journal of Criminal Justice Education, 1,* 135–151.

Meadows, Arthur Jack (1974). *Communication in science.* London: Butterworths.

Megargee, Edwin I., & Bohn, Martin J. (1979). *Classifying criminal offenders: A new system based on the MMPI.* Beverly Hills, CA: Sage.

Meho, Lokman I. (2007). The rise and rise of citation analysis. *Physics World, 20,* 32-36.

Meho, Lokman I., & Yang, Kiduk (2007). Impact of data sources on citation counts and rankings of LIS faculty: Web of Science versus Scopus and Google Scholar. *Journal of the American Society for Information Science and Technology, 58* (13), 2105-2125.

Merton, Robert K. (1938). Social structure and anomie. *American Sociological Review, 3,* 672–682.

Mijares, Tomas & Blackburn, Robert (1990). Evaluating criminal justice programs: Establishing criteria. *Journal of Criminal Justice, 18,* 33–41.

Moed, Henk F. (2005). Citation analysis of scientific journals and journal impact measures. *Current Science, 89* (12), 1990-1996.

Moffitt, Terrie E. (1993). Adolescence-limited and life-course-persistent antisocial behavior: A developmental taxonomy. *Psychological Review, 100,* 674-701.

Moffitt, Terrie E., Caspi, Avshalom, Rutter, Michael, & Silva, Phil A. (2001). *Sex differences in antisocial behaviour: Conduct disorder, delinquency, and violence in the Dunedin Longitudinal Study.* Cambridge, UK: Cambridge University Press.

Mullens, Nicholas C., Hargens, Lowell L., Hecht, Pamela K., & Kick, Edward L. (1977). The group structure of co-citation clusters: A comparative study. *American Sociological Review, 42,* 552–562.

Murphy, Penelope (1996). *Determining measures of the quality and impact of journals* (National Board of Employment, Education and Training Commissioned Report no 49). Canberra: Australian Government Publishing Service.

Myers, C. Roger (1970). Journal citations and scientific eminence in contemporary psychology. *American Psychologist, 25*,1041–1048.

Nagin, Daniel S., & Farrington, David P. (1992). The stability of criminal potential from childhood to adulthood. *Criminology, 30*, 235-260.

Nagin, Daniel S., & Land, Kenneth C. (1993). Age, criminal careers, and population heterogeneity: Specification and estimation of a nonparametric, mixed Poisson model. *Criminology, 31*, 327–362.

Nagin, Daniel S., & Paternoster, Raymond (1993). Enduring individual differences and rational choice theories of crime. *Law and Society Review*, 27, 467-496.

Nagin, Daniel S., & Paternoster, Raymond (1994). Personal capital and social control: The deterrence implications of individual differences in criminal offending. *Criminology, 32*, 581-606.

Nagin, Daniel S., Farrington, David P., & Moffitt, Terrie E. (1995). Life-course trajectories of different types of offenders. *Criminology, 33*, 111-139.

Neuhaus, Christoph & Daniel, Hans-Dieter (2008). Data sources for performing citation analysis: An overview. *Journal of Documentation, 64* (2), 193-210.

Nisonger, Thomas E. (2004). Citation autobiography: An investigation of ISI data base coverage in determining author citedness. *College and Research Libraries, 65* (2), 152-163.

Oliver, Willard M., Swindell, Sam, Marks, John, & Balusek, Ken (2009). Book 'em Dano: The scholarly productivity of institutions and their faculty in criminal justice books. *Southwest Journal of Criminal Justice, 6* (1), 59-78.

Oromaner, Mark Jay (1968). The most-cited sociologists: An analysis of introductory text citations. *American Sociologist, 3*, 124–126.

Orrick, Erin A., & Weir, Henriikka (2011). The most prolific sole and lead authors in elite criminology and criminal justice journals, 2000-2009. *Journal of Criminal Justice Education, 22* (1), 24-42.

Pancheshnikov, Yelena (2007). A comparison of literature citations in faculty publications and student theses as indicators of collection use and a background for collection management at a university library. *Journal of Academic Librarianship, 33* (6), 674-683.

Pardeck, John T., Arndt, Beverly J., Light, Donna B., Mosley, Gladys F., Thomas, Stacy D., Werner, Mary A., & Wilson, Katheryn E. (1991). Distinction and achievement levels of editorial board members of psychology and social work journals. *Psychological Reports, 68*, 523–527.

Parker, L. Craig, & Goldfeder, Eileen (1979). Productivity ratings of graduate programs in criminal justice based on publication in ten critical journals. *Journal of Criminal Justice, 7*, 125–133.

Paternoster, Raymond, Brame, Robert, Mazerolle, Paul, & Piquero, Alex R. (1998). Using the correct statistical test for the equality of regression coefficients. *Criminology, 36*, 859-866.

Patsopoulos, Nikolas A., Analatos, Apostolos A., & Ioannidis, John P.A. (2005). Relative citation impact of various study designs in the health sciences. *Journal of the American Medical Association, 293* (19), 2362-2366.

Peritz, Bluma C. (1983). Are methodological papers more cited than theoretical or empirical ones? The case of sociology. *Scientometrics, 5*, 211–218.

Peterson, Ruth D., & Hagan, John L. (1984). Changing conceptions of race: Towards an account of anomalous findings in sentencing research. *American Sociological Review, 49*, 56-70.

Piquero, Alex R., Farrington, David P., & Blumstein, Alfred (2003). The criminal career paradigm. In M. Tonry (Ed), *Crime and justice, Vol. 30* (pp. 359-506). Chicago: University of Chicago Press.

Piquero, Alex R., Jennings, Wesley, and Farrington, David P. (2010). On the malleability of self-control: Theoretical and policy implications regarding a general theory of crime. *Justice Quarterly, 27*, 803-834.

Poole, Eric D., & Regoli, Robert M. (1981). Periodical prestige in criminology and criminal justice: A comment. *Criminology, 19*, 470–478.

Poyer, Robert K. (1979). Inaccurate references in significant journals of science. *Bulletin of the Medical Library Association, 67*, 396–398.

Pratt, Travis C., & Cullen, Francis T. (2000). The empirical status of Gottfredson and Hirschi's general theory of crime: A meta-analysis. *Criminology, 38*, 931-964.

Rahm, Erhard & Thor, Andreas (2005). Citation analysis of database publications. *SIGMOD Record, 34* (4), 48-53.

Reader, Diana & Watkins, David (2006). The social and collaborative nature of entrepreneurship scholarship: A co-citation and perceptual analysis. *Entrepreneurship Theory and Practice, 30* (3), 417-422.

Regoli, Robert M., Poole, Eric D., & Miracle, Andrew W. (1982). Assessing the prestige of journals in criminal justice: A research note. *Journal of Criminal Justice, 10*, 57–67.

Reiss, Albert J., and Farrington, David P. (1991). Advancing knowledge about co-offending: Results from a prospective longitudinal survey of London males. *Journal of Criminal Law and Criminology, 82*, 360-395.

Rice, Stephen K., Cohn, Ellen G., & Farrington, David P. (2005). Where are they now?: Trajectories of publication 'stars' from American criminology and criminal justice programs. *Journal of Criminal Justice Education, 16* (2), 244-264.

Rice, Stephen K., Terry, Karen J., Miller, Holly Ventura, & Ackerman, Alissa R. (2007). Research trajectories of female scholars in criminology and criminal justice. *Journal of Criminal Justice Education, 18* (3), 360-384.

Richards, J. M. (1991). Years cited: An alternative measure of scientific accomplishment. *Scientometrics, 20*, 427–438.

Roberts, Julian V. (1992). Public opinion, crime, and criminal justice. In Michael Tonry (Ed.), *Crime and justice, Vol. 16* (pp.99-180). Chicago: University of Chicago Press.

Roberts, Julian V. (2002). *The use of victim impact statements in sentencing: A review of international research findings*. Ottawa: Policy Centre for Victim Issues, Department of Justice Canada.

Roberts, Julian V., & Melchers, Ronald (2003). The incarceration of Aboriginal offenders: Trends from 1978 to 2001. *Canadian Journal of Criminology and Criminal Justice, 45*, 211-243.

Roche, Thomas and Smith, David L. (1978). Frequency of citations as criterion for the ranking of departments, journals, and individuals. *Sociological Inquiry, 48*, 49–57.

Rock, Paul (2005). Chronocentrism and British criminology. *British Journal of Sociology, 56* (3), 473-491.

Rosenberg, Milton J. (1979). The elusiveness of eminence. *American Psychologist, 34,* 723–725.

Rushton, J. Philippe (1984). Evaluating research eminence in psychology: The construct validity of citation counts. *Bulletin of the British Psychological Society, 37,* 33–36.

Rushton, J. Phillipe Littlefield, Christine H., Russell, Robin J.H., & Meltzer, Sari J. (1983). Research production and scholarly impact in British universities and departments of psychology: An update. *Bulletin of the British Psychological Society, 36,* 41–44.

Rushton, J. Phillipe, & Endler, Norman S. (1977). The scholarly impact and research productivity of departments of psychology in the United Kingdom. *Bulletin of the British Psychological Society, 30,* 369–373.

Rushton, J. Phillipe, & Endler, Norman S. (1979). More to-do about citation counts in British psychology. *Bulletin of the British Psychological Society, 32,* 107–109.

Sam, Joel, & Tackie, S. Nii Bekoe (2007). Citation analysis of dissertations accepted by the Department of Information Studies, University of Ghana, Legon. *African Journal of Library and Information Science, 17* (2), 117-124.

Sampson, Robert J., & Laub, John H. (1993). *Crime in the making: Pathways and turning points through life.* Cambridge, MA: Harvard University Press.

Sampson, Robert J., Raudenbush, Stephen W., & Earls, Felton (1997). Neighborhoods and violent crime: A multilevel study of collective efficacy. *Science, 277,* 918-924.

Schildt, Henri A., Zahra, Shaker A., & Sillanpää, Antti (2006). Scholarly communities in entrepreneurship research: A co-citation analysis. *Entrepreneurship Theory and Practice, 30* (3), 399-415.

Schmalleger, Frank (2012) *Criminology today: An integrative introduction* (6th edition). Columbus, OH: Prentice Hall.

Scopus (2011). SciVerse Scopus content coverage guide. Retrieved January 31, 2012 from http://www.info.sciverse.com/UserFiles/sciverse_scopus_content_coverage_0.pdf

Seglen, Per O. (1997). Why the impact factor of journals should not be used for evaluating research. *British Medical Journal, 314* (7079), 497.

Sherman, Lawrence W. & Berk, Richard A. (1984). The specific deterrent effects of arrest for domestic assault. *American Sociological Review, 49,* 261-272.

Sherman, Lawrence W. (1992). *Policing domestic violence: Experiments and dilemmas.* New York: Free Press.

Sherman, Lawrence W. (1993). Defiance, deterrence, and irrelevance: A theory of the criminal sanction. *Journal of Research in Crime and Delinquency, 30,* 445-473.

Sherman, Lawrence W., Gartin, Patrick R., & Buerger, Michael E. (1989). Hot spots of predatory crime: Routine activities and the criminology of place. *Criminology, 27,* 27-55.

Sherman, Lawrence W., Gottfredson, Denise C., MacKenzie, Doris L., Eck, John E., Reuter, Peter, & Bushway, Shawn D. (1998). *Preventing crime: What works, what doesn't, what's promising.* Washington, DC: National Institute of Justice.

Shichor, David (1982). An analysis of citations in introductory criminology textbooks: A research note. *Journal of Criminal Justice, 10,* 231–237.

Shichor, David (1983). Citations in introductory criminology textbooks: A response to Allen's comment. *Journal of Criminal Justice, 11,* 179.

Shichor, David, O'Brien, Robert M., & Decker, David L. (1981). Prestige of journals in criminology and criminal justice. *Criminology, 19,* 461–469.

Shutt, J. Eagle & Barnes, James C. (2008). Reexamining criminal justice 'star power' in a larger sky: A belated response to Rice et al. on sociological influence in criminology and criminal justice. *Journal of Criminal Justice Education, 19* (2), 213-226.

Smith, Adrian (1989). Citation counting. *Association of University Teachers Bulletin,* January, 5.

Smith, Derek R. (2008). Citation analysis and impact factor trends of 5 core journals in occupational medicine, 1985-2006. *Archives of Environmental and Occupational Health, 63* (3), 114-122.

Smyth, Russell (1999). A citation analysis of Australian economic journals. *Australian Academic and Research Libraries, 30* (2), 119-133.

Soler, José M. (2007). A rational indicator of scientific creativity. *Journal of Informetrics, 1,* 123-130.

Sorensen, Jonathan R. (1994). Scholarly productivity in criminal justice: Institutional affiliation of authors in the top ten criminal justice journals. *Journal of Criminal Justice, 22* (6), 535-547.

Sorensen, Jonathan R. (2009). An assessment of the relative impact of criminal justice and criminology journals. *Journal of Criminal Justice, 37,* 505-511.

Sorensen, Jonathan R., & Pilgrim, Rocky (2002). The institutional affiliations of authors in leading criminology and criminal justice journals. *Journal of Criminal Justice, 30,* 11-18.

Sorensen, Jonathan R., Patterson, Amy L., & Widmayer, Alan (1992). Publication productivity of faculty members in criminology and criminal justice doctoral programs. *Journal of Criminal Justice Education, 3,* 1–33.

Sorensen, Jonathan R., Patterson, Amy L., & Widmayer, Alan (1993). Measuring faculty productivity in a multidisciplinary field: A response to Professor Marenin. *Journal of Criminal Justice Education, 4,* 193–196.

Sorensen, Jonathan R., Snell, Clete, & Rodriguez, John J. (2006). An assessment of criminal justice and criminology journal prestige. *Journal of Criminal Justice Education, 17,* 297-322.

Stack, Steven (1987). Measuring the relative impacts of criminology and criminal justice journals: A research note. *Justice Quarterly, 4,* 475–484.

Stack, Steven (2001). The effect of field of terminal degree on scholarly productivity: An analysis of criminal justice faculty. *Journal of Criminal Justice Education, 12* (1), 19-34.

Steiner, Benjamin & Schwartz, John (2006). The scholarly productivity of institutions and their faculty in leading criminology and criminal justice journals. *Journal of Criminal Justice, 34* (4), 393-400.

Steiner, Benjamin & Schwartz, John (2007). Assessing the quality of doctoral programs in criminology in the United States. *Journal of Criminal Justice Education, 18* (1), 53-86.

Stenning, Philip & Roberts Julian V. (2001) Empty promises: Parliament, the Supreme Court, and the sentencing of aboriginal offenders. *Saskatchewan Law Review, 64,* 137-168.

Straus, Murray A., Gelles, Richard J., & Steinmetz, Suzanne K. (1980). *Behind closed doors: Violence in the American family.* New York: Doubleday.

Stryker, Jo Ellen (2002). Reporting medical information: Effects of press releases and newsworthiness on medical journal articles' visibility in the news media. *Preventive Medicine, 35,* 519-530.

Sweetland, James H. (1989). Errors in bibliographic citations: A continuing problem. *The Library Quarterly, 59,* 291–304.

Sykes, Gresham M. (1958). *The society of captives: A study of a maximum security prison.* Princeton, NJ: Princeton University Press.

Sykes, Gresham M., & Matza, David (1957). Techniques of neutralization: A theory of delinquency. *American Sociological Review, 22,* 664–670.

Taggart, William A., & Holmes, Malcolm D. (1991) Institutional productivity in criminal justice and criminology: An examination of author affiliation in selected journals. *Journal of Criminal Justice, 19,* 549-561.

Taylor, Donald (2007). Looking for a link: Comparing faculty citations pre and post Big Deals. *Electronic Journal of Academic and Special Librarianship* [on-line serial], *8* (1).

Telep, Cody W. (2009). Citation analysis of randomized experiments in criminology and criminal justice: A research note. *Journal of Experimental Criminology, 5,* 441-463.

Tenopir, Carol (2007). Measuring impact and quality. *Library Journal,* September 1, 30.

Tewksbury, Richard & Mustaine, Elizabeth Ehrhardt (2011). How many authors does it take to write an article? An assessment of criminology and criminal justice research article author composition. *Journal of Criminal Justice Education, 22* (1), 12-23.

Thomas, Charles W. (1987). The utility of citation-based quality assessments. *Journal of Criminal Justice, 15,* 165–171.

Thomas, Charles W., & Bronick, Matthew J. (1984). The quality of doctoral programs in deviance, criminology, and criminal justice: An empirical assessment. *Journal of Criminal Justice, 12,* 21–37.

Thomson Reuters (2009). *Journal citation reports: Quick reference card.* Retrieved January 31, 2012 from http://thomsonreuters.com/content/science/pdf/ssr/training/qrc_jcr_ april_ 09.pdf

Thomson Reuters (2012a). Thompson Reuters master journal list. Retrieved January 31, 2012 from http://ip-science.thomsonreuters.com/cgi-bin/jrnlst/jloptions.cgi?PC=master

Thomson Reuters (2012b). Social Science Citation Index. Retrieved January 31, 2012 from http://ip-science.thomsonreuters.com/cgi-bin/jrnlst/jloptions.cgi?PC=SS

Thomson Reuters (2012c). Journal coverage changes. Retrieved January 31, 2012 from http://ip-science.thomsonreuters.com/cgi-bin/jrnlst/jloptions.cgi?PC=master

Thomson Reuters (2012d). Journal citation reports. Retrieved January 31, 2012 from http://thomsonreuters.com/products_services/science/science_products/a-z/journal_citation_reports/

Travis, Lawrence F. (1987). Assessing the quality of doctoral programs in deviance, criminology, and criminal justice: A response to Thomas and Bronick. *Journal of Criminal Justice, 15,* 157–163.

van Driel, Mieke L., Maier, Manfred, & De Maeseneer, Jan (2007). Measuring the impact of family medicine research: Scientific citations or societal impact? *Family Practice, 24* (5), 401-402.

Vaughn, Michael S., & Del Carmen, Rolando V. (1992). An annotated list of journals in criminal justice and criminology: A guide for authors. *Journal of Criminal Justice Education, 3,* 93–142.

Vaughn, Michael S., Del Carmen, Rolando V., Perfecto, Martin, & Charand, Ka Xiong (2004). Journals in criminal justice and criminology: An updated and expanded guide for authors. *Journal of Criminal Justice Education, 15,* 61-192.

Vine, Rita (2006). Google Scholar. *Journal of the Medical Library Association, 94* (1), 97-99.

Wendl, Michael C. (2007). H-index: However ranked, citations need context. *Nature, 448,* September 27, 403.

West, Robert, & McIlwaine, Ann (2002). What do citation counts count for in the field of addiction? An empirical evaluation of citation counts and their link with peer ratings of quality. *Addiction, 97* (5), 501-504.

Williams, Frank P., McShane, Marilyn D., & Wagoner, Carl P. (1995). Differences in assessments of relative prestige and utility of criminal justice and criminology journals. *American Journal of Criminal Justice, 19,* 215-238.

Wolfgang, Marvin E., Figlio, Robert M., & Sellin, Thorsten (1972). *Delinquency in a birth cohort.* Chicago: University of Chicago Press.

Wolfgang, Marvin E., Figlio, Robert M., & Thornberry, Terence P. (1978). *Evaluating criminology.* New York: Elsevier.

Wright, Bradley R.E., Caspi, Avshalom, Moffitt, Terrie E., & Silva, Phil A. (1999). Low self-control, social bonds, and crime: Social causation, social selection, or both? *Criminology, 37,* 479-514.

Wright, Richard A. (1995a). The most-cited scholars in criminology: A comparison of textbooks and journals. *Journal of Criminal Justice, 23,* 303-311.

Wright, Richard A. (1995b). Was there a 'golden past' for the introductory sociology textbook? A citation analysis of leading journals. *American Sociologist, 26,* 41–48.

Wright, Richard A. (1996). Do introductory criminology textbooks cite the most influential criminologists? Estimating the 'match' between what journals report and what textbooks discuss. *American Journal of Criminal Justice, 20,* 225–236.

Wright, Richard A. (1997). Do introductory criminal justice textbooks cite the most influential criminal justicians? Further estimations of the 'match' between what journals report and what textbooks discuss. *Journal of Criminal Justice Education, 8,* 81–90.

Wright, Richard A. (1998). From luminary to lesser-known: The declining influence of criminology textbook authors on scholarship. *Journal of Criminal Justice Education, 9,* 104–115.

Wright, Richard A. (2000). Recent changes in the most-cited scholars in criminology: A comparison of textbooks and journals. *Journal of Criminal Justice, 28,* 117-128.

Wright, Richard A. (2002). Recent changes in the most-cited scholars in criminal justice textbooks. *Journal of Criminal Justice, 30,* 183-195.

Wright, Richard A., & Carroll, Kelly (1994). From vanguard to vanished: The declining influence of criminology textbooks on scholarship. *Journal of Criminal Justice, 22,* 559–567.

Wright, Richard A., & Cohn, Ellen G. (1996). The most-cited scholars in criminal justice textbooks, 1989 to 1993. *Journal of Criminal Justice, 24,* 459-467.

Wright, Richard A., & Friedrichs, David O. (1998). The most-cited scholars and works in critical criminology. *Journal of Criminal Justice Education, 9* (2), 211-231.

Wright, Richard A., & Miller, J. Mitchell (1998). The most-cited scholars and works in police studies. *Policing: An International Journal of Police Strategies and Management, 21* (2), 240-254.

Wright, Richard A., & Miller, J. Mitchell (1999). The most-cited scholars and works in corrections. *The Prison Journal, 79* (1), 5-22.

Wright, Richard A., & Rogers, Joseph W. (1996). An introduction to teaching criminology: Resources and issues." In Richard A. Wright (Ed.), *Teaching criminology: Resources and issues* (pp. 1-33). Washington, DC: American Sociological Association.

Wright, Richard A., & Sheridan, Cindy (1997). The most-cited scholars and works in women and crime publications. *Women and Criminal Justice, 9* (2), 41-60.

Wright, Richard A., & Soma, Colette (1995). The declining influence of dissertations on sociological research. *American Sociological Association Footnotes, 23* (1), 8.

Wright, Richard A., & Soma, Colette (1996). The most-cited scholars in criminology textbooks, 1963 to 1968, 1976 to 1980, and 1989 to 1993. *Journal of Crime and Justice, 19*, 45–60.

Wright, Richard A., Bryant, Kevin M., & Miller, J. Mitchell (2001). Top criminals/top criminologists: The most-cited authors and works in white-collar crime. *Journal of Contemporary Criminal Justice, 17* (4), 383-399.

Wyles, Dana F. (2004). Citation errors in two journals of psychiatry: A retrospective analysis. *Behavioral and Social Sciences Librarian, 22* (2), 27-51.

Yoels, William C. (1973). The fate of the Ph.D. dissertation in sociology: An empirical examination. *American Sociologist, 8*, 87–89.

Name Index

A

Accomazzi, Alberto, 19, 161
Ackerman, Alissa R., 131, 165
Adam, David, 5, 7, 155
Aebi, Marcelo F., 141, 142, 143
Ageton, Suzanne S., 48
Agnew, Robert, 71, 72, 73, 75, 77, 78, 81, 84, 85, 90, 98, 112, 113, 116, 148
Akers, Ronald L., 71, 73, 75, 77, 78, 80, 97
Alarid, Leanne F., 141, 143
Albanese, Jay S., 145
Allen, Harry E., 48, 155
Allison, Paul D., 13, 163
Alpert, Geoffrey P., 81
Analatos, Apostolos A., 18, 164
Anderson, Elijah, 71
Andrews, Don A., 82, 83, 84, 90, 91, 92, 98, 101, 108, 110, 111, 113, 114, 115, 116, 117, 118, 119, 120, 148, 149, 150, 152, 154, 155
Anglin, M. Douglas, 83, 110
Applegate, Brandon K., 133, 137
Arndt, Beverly J., 164
Arneklev, Bruce J., 73, 74, 75, 90
Ashworth, Andrew, 86
Atkins, Helen, 12, 158

B

Bacchetti, Peter, 1, 162
Bagby, R. Michael, 2, 25, 30, 155
Bain, Read, 47, 155
Bakkalbasi, Nisa, 14, 15, 155
Bala, Nicholas, 90
Balusek, Ken, 126, 129, 137, 164
Bandura, Albert, 87
Banks, Michael, 11
Banks, Steven, 83

Barbaree, Howard E., 82, 83, 90, 155, 163
Barbui, Corrado, 1, 155
Barnes, James C., 64, 121, 125, 129, 131, 134, 135, 162, 167
Bauer, Kathleen, 14, 15, 155
Bayley, David H., 42, 81, 87, 98, 110, 115
Beaver, Kevin M., 135, 161
Béchard, Jean-Pierre, 34, 160
Bentler, Peter M., 73, 75
Berk, Richard A., 13, 48, 57, 118, 166
Bero, Lisa A., 1, 162
Biderman, Albert D., 73
Black, Donald J., 71, 78
Blackburn, Richard S., 2, 25, 35, 155
Blackburn, Robert, 3, 163
Blumstein, Alfred, 40, 41, 43, 44, 45, 64, 71, 73, 75, 76, 77, 78, 79, 80, 81, 87, 93, 94, 97, 98, 104, 107, 116, 149, 150, 155, 165
Boggess, Lyndsay N., 131, 134, 163
Bohn, Martin J., 82, 163
Bonta, James L., 82, 83, 84, 90, 91, 92, 110, 111, 112, 113, 114, 115, 116, 117, 118, 119, 120, 149, 150, 152, 154, 155
Bornmann, Lutz, 18, 155
Bott, David M., 2, 25, 32, 156
Bottoms, Anthony E., 87, 88, 89
Bowers, Kate, 143
Bowling, Benjamin, 89
Braithwaite, John, 40, 42, 43, 78, 86, 88, 89, 92, 93, 94, 98, 108, 110, 111, 112, 113, 114, 115, 116, 117, 148, 150, 151, 154, 156
Brame, Robert, 71, 73, 75, 77, 78, 81, 98, 102, 131, 134, 135, 142, 143, 144, 164
Brody, Tim, 9, 156
Bronick, Matthew J., 51, 52, 168
Brown, David, 65, 86, 87
Bryant, Kevin M., 42, 47, 170
Buchanan, Robert A., 14, 156
Buerger, Michael E., 79, 166

Bugeja, Michael, 19, 156
Bursik, Robert J., 70, 71, 73, 75, 77, 78, 80, 81, 84, 85, 90, 98, 110, 113, 114, 115, 116, 148, 150
Burton, Velmer S., 75, 81, 143, 144
Bury, Alison S., 2, 30, 155
Bushway, Shawn D., 87, 166
Buss, Allan R., 24, 30, 156
Bynum, Timothy S., 3, 160

C

Callaham, Michael, 1, 156
Campbell, Jacqueline C., 110, 112, 113, 115, 141, 143
Cano, V., 2, 27, 35, 156
Cantor, David, 72, 73
Cao, Liqun, 143, 145
Carlen, Pat, 87
Carr, Leslie, 9, 156
Carrington, Peter J., 90
Carroll, Kelly, 49, 169
Caspi, Avshalom, 70, 71, 72, 73, 75, 77, 98, 110, 115, 163, 169
Chamlin, Mitchell B., 110, 114, 115, 143
Chan, Janet B.L., 87
Chan, Matthew T.V., 14, 162
Chapman, Antony J., 13, 17, 18, 156
Charand, Ka Xiong, 60, 107, 168
Chatterton, Michael R., 88, 159
Chesney-Lind, Meda, 42, 145
Chew, Mabel, 6, 7, 156
Chikate, R.V., 2, 29, 37, 156
Chiricos, Theodore G., 78
Christenson, James A., 1, 156
Cipriani, Andrea, 1, 155
Clarke, Ronald V., 87, 89, 90, 92, 93, 98, 108, 110, 150, 151, 154, 157
Clear, Todd R., 135, 141, 159
Clinard, Marshall B., 42, 48
Cloward, Richard A., vii, 18, 156
Cochran, John K., 141, 143
Cohen, Albert K., 18, 48, 156
Cohen, Jacob, 13, 65
Cohen, Jacqueline, 13, 48, 64, 65, 71, 72, 73, 75, 87, 93, 107, 112, 116, 150, 155
Cohen, Joseph, 13, 65
Cohen, Lawrence E., 41, 65, 71, 72, 73, 74, 75, 77, 78, 81, 89, 98, 113, 115, 148
Cohen, Stanley, 40, 86, 87, 88, 89, 92, 93, 104, 110, 148, 156
Cohn, Alvin, 141, 143
Cohn, Ellen G., iii, iv, viii, ix, 2, 5, 12, 13, 17, 18, 30, 31, 39, 40, 41, 42, 43, 44, 45, 46, 47, 48, 49, 50, 51, 53, 60, 61, 62, 64, 66, 67, 69, 107, 108, 123, 127, 128, 129, 130, 131, 134. 135. 136, 140, 150, 151, 156, 157, 165, 169
Cohn, Ellen S., 13
Cole, Jonathan, 2, 3, 4, 17, 18, 157
Cole, Stephen, vii, 2, 3, 4, 17, 18, 157
Cormier, Catherine A., 83
Cornish, Derek B., 108, 151, 157
Courtney, John C., 17, 27, 34, 158
Crawford, Adam, 87, 89
Cressey, Donald R., 42, 48
Cronin, Blaise, 12, 158
Cullen, Francis T., ix, 41, 42, 43, 46, 71, 73, 74, 75, 77, 78, 79, 80, 81, 82, 83, 84, 85, 90, 91, 94, 97, 98, 99, 100, 101, 102, 103, 108, 110, 111, 112, 113, 114, 115, 116, 117, 118, 119, 120, 132, 136, 141, 142, 143, 144, 145, 148, 149, 150, 151, 152, 154, 155, 158, 165
Cunneen, Chris, 87
Cusson, Maurice, 90

D

Daigle, Leah E., 131
Daly, Kathleen, 42, 86, 89, 92, 93, 98, 110, 148
Davis, Jaya, 125, 130, 158
Davis, Richard, 141
De Lacey, Gerald, 14, 158
De Leon, George, 83
De Maeseneer, Jan, 6, 8, 9, 168
Decker, David L., 4, 54, 61, 166
Decker, Scott H., 75, 78, 81, 88, 89, 98, 143, 144, 145
Del Carmen, Rolando V., 46, 60, 107, 168
Dembo, Richard, 43, 49, 50, 141, 143
Déry, Richard, 34, 160
Dess, Howard M., 16, 158
DeZee, Matthew R., 3, 51, 52, 122, 126, 158
Diamond, Arthur M., 3, 158
Dignan, James, 89
Dimitrova, Daniela V., 19, 156
Dishion, Thomas J., 151, 158
Ditton, Jason, 89
Dixon, David, 87
Dobash, Rebecca E., 42, 89
Dobash, Russell P., 42, 89
Doerner, William G., 3, 158
Doherty, Elaine E., 131
Doob, Anthony N., 90, 91, 92, 158
Douglas, Kevin S., 83
Douglas, Robert J., 17, 158
Dowds, Lizanne, 88, 163
Dumé, Belle, 11, 158

Dunaway, R. Gregory, 75
Duncanson, John, 90, 91
Dunford, Franklyn W., 57, 158
Durkheim, Emile, 48
Duy, Joanna, 3, 158

E

Earls, Felton, 71, 119, 151, 166
Eaves, David, 83
Eck, John E., 90, 166
Egghe, Leo, 10, 158
Eichhorn, Guenther, 19, 161
Elliott, David, 88, 163
Elliott, Delbert S., 41, 44, 57, 70, 71, 73, 75, 77, 78, 85, 98, 104, 110, 116, 149, 158
Endler, Norman S., 3, 13, 24, 30, 158, 159, 166
Engel, Robin S., 131, 132, 136
Engels, Friedrich, 110
Erez, Edna, 143
Erickson, Patricia, 90
Ericson, Richard V., 40, 43, 89, 90, 92, 98, 108, 112, 113, 114
Esbensen, Finn-Age, 143
Eskridge, Chris, 140
Evans, T. David, 75, 143, 144
Eysenbach, Gunther, 19, 159
Eysenck, Hans, 43

F

Fabianic, David A., 3, 61, 122, 123, 124, 126, 127, 128, 133, 137, 159
Fagan, Jeffrey A., 78, 110, 141, 143
Farkas, Mary A., 141, 143, 144, 145
Farrington, David P., iii, iv, viii, ix, 2, 5, 12, 13, 17, 18, 30, 31, 39, 40, 41, 43, 44, 45, 46, 47, 48, 49, 50, 51, 53, 60, 61, 62, 64, 66, 67, 71, 72, 73, 75, 76, 77, 78, 79, 81, 83, 84, 85, 86, 88, 89, 90, 92, 93, 94, 97, 98, 99, 100, 101, 102, 103, 107, 108, 110, 111, 112, 113, 114, 115, 116, 118, 119, 120, 123, 127, 128, 129, 130, 131, 134, 141, 142, 143, 144, 145, 148, 149, 150, 151, 152, 156, 157, 159, 164, 165
Felson, Marcus, 74, 87, 89, 110, 113, 115
Ferber, Marianne A., 1, 2, 18, 26, 33, 159
Ferraro, Kathleen F., 78
Fingerman, Susan, 16, 159
Finkelhor, David, 110, 115, 116, 117
Flanagan, Timothy J., 42
Forrester, David H., 88, 159
Forth, Adele E., 83

Foucault, Michel, 42, 87, 89, 92, 98, 108, 112, 113, 114, 116
Fox, Richard G., 86, 159
Frank, James, 80, 81, 131, 134, 143, 158
Freiberg, Arie, 86, 87, 159
Friedrichs, David O., 42, 46, 47, 107, 169
Frost, Natasha A., 132, 135, 136, 159
Funkhouser, Edward T., 12, 159

G

Gabbidon, Shaun L., 55, 56, 159
Gabor, Thomas, 90
Gainey, Randy R., 141, 142, 143, 144, 145, 152
Garfield, Eugene, 2, 3, 4, 6, 7, 13, 17, 18, 19, 23, 24, 39, 159, 160
Garland, David, 40, 43, 86, 89, 92, 98, 108, 110, 113, 114, 115, 116, 117
Garofalo, James, 161
Gartin, Patrick R., 79, 166
Gastwirth, Joseph L., 10, 160
Geis, Gilbert, 13, 42, 160
Gelles, Richard J., 91, 110, 112, 113, 115, 167
Gelsthorpe, Loraine R., 89
Gendreau, Paul, 83, 90, 91, 92, 98, 110, 113, 114, 115, 116, 117, 150, 155
Giblin, Matthew J., 43, 50, 160
Gibson, Chris L., 135, 161
Giddens, Anthony, 89, 93
Gilbert, G. Nigel, 19, 160
Gilbert, Karen E., 79, 108, 150, 158
Glänzel, Wolfgang, 2, 160
Glueck, Sheldon E., 41
Goggin, Claire E., 83, 90
Goldfeder, Eileen, 3, 61, 121, 122, 126, 164
Goldstein Herman, 42
Gondolf, Edward W., 141, 142, 143, 144, 145
Goodrich, June E., 14, 160
Gordon, Randall A., 3, 25, 31, 121, 160
Gorenflo, David W., 25, 30, 31, 160
Gottfredson, Denise C., 90, 110, 166
Gottfredson, Michael R., 40, 41, 43, 44, 45, 70, 71, 73, 74, 75, 76, 77, 78, 81, 84, 85, 87, 89, 90, 92, 97, 98, 99, 100, 101, 102, 103, 108, 110, 113, 114, 115, 116, 118, 120, 148, 149, 151, 152, 154, 160, 161
Gover, Angela R., 131, 135
Grant, Carolyn, 19, 161
Grasmick, Harold G., 70, 71, 75, 76, 77, 78, 79, 81, 84, 85, 90, 98, 110, 113, 114, 115, 116, 148, 150
Greenberg, David F., 73
Greene, Helen T., 55, 56, 159
Greene, Jack R., 3, 141, 143, 160

Grégoire, Denis A., 27, 34, 160
Grisso, Thomas, 82, 83

H

Haddow, Gaby, 9, 160
Hagan, John L., 70, 71, 73, 74, 75, 77, 78, 79, 80, 81,
    84, 85, 90, 97, 98, 104, 116, 148, 149, 160, 165
Haggerty, Kevin D., 90
Hall, Stuart, 89
Hall, Wayne, 87
Hamermesh, Daniel S., 3, 161
Hamilton, David P., 2, 111, 161
Hans, Valerie, 141, 143
Hanson, David J., 26, 32, 161
Hanson, R. Karl, 82, 83, 90, 91
Hare, Robert D., 82, 83, 84, 110, 112, 113, 114, 115,
    116, 117, 150
Hargens, Lowell L., 2, 25, 32, 156, 163
Harnad, Stevan, 9, 156
Harris, Grant T., 83, 84
Hart, Stephen D., 83, 84, 110
Hawkins, J. David, 72, 73, 87
Haynes, R. Brian, 2, 163
Hecht, Pamela K., 2, 163
Heilbrun, Kirk, 83
Heinzkill, Richard, 2, 29, 37, 161
Hemmens, Craig T., 141, 142, 143, 144, 145
Henneken, Edwin A., 19, 28, 36, 161
Hepburn, John R., 81
Herzog, Sergio, 143, 145
Hickman, Laura J., 131
Higgins, George E., 55, 56, 161, 162
Hiller, Matthew L., 143
Hindelang, Michael J., 40, 41, 44, 72, 73, 74, 75, 77,
    78, 93, 101, 104, 116, 148, 149, 154, 161
Hirsch, J.E., 9, 10, 161
Hirschi, Travis, 13, 40, 41, 42, 43, 44, 45, 46, 65, 70,
    71, 72, 73, 74, 75, 76, 77, 78, 79, 81, 82, 84, 85,
    87, 89, 90, 92, 94, 97, 98, 99, 100, 101, 102, 103,
    104, 108, 110, 111, 112, 113, 114, 115, 116, 117,
    118, 119, 120, 148, 149, 150, 151, 152, 154, 160,
    161
Hobbs, Dick, 89
Hoffmann, John P., 143
Hoge, Robert D., 83, 155
Holmes, Malcolm D., 122, 126, 127, 168
Homel, Ross J., 86, 87, 92
Hong, Hyehyun, 19, 156
Hope, Tim, 90, 110
Hough, J. Michael, 88, 89, 161
Hughes, Gordon, 87
Hughes, Lorine A., 145

Huizinga, David, 57, 70, 71, 73, 75, 77, 78, 85, 98,
    158
Hutson, Scott R., 29, 37, 161

I

Inciardi, James A., 141, 143
Indermauer, David, 87
Ioannidis, John P.A., 18, 164

J

Jang, Sun Joon, 145
Jascó, Peter, 14, 15, 16, 161
Jefferson, Tony, 87, 89, 92
Jennings, Wesley G., 55, 56, 131, 132, 133, 134,
    135, 136, 137, 151, 161, 162, 163, 165
Johnson, George E., 3, 161
Johnson, Shane D., 141, 143
Johnston, Les, 89
Jones, Alan Wayne, 28, 35, 162
Jones, Trevor, 87
Jurik, Nancy C., 81

K

Kappeler, Victor E., 81, 133, 137
Kawchuk, Karman B., 17, 34, 158
Kelling, George L., 42, 75, 78
Kennedy, Leslie W., 90
Khey, David N., 55, 56, 131, 135, 161, 162
Kick, Edward L., 2, 163
Killias, Martin, 141, 142, 143
Kleck, Gary, 73, 121, 125, 129, 162
Knight, Raymond A., 90
Koss, Mary P., 110, 115
Kramer, John H., 71, 73
Krohn, Marvin D., 48, 71, 73, 75, 77, 78, 98
Kurtz, Michael J., 19, 161

L

Lab, Steven P., 3, 158
Laband, David N., 1, 111, 162
LaBonte, Kristen B., 2, 162
LaFree, Gary, 133
Lambert, Eric G., 141, 143, 144
Land, Kenneth C., 71, 72, 73, 75, 76, 77, 78, 81, 98,
    162, 164
Landreville, Pierre, 90
Lane, Jodi, 143, 144

Langton, Lynn, 162
Latessa, Edward J., 141, 142
Laub, John H., 43, 51, 70, 71, 72, 73, 7475, 76, 77, 78, 79, 81, 84, 85, 87, 93, 94, 97, 98, 99, 100, 101, 102, 104, 108, 110, 111, 112, 113, 114, 115, 116, 117, 118, 119, 145, 148, 149, 150, 151, 154, 162, 166
Lauritsen, Janet L., 71, 78, 79, 98
Lawrence, Steve, 19, 162
Lea, John, 42, 87
LeBlanc, Marc, 90, 110, 112, 113
Lee, Kirby P., 1, 162
Lenton, Rhonda L., 91, 162
Leukefeld, Carl, 141, 143, 144
Levi, Michael, 40, 89, 110, 113, 115, 150, 162
Liebling, Alison, 87
Light, Donna B., 164
Lind, Bronwyn, 87
Lind, N.C., 2, 27, 35, 156
Lindsey, Duncan, 14, 162
Link, Bruce G., 42, 80, 158
Liska, Allen E., 71, 78
Littlefield, Christine H., 3, 166
Liu, Jianhong, 141, 143, 145
Lizotte, Alan J., 78
Loeber, Rolf, 71, 73, 74, 75, 77, 78, 81, 83, 84, 89, 98, 115, 116
Logan, Elisabeth L., 2, 162
Lok, Candy K.W., 14, 162
Lokker, Cynthia, 2, 163
Long, Heather, 131, 134, 135, 163
Long, J. Scott, 13, 163
Lotz, Roy, 80, 163
Lynam, Donald R., 141, 143
Lynch, James P., 73
Lynch, Michael J., 141, 143

M

Mabrey, Daniel J., 141
MacKenzie, Doris L., 80, 81, 83, 84, 90, 98, 110, 111, 115, 141, 143, 144, 145, 166
MacLean, Brian D., 42
Maguire, Kathleen F., 43
Maguire, Mike, 89
Mahoney, Margaret, 137, 161
Maier, Manfred, 6, 8, 168
Makkai, Toni, 87
Malvini, Lara, 1, 155
Manning, Peter K., 80
Marenin, Otwin, 53, 163
Marks, John, 126, 129, 137, 164
Marquart, James W., 141, 143, 144, 145

Marshall, William L., 82, 83, 90, 110, 115, 155, 163
Martinson, Ida M., 14, 162
Mastrofski, Stephen D., 81, 110, 113, 115
Matza, David, 50, 89, 110, 168
Maxwell, Gabrielle, 87, 89
Maxwell, Sheila R., 141, 143, 144, 145
Mayhew, Patricia M., 87, 88, 89, 90, 92, 93, 148, 161, 163
Mazerolle, Paul J., 70, 71, 73, 75, 77, 78, 81, 98, 102, 143, 144, 164
McCall, Patricia L., 71, 72, 73, 162
McCluskey, John D., 143
McConnell, James V., 25, 30, 31, 160
McCord, Joan, 151, 158
McElrath, Karen, 3, 163
McGinnis, Robert, 13, 163
McGloin, Jean M., 131
McIlwaine, Ann, 18, 169
McKibbon, K. Ann, 2, 163
McKinlay, R. James, 2, 163
McShane, Marilyn D., 4, 46, 169
Meadows, Arthur Jack, 1, 163
Mears, Daniel P., 132, 137
Meehl, Paul E., 83
Megargee, Edwin I., 82, 83, 163
Meho, Lokman I., 1, 6, 7, 9, 10, 12, 163
Meier, Robert F., 13, 160
Melchers, Ronald, 91, 165
Meltzer, Sari J., 3, 166
Merton, Robert K., vii, 17, 18, 163
Messner, Steven F., 71, 75, 76, 77, 78, 81, 89, 98, 110, 112, 133, 137, 141, 143, 144, 145
Mieczkowski, Thomas, 43, 50
Miethe, Terance D., 71, 73, 75, 89
Mijares, Tomas, 3, 163
Miller, J. Mitchell, 42, 47, 107, 110, 133, 137, 141, 143, 144, 169, 170
Miller, Holly Ventura, 131, 165
Miracle, Andrew W., 3, 61, 165
Mitchell, Michelle, 2, 27, 35, 155
Moed, Henk F., 7, 163
Moffitt, Terrie E., 6, 8, 44, 70, 71, 72, 73, 74, 75, 76, 77, 78, 80, 81, 83, 84, 85, 87, 90, 92, 93, 94, 97, 98, 99, 100, 101, 102, 103, 104, 108, 110, 111, 112, 113, 114, 115, 116, 117, 118, 119, 120, 141, 143, 147, 148, 149, 150, 151, 152, 154, 163, 164, 169
Monahan, John T., 82, 83, 84
Moon, Byongook, 141, 143, 144, 145
Morris, Allison M., 87, 88, 89, 92, 93, 98, 148
Mosley, Gladys F., 164
Motiuk, Lawrence L., 83, 90
Moyer, Sharon, 90, 91

Mullens, Nicholas C., 2, 163
Mulvey, Edward P., 82, 83, 143
Murphy, Penelope, 2, 163
Murray, Stephen S., 19, 161
Myers, C. Roger, 2, 3, 164

N

Nagin, Daniel S., 71, 72, 73, 74, 75, 76, 77, 78, 80, 81, 84, 94, 97, 98, 99, 100, 101, 102, 103, 104, 110, 112, 113, 114, 115, 116, 118, 119, 120, 141, 143, 144, 145, 148, 149, 150, 162, 164
Neuhaus, Christoph, 12, 14, 15, 164
Newburn, Tim, 87, 88, 89, 110
Nisonger, Thomas E., 7, 164
Noël, Martin X., 34, 160

O

O'Leary, Kent D., 110, 112, 113, 115
O'Malley, Patrick, 65, 86, 87, 89, 92
Oakshot, Michael, 87
Ohlin, Lloyd E., 18, 108, 151, 156, 159
Oliver, Willard M., 125, 126, 129, 130, 133, 151, 164
Orrick, Erin A., 132, 136, 164
Osgood, D. Wayne, 71, 73, 75, 78
Ouimet, Marc, 90

P

Pancheshnikov, Yelena, 28, 36, 164
Paoline, Eugene A., 141, 143, 144
Pardeck, John T., 25, 31, 164
Park, Robert E., 89
Parker, James D.A., 2, 30, 155
Parker, L. Craig, 3, 61, 121, 122, 126, 164
Parks, Roger B., 81
Pastore, Ann L., 43
Patchin, Justin, 133
Paternoster, Raymond, 41, 43, 44, 70, 71, 72, 73, 75, 76, 77, 78, 80, 81, 84, 85, 94, 97, 98, 99, 100, 101, 102, 110, 111, 114, 115, 116, 118, 141, 142, 143, 144, 145, 148, 149, 164
Patil, Suresh Krishna, 2, 29, 37, 156
Patsopoulos, Nikolas A., 18, 164
Patterson, Amy L., 46, 51, 52, 53, 121, 123, 127, 167
Patterson, Gerald R., 75
Payne, Brian, 141, 142, 143, 144, 145, 152
Pearson, Geoffrey, 89
Pease, Ken, 40, 86, 88, 89, 92, 159

Perfecto, Martin, 60, 107, 168
Peritz, Bluma C., 17, 164
Petersilia, Joan, 42, 43, 81, 110, 111, 114, 115, 116, 131, 134
Peterson, Ruth D., 71, 79, 165
Piette, Michael J., 1, 26, 33, 111, 162
Pilgrim, Rocky, 124, 128, 129, 130, 136, 137, 167
Piquero, Alex R., xii, 70, 71, 72, 73, 75, 77, 78, 79, 81, 84, 94, 98, 102, 103, 104, 110, 111, 113, 114, 115, 116, 118, 129, 131, 132, 134, 135, 136, 137, 141, 142, 143, 144, 145, 148, 149, 151, 152, 154, 164, 165
Piquero, Nicole L., 131, 135
Pogarsky, Greg, 132, 136, 143, 144, 145
Poole, Eric D., 3, 54, 55, 56, 61, 80, 85, 165
Poulin, François, 151, 158
Poyer, Robert K., 165
Pratt, John, 87, 92
Pratt, Travis C., 101, 102, 118, 149, 165
Prendergast, Michael L., 141, 143
Prentky, Robert A., 90
Prenzler, Tim, 87
Pridemore, William A., 141, 143

Q

Quinn, Jennifer, 90, 91
Quinney, Richard, 42, 48
Quinsey, Vernon L., 83, 84, 110, 113, 115

R

Rahm, Erhard, 6, 165
Raudenbush, Stephen W., 70, 71, 73, 74, 75, 77, 78, 81, 84, 98, 116, 119, 148, 151, 166
Reader, Diana, 27, 34, 165
Record, Carol, 14, 158
Regoli, Robert M., 3, 54, 55, 56, 61, 80, 81, 85, 163, 165
Reiner, Robert, 89, 92
Reisig, Michael D., 81, 141, 143, 144
Reiss, Albert J., 71, 73, 78, 81, 90, 98, 110, 151, 165
Reuter, Peter, 87, 90, 110, 166
Rice, Marnie E., 82, 83, 84, 110, 113, 115, 150
Rice, Stephen K., 64, 131, 134, 135, 140, 165
Roach, Kent, 90
Robbins, Pamela C., 83
Roberson, Cliff, 133, 137
Roberts, Julian V., 90, 91, 92, 94, 141, 142, 143, 145, 158, 165
Robinson, David D., 83
Robinson, Matthew B., 141, 143, 145

Roche, Thomas, 3, 25, 32, 165
Rock, Paul, 43, 55, 56, 165
Rodriguez, John J., 4, 56, 134, 167
Roediger, Henry L., 3, 13, 159
Rogers, Joseph W., 46, 170
Rogers, Robert D., 83
Roland, Charles G., 14, 160
Rosenberg, Milton J., 13, 166
Rosenberg, Morris, 13
Rosenfeld, Richard, 71, 75
Ross, Robert R., 82, 83
Roth, Jeffrey A., 107, 155
Roth, Loren H., 82, 83
Rubin, Donald B., 73
Ruddell, Rick K., 141
Rumgay, Judith, 145
Rushton, J. Phillipe, 2, 3, 13, 18, 24, 30, 70, 159, 166
Russell, Robin J.H., 3, 166
Russell-Brown, Katheryn K., 134
Rutter, Michael, 163

S

Salekin, Randall T., 83
Sam, Joel, 29, 36, 37, 166
Sampson Robert J., xii, 40, 41, 43, 44, 46, 48, 65, 70, 71, 72, 73, 74, 75, 76, 77, 78, 79, 80, 81, 84, 85, 86, 89, 90, 92, 93, 94, 97, 98, 99, 100, 101, 102, 103, 104, 108, 110, 111, 112, 113, 114, 115, 116, 117, 118, 119, 148, 149, 150, 151, 154, 162, 166
Schafer, Joseph A., 43, 50, 141, 143, 144, 145, 160
Schildt, Henri A., 2, 27, 34, 166
Schmalleger, Frank, 59, 133, 137, 166
Schoepfer, Andrea, 162
Schotland, Marieka, 1, 162
Schreck, Christoper J., 137, 161
Schuck, Arnie M., 141, 144, 145
Schwartz, John, 64, 121, 124, 125, 128, 129, 130, 132, 136, 167
Schwartz, Martin D., 143, 145
Seglen, Per O., 7, 166
Sellin, Thorsten, 23, 48, 72, 107, 169
Serin, Ralph C., 83
Sewell, Kenneth W., 83
Shearing, Clifford D., 87, 88, 89, 92, 98, 108, 110, 112, 113, 114, 115, 116, 117, 150
Shepard, Michelle, 90, 91
Sheridan, Cindy, 42, 46, 47, 107, 170
Sherman, Lawrence W., 40, 41, 42, 43, 45, 57, 73, 75, 78, 79, 80, 81, 84, 86, 89, 90, 92, 93, 94, 97, 98, 99, 100, 101, 102, 108, 110, 111, 112, 113, 114, 115, 116, 118, 119, 120, 148, 149, 150, 151, 152, 154, 166

Shichor, David, 3, 42, 47, 48, 54, 56, 61, 166
Shutt, J. Eagle, 64, 131, 134, 135, 167
Siegel, Larry J., 133, 137
Sigelman, Lee, 1, 156
Sigler, Robert T., 141, 143
Sillanpää, Antti, 2, 34, 166
Silva, Phil A., 71, 73, 75, 77, 81, 163, 169
Silver, Eric, 83, 141, 143
Simon, Jonathan, 87, 89
Simourd, David J., 83
Skogan, Wesley G., 73, 75, 78, 79, 80, 81, 84, 89, 94, 98, 110
Skolnick, Jerome H., 42, 81
Smart, Carol, 42
Smith, Adrian, 12, 17, 167
Smith, David L., 3, 25, 32, 165
Smith, Derek R., 1, 18, 28, 35, 36, 167
Smith, Douglas A., 70, 74, 77, 80, 81, 93, 97, 104, 149
Smyth, Russell, 26, 33, 167
Snell, Clete, 4, 56, 134, 167
Snyder, Herbert, 12, 158
Snyder, Howard N., 141
Soler, José M., 11, 167
Soma, Colette, 26, 32, 42, 44, 48, 49, 170
Sorensen, Jonathan R., 4, 30, 46, 51, 52, 53, 54, 55, 56, 61, 121, 123, 124, 125, 127, 128, 129, 130, 131, 134, 136, 137, 157, 158, 167
Spafford, Duff, 17, 34, 158
Sparks, J. Richard, 89
Spohn, Cassia, 71, 73, 113
Sprott, Jane B., 90, 91
Stack, Steven, 43, 46, 50, 54, 55, 56, 61, 132, 136, 167
Stanko, Elizabeth A., 89
Steadman, Henry J., 82, 83
Steffensmeier, Darrell J., 71, 72, 73, 75, 77, 78, 98, 110, 116
Steiner, Benjamin, 64, 121, 124, 125, 128, 129, 130, 132, 136, 167
Steinmetz, Suzanne K., 92, 167
Stenning, Philip C., 90, 91, 92, 110, 111, 112, 113, 167
Stevens, Dennis J., 141
Stockwell, Tim, 87
Stouthamer-Loeber, Magda, 71, 75
Strang, Heather, 86, 87, 92, 110
Straus, Murray A., 91, 110, 111, 112, 113, 114, 115, 167
Stryker, Jo Ellen, 1, 167
Sturtz, Michael, 137, 161
Sung, Hung-en, 141, 143
Sutherland, Edwin H., 42, 43, 48, 89

Sweetland, James H., 13, 14, 167
Swindell, Sam, 126, 129, 137, 164
Sykes, Gresham M., 48, 50, 168

T

Tackie, S. Nii Bekoe, 29, 36, 37, 166
Taggart, William A., 122, 126, 127, 168
Tansella, Michele, 1, 155
Tark, Jongyeon, 125, 129, 162
Taxman, Faye S., 141
Taylor, Donald, 19, 168
Taylor, Ralph B., 74, 75, 81
Taylor, Terrance J., 143
Telep, Cody W., 55, 57, 168
Tenopir, Carol, 5, 168
Terrill, William C., 141, 143, 145
Terry, Karen J., 131, 165
Tewksbury, Richard, 121, 131, 135, 168
Thomas, Charles W., 51, 52, 168
Thomas, Stacy D., 164
Thompson, Donna, 19, 161
Thor, Andreas, 6, 165
Thornberry, Terence P., 2, 4, 39, 44, 71, 73, 75, 77, 78, 98, 169
Tibbetts, Stephen G., 81, 141, 143, 144
Tilley, Nick, 87
Tittle, Charles R., 70, 71, 73, 74, 75, 78, 81, 98
Tonry, Michael H., 63, 80, 90, 110, 141, 143
Travis, Lawrence F., 17, 52, 168
Tremblay, Richard E., 73, 143
Turner, Susan F., 73, 81

U

Uggen, Christopher J., 141, 143, 145
Ulmer, Jeffrey T., 71, 113
Unnever, James D., 143
Unnithan, N. Prabha, 143

V

Van Der Weyden, Martin B., 6, 156
van Driel, Mieke L., 6, 8, 9, 168
Vaughan, Liwen, 3, 158
Vaughn, Michael S., 46, 60, 107, 131, 134, 141, 143, 168
Vicari, Pamela J., 3, 25, 31, 121, 160
Villanueva, Elmer V., 6, 156
Vine, Rita, 14, 168
Visher, Christy A., 74, 77, 97, 107, 155

Vold, George B., 48

W

Wade, Jenny, 14, 158
Wagoner, Carl P., 4, 46, 169
Walker, Samuel, 42, 43, 78, 81
Walters, Glenn D., 132
Wang, Shun-Yung K., 125, 129, 162
Ward, Jeffrey T., 136, 161
Warr, Mark, 71, 78, 81, 84, 98
Watkins, David, 27, 34, 165
Wears, Robert L., 1, 156
Weatherburn, Don, 87
Webb, David W., 141
Webb, Vincent J., 3, 160
Weber, Ellen, 1, 156
Webster, Christopher D., 83
Weir, Henriikka, 132, 136, 164
Weis, Joseph G., 77, 161
Weisbrod, Burton A., 3, 161
Weisburd, David, 64, 78
Weitzer, Ronald, 141, 143, 145
Welch, Michael, 141, 143
Welljams-Dorof, Alfred, 23, 24, 160
Welsh, Brandon C., 90, 110, 111
Welsh, Wayne N., 143, 144
Wendl, Michael C., 10, 169
Werner, Mary A., 164
West, Donald J., 41
West, Robert, 18, 169
Wheeler, Stanton, 42
White, Rob, 86, 87
Whitehead, John T., 81, 143
Widmayer, Alan, 46, 51, 52, 53, 121, 123, 167
Widom, Cathy S., 75, 110
Wilcox, Pamela, 131
Wilczynski, Nancy L., 2, 163
Williams, Frank P., 4, 46, 56, 169
Williams, Kirk R., 73
Wilson, James Q., 40, 42, 43, 48, 73, 75, 78, 79, 81, 84, 87, 94, 97, 98, 104, 107, 108, 149, 151, 159
Wilson, Katheryn E., 164
Wilson, William J., 71, 74, 75, 76, 77, 78, 98
Winfree, L. Thomas, 143
Witte, Ann, 43, 50
Wolfe, Nancy T., 42, 158
Wolfgang, Marvin E., viii, xii, 2, 4, 23, 39, 40, 41, 42, 43, 44, 45, 46, 48, 55, 70, 72, 78, 80, 81, 85, 87, 93, 97, 104, 107, 111, 112, 113, 115, 116, 148, 149, 150, 154, 169
Wong, Stephen, 83
Worden, Robert E., 78, 81, 84, 98, 110, 113

Wormith, J. Stephen, 83
Worrall, John L., 132, 142, 143, 145
Wright, Bradley R.E., 101, 169
Wright, Kevin N., 81
Wright, Richard A., viii, 2, 5, 26, 31, 32, 33, 41, 42,
    43, 44, 45, 46, 47, 48, 49, 50, 62, 107, 143, 156,
    169, 170
Wright, Richard T., 88, 89, 110
Wyles, Dana F., 14, 170

Y

Yacoubian, George S., 142, 143
Yang, Kiduk, 6, 12, 163

Yeager, Peter C., 42
Yoels, William C., 26, 32, 170
Young, Jock, 42, 47, 86, 87, 89, 92, 93, 98, 104, 108,
    110, 115, 116

Z

Zahra, Shaker A., 2, 34, 166
Zhang, Lening, 141, 143, 144
Zhao, Jihong S., 143, 144
Zimmer, Lynn E., 42
Zinger, Ivan, 90, 155

SUBJECT INDEX

A

"A comparison of Poisson, negative binomial, and semiparametric mixed Poisson regression models with empirical applications to criminal careers research," (Land, McCall, and Nagin), 72, 162

A General Theory of Crime (Gottfredson and Hirschi), 70, 74, 76, 85, 101, 108, 118, 120, 148, 149, 151, 160

Academic productivity. *See* productivity

Academy of Criminal Justice Sciences (ACJS), 3, 126, 130, 132, 133, 135, 137

ACJS. *See* Academy of Criminal Justice Sciences

"Adolescence-limited and life-course persistent antisocial behavior" (Moffitt), 6, 76, 101, 102, 108, 118, 147, 148, 149, 163

African American scholarship, 55, 56

"Age and crime" (Farrington), 76, 93, 99, 101, 118,148, 159

"Age, criminal careers, and population heterogeneity," (Nagin and Land), 72, 164

AHCI. *See* Arts and Humanities Citation Index

American Association of Doctoral Programs in Criminology and Criminal Justice, 125

American Chemical Society, 14

American Journal of Drug and Alcohol Abuse, 60

American Journal of Police, 42

American Journal of Sociology, 26, 27, 32, 33

American Psychological Association, 3, 16, 30

American Society of Criminology (ASC) viii, xi, 45, 60, 63, 116, 126, 132, 133, 135, 137, 139, 140, 141, 142, 145, 152

American Sociological Association, 26

American Sociological Review, 26, 27, 32, 33, 57, 60

American University, 51, 53, 122

American University Law Review, 127

ANZ. *See Australian and New Zealand Journal of Criminology*

Arizona State University, 51, 53, 125

Article, defined, 63

Arts and Humanities Citation Index (AHCI), 4, 20

arXiv, 28, 36

ASC. *See* American Society of Criminology

Attribution theory, 25, 31

Australian and New Zealand Journal of Criminology (ANZ), 40, 41, 60, 62, 63, 85, 86, 91, 92, 94, 97, 99, 100, 109, 110, 116, 131, 135, 148

Australian Economic Papers, 26

Australian Economic Review, 26

B

Behavioral Sciences and the Law, 60

Behind Closed Doors (Straus, Gelles, and Steinmetz), 91, 167

Bibliometric research, 12

Big Deals, 19

BJC. *See British Journal of Criminology*

Boise State University, 125, 130

Bowling Green University, 51, 53

Breadth of scholarship,

British Journal of Criminology (BJC), xi, xii, 39, 40, 41, 43, 55, 56, 60, 62, 63, 85, 88, 89, 92, 94, 97, 100, 109, 110, 116, 122, 123, 127, 140, 144

British Journal of Delinquency, 43, 55, 56

C

CAJ. *See Crime and Justice*

California State University-San Bernardino, 125, 130

Cambridge University, 142

Canadian Journal of Criminology/Canadian Journal of Criminology and Criminal Justice (CJC), 40,

41, 60, 62, 63, 85, 90, 91, 92, 94, 99, 100, 109, 110, 111, 116, 140, 144, 148

Canadian Journal of Political Science/Revue canadienne de science politique (CJPS/Rcsp), 27, 34

Carnegie research classification, 134, 135

Causes of Delinquency (Hirschi), 70, 72, 74, 101, 102, 118, 120, 150

CD. *See Crime and Delinquency*

"Changing conceptions of race" (Peterson and Hagan), 79, 165

Chicago School, vii, 56

Child Maltreatment, 60

Citation: careers, 45, 70, 94, 152, 153; classics, 27, 35; frequency, 3, 25, 32, 35, 52, 54, 61, 66, 70, 74, 79, 99, 117, 119, 120; gender differences in, 26, 29, 33, 37; inflation of citation counts, 7, 13, 15, 18, 19; prevalence, 66, 70, 74, 79, 91, 99, 100, 101, 103, 117, 119, 153; reliability, 3, 4, 20, 120; studies (*see* Journals, ranking of); validity, xii, 3, 4, 20, 21, 67, 120, 147, 148, 153, 154

Citations in: archeology, 29, 37; astronomy, 19, 28, 36; biochemistry, 2, 35; chemistry, 17; computer science, 19; economics, 2, 26, 33; entrepreneurship, 2, 27, 34; general studies, 23, 24; history, 19; library and information science, 2, 16, 28, 29, 36; literature, 2, 29, 37; medicine, 2, 14, 27, 28, 35, 36; organizational science, 2, 27, 35; physics, 2, 9, 19, 28, 36; psychology, 2, 3, 17, 24, 25, 30, 31; social work, 25, 31; sociology 2, 17, 18, 25, 26, 32, 33

Cited half-life, 5

CiteSeer[X], 5

Citing half-life, 5

CJA. *See Criminal Justice Abstracts*

CJB. *See Criminal Justice and Behavior*

CJC. *See Canadian Journal of Criminology/ Canadian Journal of Criminology and Criminal Justice*

CJPI. *See Criminal Justice Periodical Index*

CJPS/Rcsp. *See Canadian Journal of Political Science/Revue canadienne de science politique*

CJR. *See Criminal Justice Review*

Classifying Criminal Offenders (Megargee and Bohn), 82, 163

CLSC. *See Crime, Law, and Social Change*

Co-author citations, 64, 67

Co-citation analysis, 1, 2, 34

Co-citation networks, 34

Cognitive dissonance theory, 25, 30

Complementarity. *See* Criminology and criminal justice, relations between

Contemporary Crises (see *Crime, Law and Social Change*)

Contemporary Psychology, 17

Convergence. *See* Criminology and criminal justice, relations between

Creativity index (C_a), 11

CRGE. *See Criminologie*

CRIM. *See Criminology*

Crime and Delinquency (CD), 61, 62, 109, 110, 122, 123, 124, 125, 132, 140, 144

Crime and Justice: A Review of Research (CAJ), 12, 41, 44, 45, 47, 62, 63, 109, 110

Crime in the Making (Sampson and Laub), 70, 74, 76, 79, 85, 93, 101, 102, 108, 117, 118, 148, 149, 151, 166

Crime, Law, and Social Change (CLSC), 42, 60, 62, 63, 109, 110

Crime, Shame and Reintegration (Braithwaite), 86, 88, 93, 148, 151, 156

Criminal Justice Abstracts (CJA), 123, 125, 127

Criminal Justice and Behavior (CJB), 40, 41, 51, 61, 62, 63, 64, 79, 82, 83, 84, 94, 97, 99, 100, 109, 110, 116, 123, 124, 125, 132, 140, 144, 154

Criminal Justice History, 63

Criminal Justice Periodical Index (CJPI), 123, 125, 127, 129, 131, 133, 139, 140, 152

Criminal Justice Review (CJR), 61, 62, 109, 110, 140, 144

Criminal justice, defined, 59

Criminologie (CRGE), 62, 63, 109, 110

Criminology (CRIM), 57, 60, 61, 62, 65, 66, 67, 69, 70, 71, 72, 74, 77, 99, 100, 109, 110, 111, 112, 116, 140, 144

Criminology and criminal justice, relations between: complementarity, 50; convergence, 50; divergence, 50

Criminology and Public Policy, 12, 55, 56, 60, 67, 153

Criminology, globalization of, 94

Criminology: defined, 59

Cross-pollination index, 35

CrossRef, 5

Current Contents, 4, 7

D

"Defiance, deterrence, and irrelevance" (Sherman), 101, 166

Delinquency in a Birth Cohort (Wolfgang, Figlio, and Sellin), 72, 169

Development and Psychopathology, 60

Deviant Behavior, 60

Divergence. *See* Criminology and criminal justice, relations between

"Does correctional treatment work? A clinically relevant and psychologically informed meta-analysis" (Andrews et al.), 84, 101, 108, 118, 148, 155

Download counts, 9

E

East Texas State University, 122
Economic Analysis & Policy, 26
Economic Papers, 26
Economic Record, 26
Electronic: alerts, 8; journals, 3; pre-prints, 19; publication, 8
Elsevier, 5, 14, 15, 16, 19
"Empty promises" (Stenning and Roberts), 91, 167
"Enduring individual differences and rational choice theories of crime" (Nagin and Paternoster), 76, 101, 102, 118, 148
"Erectile responses among heterosexual child molesters, father-daughter incest offenders and matched nonoffenders" (Barbaree and Marshall), 82, 155
European Journal of Criminology, 59, 67, 93, 153
"Explaining and preventing crime" (Farrington), 148, 159
"Extra-legal attributes and criminal sentencing" (Hagan), 80, 160

F

Federal Probation (FP), 61, 109, 110, 122
Florida State University, 51, 52, 123, 125, 128, 129, 130
FP. *See Federal Probation*
Frontiers of Entrepreneurship Research, 27, 34

G

g-index, 10, 134
Gini coefficient, 11, 152
Global Options, 63
Google Scholar (GS), viii, 5, 6, 9, 14, 15, 16, 20, 55, 57, 67, 68, 107, 134, 147
GS. *See* Google Scholar

H

Harvard University, 70

Harzing Publish or Perish software program, 131, 134, 135
h-b-index, 11
Hebrew University-Jerusalem, 64
h-index. *See* Hirsch index
Hirsch index (*h*-index), 9, 10, 11, 15, 135
HJCJ. *See Howard Journal of Criminal Justice*
Home Office (UK), 63
Homicide Studies, 60, 67
"Hot spots of predatory crime" (Sherman, Gartin, and Buerger), 79, 166
Howard Journal of Criminal Justice (HJCJ), 62, 140

I

IJCA. *See International Journal of Comparative and Applied Criminal Justice*
IJOT. *See International Journal of Offender Therapy and Comparative Criminology*
Impact factor score. 36, 54
Impact factor. *See* Journal impact factor
Index to Legal Periodicals, 123, 127
Indiana State University, 122, 126
Indiana University, 123, 127
Inflation of citation counts. *See* Citations
Inside-outside index, 35
Institute for Scientific Information (ISI), 4, 5, 6, 7, 8, 9, 12, 13, 14, 20, 23, 24, 28, 29, 35, 125
International Association for Correctional and Forensic Psychology, 63
International Journal of Comparative and Applied Criminal Justice (IJCA), 61, 62, 63, 109, 110, 140, 144
International Journal of Legal Medicine, 35
International Journal of Offender Therapy and Comparative Criminology (IJOT), 61, 62, 63, 109, 110, 140, 144
ISI. *See* Institute for Scientific Information

J

JCCJ. *See Journal of Contemporary Criminal Justice*
JCJ. *See Journal of Criminal Justice*
JCJE. *See Journal of Criminal Justice Education*
JCLC. *See Journal of Criminal Law and Criminology*
JCR. *See* Journal Citation Reports
JIF. *See* Journal impact factor
JIV. *See Journal of Interpersonal Violence*
JoCJ. *See Journal of Crime and Justice*

John Jay College of Criminal Justice, 51, 52, 122, 125, 126

Journal Citation Reports (JCR), 5, 8, 28, 36, 55, 56

Journal immediacy index, 5

Journal impact factor (JIF), xii, 4, 5, 6, 7, 8, 9, 35, 55, 147

Journal of Adolescence, 60

Journal of Contemporary Criminal Justice (JCCJ), 140, 144

Journal of Crime and Justice (JoCJ), 62, 140, 144

Journal of Criminal Justice (JCJ), 40, 41, 42, 61, 62, 79, 80, 81, 84, 94, 99, 100, 109, 110, 116, 122, 123, 124, 125, 126, 127, 132, 140, 144

Journal of Criminal Justice Education (JCJE), 42, 140, 144

Journal of Criminal Law and Criminology (JCLC), 61, 122, 123, 124, 125, 132, 140, 144

Journal of Economic Literature, 26, 33

Journal of Elder Abuse and Neglect, 67

Journal of Experimental Criminology, 55, 59, 67, 153

Journal of Experimental Social Psychology, 25

Journal of Fertility and Sterility, 24, 30

Journal of Human Justice, 42

Journal of Interpersonal Violence (JIV), 62, 109, 110, 112, 140, 144

Journal of Occupational and Environmental Medicine, 28, 36

Journal of Personality and Social Psychology, 25,

Journal of Police Science and Administration, 62

Journal of Quantitative Criminology (JQC), 40, 41, 51, 55, 60, 62, 67, 69, 72, 73, 76, 77, 99, 100, 109, 110, 112, 116, 123, 124, 125, 132, 140, 144

Journal of Research in Crime and Delinquency (JRCD)

Journal of Threat Assessment, 60

Journal of Youth and Adolescence, 60

JQ. *See Justice Quarterly*

JQC. *See Journal of Quantitative Criminology*

JRCD. *See Journal of Research in Crime and Delinquency*

Justice Quarterly (JQ), 40, 41, 42, 47, 51, 55, 56, 61, 62, 66, 78, 79, 84, 94, 99, 100, 109, 110, 116, 122, 123, 124, 125, 126, 127, 132, 140, 144

Juvenile and Family Court Journal, 60, 62

L

Law and Human Behavior, 60

Law and Social Inquiry, 60

Law and Society Review, 42, 60, 123, 125, 131, 132

"Life-course trajectories of different types of offenders" (Nagin, Farrington, and Moffitt), 84, 99, 101, 148, 149, 164

Longevity, 49

"Low self-control, social bonds, and crime" (Wright et al.), 101, 169

Luminaries technique, 46

M

Max Planck Institute, 11

Mean citation index, 31

Measuring Delinquency (Hindelang, Hirschi, and Weis), 77, 161

Medline, 8

Mendel syndrome, 17

Michigan State University, 122, 123, 124, 125, 127, 128

Minneapolis Domestic Violence Experiment, 57

N

National Academy of Sciences, 3

National Institute of Justice, xii, 63,

"Neighborhoods and violent crime" (Sampson et al.), 101, 118, 119, 166

New York University, 51, 52,

Nobel Prize, 3, 19,

Normandale Community College, 125, 130

O

Obliteration by incorporation, 18,

Occupational and Environmental Medicine, 28, 36

Ohio State University, 122

Omaha Police Experiment, 57

Open Access journals, 16

Open Citation Project, 5

Ottawa University, 142

Oxford University, 24, 30, 142

P

Pennsylvania State University, 122, 124, 125, 127, 128, 129, 130, 152

Perseverance, 49

"Personal capital and social control" (Nagin and Paternoster), 118, 164

Personality and Social Psychology Bulletin, 25

Police Chief, The, 62, 122, 127

"Police cynicism and professionalism" (Lotz and Regoli), 80, 163

Police Forum, 42

Police Studies, 42, 62

Policing and Society, 42

Policing Domestic Violence (Sherman), 108, 151, 166

Policing: An International Journal of Police Strategies and Management, 60, 62

Population Association of America. 24, 30

Portland State University, 51, 52, 122

Preventing Crime (Sherman et al.), 86, 93, 101, 102, 118, 148, 149, 152, 166

Prison Journal, The, 42, 62

Producer-consumer index, 35

Project Muse, 19

PsycINFO, 25, 31

R

Reaffirming Rehabilitation (Cullen and Gilbert), 79, 150, 158

Reductionism, 52

Royal Society of London, 3

Rutgers University, 51, 53, 122, 123, 125, 126, 127, 130

S

Sam Houston State University, 123, 124, 125, 127, 128

SCI. *See* Science Citation Index

SCJA. *See* Southern Criminal Justice Association

Science Citation Index (SCI), 4, 7, 12, 13, 14, 17, 20, 23, 24, 25, 28, 29, 30, 35, 36, 39, 55

SciVerse Scopus. *See* Scopus

Scopus, viii, 5, 6, 14, 15, 16, 20, 67, 68, 107, 147

Self-citations, xii, 7, 10, 11, 14, 18, 20, 21, 31, 32, 33, 46, 54, 63, 64, 65, 68, 69, 72, 74, 79, 80, 82, 85, 88, 91, 108, 111, 117, 147, 148, 154

Self-feeding index, 35

Self-selection bias, 19

Sellin-Glueck Award, 116

Sentencing (Doob and Roberts), 91, 158

Sentencing (Fox and Freiberg), 86, 159

"Sex differences in antisocial behavior" (Moffitt et al.), 118, 163

Sexual Abuse, 67

Shared Beginnings, Divergent Lives (Laub and Sampson), 118, 162

SJ. *See Social Justice*

Social Forces, 26, 33, 60,

Social Justice (SJ), 42, 62, 63, 109, 110, 111, 140

Social Problems, 60, 122

Social Science Citation Index (SSCI), vii, 4, 12, 13, 14, 20, 23, 24, 25, 27, 29, 30, 31, 32, 34, 39, 43, 45, 47, 49, 51, 52, 53, 54, 55, 57, 61, 63, 93, 107, 125, 123, 127, 132, 136

Southern Criminal Justice Association (SCJA), 137

Specialization, 18, 66, 70, 74, 79, 99, 101, 103, 107, 118, 119, 153

Springer, 19

SSCI. *See* Social Sciences Citation Index

Stockholm Prize in Criminology, 117,

SUNY-Albany *See* University at Albany, The

T

Temple University, 124, 128

Texas A & M University, 125, 130

The 1988 British Crime Survey (Mayhew, Elliott, and Dowds), 88, 163

The British Crime Survey (Hough and Mayhew), 88, 161

"The criminal career paradigm" (Piquero et al.), 118, 165

"The development of offending and antisocial behavior from childhood" (Farrington), 108, 159

"The empirical status of Gottfredson and Hirschi's general theory of crime: A meta analysis" (Pratt and Cullen), 101, 102, 118, 149, 165

"The incarceration of Aboriginal offenders" (Roberts and Melchers), 91, 165

The Kirkholt Burglary Prevention Project (Forrester, Chatterton, and Pease), 88, 159

"The long-term evaluation of a behavioral treatment program for child molesters" (Marshall and Barbaree), 82, 163

The Psychology of Criminal Conduct (Andrews and Bonta), 82, 91, 118, 152, 155

The Reasoning Criminal (Cornish and Clarke), 151, 157

"The social dimensions of correctional officer stress" (Cullen, Link, Wolfe, and Frank), 80, 158

"The specific deterrent effects of arrest for domestic assault" (Sherman and Berk), 118, 166

"The stability of criminal potential from childhood to adulthood" (Nagin and Farrington), 72, 164

The Use of Victim Impact Statements in Sentencing (Roberts), 91, 166

Theoretical Criminology, 55

Thomson Reuters, 4, 5, 8, 11, 12, 28, 35,

Thomson Scientific. *See* Thomson Reuters

"Trajectories of change in criminal offending," (Laub, Nagin, and Sampson), 72, 101, 162

U

U.S. News and World Report, 137
Understanding and Controlling Crime (Farrington, Ohlin, and Wilson), 108, 151, 159
University at Albany, The, 51, 52, 53, 122, 123, 124, 125, 126, 127, 128, 129, 130, 136, 152
University departments, citations and, 1, 3, 39, 51, 52, 53, 57. *See also* individual universities
University of Alabama-Birmingham, 122, 127
University of California-Berkeley, 51, 52, 53, 123, 127
University of California-Irvine, 51, 123, 127, 128
University of Central Florida, 124, 128
University of Chicago, 56
University of Cincinnati, 51, 53, 123, 125, 127, 128, 129, 130, 136, 152
University of Florida, 123, 124, 125, 127, 129, 130
University of Ghana, 36
University of Illinois, 123, 128
University of Lausanne, 142
University of London, 24, 30
University of Maryland, 51, 52, 53, 64, 123, 124, 125, 127, 128, 129, 130, 136, 152
University of Massachusetts-Boston, 125, 130
University of Missouri-St. Louis, 123, 124, 127, 128
University of New Haven, 122
University of North Carolina, 123, 128
University of Pennsylvania, 51, 52, 53, 122
University of Pune, 37
University of Saskatchewan, 36

University of South Carolina, 129
University of Southern California, 122, 126
University of Tennessee-Knoxville, 51, 53
University of Wisconsin, 123
"Using the correct statistical test for the equality of regression coefficients" (Paternoster, Brame, Mazerolle, and Piquero), 101, 102, 164

V

Vanderbilt University, 51, 52
Versatility, 18, 66, 70, 74, 79, 80, 99, 101, 102, 103, 118, 119, 153
Victimology, 62,
Victims of Personal Crime (Hindelang et al), 101, 161
Violence and Victims (VAV), 62, 109, 110
Visions of Social Control (Cohen), 88, 156
VAV. *See Violence and Victims*

W

Washington State University (WSU), 53, 123, 127
WCJ. *See Women and Criminal Justice*
Web of Science (WoS), viii, 4, 6, 9, 11, 12, 13, 14, 15, 16, 20, 67, 68, 107, 125, 129, 147
Women and Criminal Justice (WCJ), 140, 144
WoS. *See* Web of Science
WSU. *See* Washington State University

Y

Yale University, 51, 52